Communism, Nationalism and Ethnicity in Poland, 1944–50

This book fills a significant gap in the study of the establishment of communist rule in Poland in the key period of 1944–50. It shows that nationalism and nationality policy were fundamentally important in the consolidation of communist rule, acting as a crucial nexus through which different groups were both coerced and were able to consent to the new unfolding social and political order. Drawing on extensive archival research, including national and regional archives in Poland, it provides a detailed and nuanced understanding of the early years of communist rule in Poland. It shows how, after the war, the communist Polish Workers' Party (PPR) was able to redirect widespread anger resulting from the actions of the People's Commissariat for Internal Affairs (NKVD), Soviet Army and the communists to more 'realistic' targets such as minority communities, and that this displacement of anger helped the party to connect with a broader constituency and present itself as the only party able to protect Polish interests. It considers the role played by the West, including the endorsement by the Grand Alliance of homogenizing policies, such as population transfer. It also explores the relationship between the communists and other powerful institutions in Polish society, such as the Catholic Church, which was treated fairly liberally until late 1947 as it fulfilled an important function in identifying who was Polish. Finally, the book considers important episodes – hitherto neglected by scholars – that shed new light on the emergence of the Cold War and the contours of Cold War geopolitics, such as the 'Westphalian incident' of 1947–48, and the arrival of Greek refugees in Poland in the period 1948–50.

Michael Fleming is Associate Professor at the Academy of Humanities and Economics, Lodz, Poland; and Lecturer at the Polish University Abroad in London, UK. He is the author of *National Minorities in Post-Communist Poland* (2003).

BASEES/Routledge Series on Russian and East European Studies

Series editor: Richard Sakwa
Department of Politics and International Relations, University of Kent

Editorial committee:
  Julian Cooper, Centre for Russian and East European Studies, University of Birmingham; Terry Cox, Department of Central and East European Studies, University of Glasgow; Rosalind Marsh, Department of European Studies and Modern Languages, University of Bath; David Moon, Department of History, University of Durham; Hilary Pilkington, Department of Sociology, University of Warwick; Stephen White, Department of Politics, University of Glasgow.
Founding editorial committee member:
  George Blazyca, Centre for Contemporary European Studies, University of Paisley

This series is published on behalf of BASEES (the British Association for Slavonic and East European Studies). The series comprises original, high-quality, research-level work by both new and established scholars on all aspects of Russian, Soviet, post-Soviet and East European Studies in humanities and social science subjects.

1. Ukraine's Foreign and Security Policy, 1991–2000
Roman Wolczuk

2. Political Parties in the Russian Regions
Derek S. Hutcheson

3. Local Communities and Post-Communist Transformation
Edited by Simon Smith

4. Repression and Resistance in Communist Europe
J.C. Sharman

5. Political Elites and the New Russia
Anton Steen

6. Dostoevsky and the Idea of Russianness
Sarah Hudspith

7. Performing Russia – Folk Revival and Russian Identity
Laura J. Olson

8. Russian Transformations
Edited by Leo McCann

9. Soviet Music and Society under Lenin and Stalin
The Baton and Sickle
Edited by Neil Edmunds

10. State Building in Ukraine
The Ukranian Parliament, 1990–2003
Sarah Whitmore

11. Defending Human Rights in Russia
Sergei Kovalyov, Dissident and Human Rights Commissioner, 1969–2003
Emma Gilligan

12. Small-Town Russia
Postcommunist Livelihoods and Identities: A Portrait of the Intelligentsia in
Achit, Bednodemyanovsk and Zubtsov, 1999–2000
Anne White

13. Russian Society and the Orthodox Church
Religion in Russia after Communism
Zoe Knox

14. Russian Literary Culture in the Camera Age
The Word as Image
Stephen Hutchings

15. Between Stalin and Hitler
Class War and Race War on the Dvina, 1940–46
Geoffrey Swain

16. Literature in Post-Communist Russia and Eastern Europe
The Russian, Czech and Slovak Fiction of the Changes 1988–98
Rajendra A. Chitnis

17. Soviet Dissent and Russia's Transition to Democracy
Dissident Legacies
Robert Horvath

18. Russian and Soviet Film Adaptations of Literature, 1900–2001
Screening the Word
Edited by Stephen Hutchings and Anat Vernitski

19. Russia as a Great Power
Dimensions of Security Under Putin
Edited by Jakob Hedenskog, Vilhelm Konnander, Bertil Nygren, Ingmar
Oldberg and *Christer Pursiainen*

20. Katyn and the Soviet Massacre of 1940
Truth, Justice and Memory
George Sanford

21. Conscience, Dissent and Reform in Soviet Russia
Philip Boobbyer

22. The Limits of Russian Democratization
Emergency Powers and States of Emergency
Alexander N. Domrin

23. The Dilemmas of De-Stalinization
A Social and Cultural History of Reform in the Khrushchev Era
Edited by Polly Jones

24. News Media and Power in Russia
Olessia Koltsova

25. Post-Soviet Civil Society
Democratization in Russia and the Baltic States
Anders Uhlin

26. The Collapse of Communist Power in Poland
Jacqueline Hayden

27. Television, Democracy and Elections in Russia
Sarah Oates

28. Russian Constitutionalism
Historical and Contemporary Development
Andrey N. Medushevsky

29. Late Stalinist Russia
Society Between Reconstruction and Reinvention
Edited by Juliane Fürst

30. The Transformation of Urban Space in Post-Soviet Russia
Konstantin Axenov, Isolde Brade and Evgenij Bondarchuk

31. Western Intellectuals and the Soviet Union, 1920–40
From Red Square to the Left Bank
Ludmila Stern

32. The Germans of the Soviet Union
Irina Mukhina

33. Re-constructing the Post-Soviet Industrial Region
The Donbas in Transition
Edited by Adam Swain

34. Chechnya – Russia's "War on Terror"
John Russell

35. The New Right in the New Europe
Czech Transformation and Right-Wing Politics, 1989–2006
Seán Hanley

36. Democracy and Myth in Russia and Eastern Europe
Edited by Alexander Wöll and Harald Wydra

37. Energy Dependency, Politics and Corruption in the Former Soviet Union
Russia's Power, Oligarchs' Profits and Ukraine's Missing Energy Policy,
1995–2006
Margarita M. Balmaceda

38. Peopling the Russian Periphery
Borderland Colonization in Eurasian History
Edited by Nicholas B. Breyfogle, Abby Schrader and Willard Sunderland

39. Russian Legal Culture Before and After Communism
Criminal justice, politics and the public sphere
Frances Nethercott

40. Political and Social Thought in Post-Communist Russia
Axel Kaehne

41. The Demise of the Soviet Communist Party
Atsushi Ogushi

42. Russian Policy towards China and Japan
The El'tsin and Putin Periods
Natasha Kuhrt

43. Soviet Karelia
Politics, Planning and Terror in Stalin's Russia, 1920–39
Nick Baron

44. Reinventing Poland
Economic and Political Transformation and Evolving National Identity
Edited by Martin Myant and Terry Cox

45. The Russian Revolution in Retreat, 1920–24
Soviet Workers and the New Communist Elite
Simon Pirani

46. Democratization and Gender in Contemporary Russia
Suvi Salmenniemi

47. Narrating Post/Communism
Colonial Discourse and Europe's Borderline Civilization
Natała Kovačević

48. Globalization and the State in Central and Eastern Europe
The Politics of Foreign Direct Investment
Jan Drahokoupil

49. Local Politics and Democratization in Russia
Cameron Ross

50. The Emancipation of the Serfs in Russia
Peace Arbitrators and the Development of Civil Society
Roxanne Easley

51. Federalism and Local Politics in Russia
Edited by Cameron Ross and Adrian Campbell

52. Transitional Justice in Eastern Europe and the former Soviet Union
Reckoning with the Communist Past
Edited by Lavinia Stan

53. The Post-Soviet Russian Media
Conflicting Signals
Edited by Birgit Beumers, Stephen Hutchings and Natalia Rulyova

54. Minority Rights in Central and Eastern Europe
Edited by Bernd Rechel

55. Television and Culture in Putin's Russia: Remote Control
Stephen Hutchings and Natalia Rulyova

56. The Making of Modern Lithuania
Tomas Balkelis

57. Soviet State and Society Under Nikita Khrushchev
Melanie Ilic and Jeremy Smith

58. Communism, Nationalism and Ethnicity in Poland, 1944–50
Michael Fleming

59. Democratic Elections in Poland, 1991–2007
Frances Millard

Communism, Nationalism and Ethnicity in Poland, 1944–50

Michael Fleming

 Routledge
Taylor & Francis Group

LONDON AND NEW YORK

First published 2010
by Routledge
2 Park Square, Milton Park, Abingdon, Oxon OX14 4RN

Simultaneously published in the USA and Canada
by Routledge
270 Madison Avenue, New York, NY 10016

Routledge is an imprint of the Taylor & Francis Group, an informa business

Typeset in Times New Roman by
Book Now Ltd, London
Printed and bound in Great Britain by
MPG Books Group in the UK

British Library Cataloguing in Publication Data
A catalogue record for this book is available from the British Library

Library of Congress Cataloging in Publication Data
Fleming, Michael, 1974–
Communism, nationalism and ethnicity in Poland,
1944–1950/Michael Fleming.—1st ed.
    p. cm.—(Basees/Routledge series on Russian and East European studies)
Includes bibliographical references and index.
1. Communism—Poland—History—20th century. 2. Nationalism—
Poland—History—20th century. 3. Poland—Politics and government—
1945–1980. I. Title.

HX315.7.A6F54 2009
943.805′4—dc22   2009006099

ISBN10: 0–415–47651–8 (hbk)
ISBN10: 0–203–87274–6 (ebk)

ISBN13: 978–0–415–47651–5 (hbk)
ISBN13: 978–0–203–87274–1 (ebk)

Contents

List of illustrations		xi
Acknowledgements		xiii
List of abbreviations		xv
1	Introduction	1
2	Ethnicity and nation: the international consensus	22
3	Manipulating social anger	52
4	Violence	76
5	Securing the Church	101
6	Rupturing homogeneity? Class and national identities	125
7	Conclusion	143
Notes		150
Bibliography		178
Index		195

Illustrations

Maps

2.1 Polish frontiers proposed by Fred Savery, January 1940   24
2.2 Poland's frontiers 1921–39   32
2.3 Poland's frontiers after the Second World War   33

Tables

2.1 Distribution of PUR employees 7 June 1946   35
3.1 Nationalities in Poland 1931–50   69
6.1 Allocation of influence according to the 'naughty document'   136
6.2 Refugees to Poland 1948–50 according to role played in the
     Civil War   138

Figures

2.1 Population movements to and from Poland 1944–49   47
4.1 Population in Opole Silesia according to origin (31 May 1949)   94

Acknowledgements

In the course of pursuing the research for this book I have benefited from the generous support of a number of institutions and people. The research received funding from the British Academy and the Polish Government through its embassy in London. The Polish Government grant facilitated a period of research at archives in Warsaw while affiliated to the Pułtusk School of Humanities, Institute of European Culture. The former director of the Institute, Professor Halina Taborska, not only helped to make my stay productive, but provided useful criticism as the work took shape. The British Academy grant funded a three-month stay at the Polish Academy of Sciences, Institute of History, Warsaw, in autumn 2006. I thank Professor Adam Manikowski for his hospitality and assistance.

I also express my gratitude to the staff and archivists of the various archives visited during the course of research, most notably in Warsaw – the New Documents Archive and the archive of the Ministry of Foreign Affairs, in London – the National Archives, the Polish Institute and General Sikorski Museum and in Łódź – the State Archives.

I am also indebted to participants at the annual Belarusian Trialog conference which takes place in Krynki in north-east Poland who have helped to frame my understanding of the Belarusian minority in Poland and have provided excellent criticism of work in progress over a number of years. I would particularly like to thank Sokrat Janowicz and Jerzy Chmielewski. Further thanks are due to those participants at the 2006 and 2008 Institute of British Geographers–Royal Geographical Society conferences in London, the 2007 Association for the Study of Ethnicity and Nationalism conference in London, the 2007 Refugees and the End of Empire conference, Leicester, the 2007 and 2008 Warsaw East European conferences in Warsaw, who engaged with and criticized early attempts to articulate the various arguments made in this book.

Thanks are also due to Dariusz Libionka who helped me to clarify the origins of Roman Knoll's letter to Tadeusz Romer, Wanda Jarząbek who discussed the reception of Marcin Zaremba's book in Poland with me, and Ian Byrnes for work on the outline maps in Chapter 2.

I am extremely grateful to Colin Clarke, Adrian Kelly and Marian Turski for their very useful comments and suggestions. I would also like to thank Anna Taborska who not only patiently read and criticized the text as it took shape, but also encouraged the entire enterprise.

None of the above bears any responsibility for the shortcomings of the text or for any errors (hopefully minor) contained within, though without their input the study and argument would have been much impoverished.

The publishers and author would like to thank the National Archives for permission to reprint map FO 371/24470/355, printed here as Map 2.1.

Abbreviations

AAN	New Documents Archive – Archiwum Akt Nowych
AJDC	American Jewish Joint Distribution Committee
AK	Home Army – Armia Krajowa
APB	State Archive in Białystok – Archiwum Państwowe w Białymstoku
APŁ	State Archive in Łódź – Archiwum Państwowe w Łodzi
CAB	Cabinet Office
CCG (BE)	Control Commission for Germany (British Element)
CKŻP	Central Committee of Jews in Poland – Centralny Komitet Żydów w Polsce
CRE	Combined Repatriation Executive
DP	Displaced Persons
DPSR	Documents on Polish Soviet Relations
Dz.U	Journal of Laws – Dziennik Ustaw Rzesczypospolitej Polskiej
FO	Foreign Office
FRUS	Foreign Relations of the United States
FRPS	Foreign Research and Press Service
IPN	Institute of National Remembrance – Instytut Pamięci Narodowej
KC	Central Committee – Komitet Centralny
KPP	Communist Party of Poland – Komunistyczna Partia Polski
KPRP	Communist Workers' Party of Poland – Komunistyczna Partia Robotnicza Polski
KRN	Homeland National Council – Krajowa Rada Narodowa
MAP	Ministry of Public Administration – Ministerstwo Administracji Publicznej
MBP	Ministry of Public Security – Ministerstwo Bezpieczeństwa Publicznego
MO	Citizens' Militia – Milicja Obywatelska
MSW	Ministry of Internal Affairs – Ministerstwo Spraw Wewnętrznych

MSZ	Ministry of Foreign Affairs – Ministerstwo Spraw Zagranicznych
MZO	Ministry of Recovered Territories – Ministerstwo Ziem Odzyskanych
NA	National Archives (London)
NKVD	People's Commissariat for Internal Affairs – Narodnyi Kommissariat Vnutrennikh D'el
NSDAP	National Socialist German Workers' Party – Nationalsozialistische Deutsche Arbeiterpartei
NSZ	National Armed Forces – Narodowe Siły Zbrojne
OUN–UPA	Organisation of Ukrainian Nationalists – Ukrainian Insurgent Army – Ukraińska Powstańcza Armia
PAP	Polish Press Agency – Polska Agencja Prasowa
PAS–NZW	Special Action Group National Army Association – Pogotowie Akcji Specjalnej – Narodowy Związek Wojskowy
PAN	Polish Academy of Science – Polska Akademia Nauk
PISM	Polish Institute and General Sikorski Museum
PKN	Polish National Committee – Polski Komitet Narodowy
PKWN	Polish Committee of National Liberation – Polski Komitet Wyzwolenia Narodowego
PPR	Polish Workers' Party – Polska Partia Robotnicza
PPS	Polish Socialist Party – Polska Partia Socjalistyczna
PRL	Polish People's Republic – Polska Rzeczpospolita Ludowa
PSL	Polish People's (Peasant) Movement – Polskie Stronnictwo Ludowe
PUR	State Repatriation Office – Państwowy Urząd Repatriacyjny
PUST	Polish Underground Movement (1939–45) Study Trust
PWDP	Prisoners of War and Displaced Persons
PZPR	Polish United Workers' Party – Polska Zjednoczona Partia Robotnicza
PZZ	Polish Western Union – Polski Związek Zachodni
RJN	Council of National Unity – Rada Jedności Narodowej
RTRP	Provisional Government of the Polish Republic – Rząd Tymczasowy Rzeczypospolitej Polskiej
SEN	Save Europe Now
SL	People's (Peasant) Movement – Stronnictwo Ludowe
SN	National Movement – Stronnictwo Narodowe
TRJN	Provisional Government of National Unity – Tymczasowy Rząd Jedności Narodowej
TSKŻ	Social Cultural Organisation of Jews in Poland – Towarzystwo Społeczno-Kulturalne Żydów w Polsce
UBP	Office of Public Security – Urząd Bezpieczeństwa Publicznego
UNRRA	United Nations Relief and Rehabilitation Administration
UPA	Ukrainian Insurgent Army – Ukraińska Powstańcza Armia

USSR	Union of Soviet Socialist Republics
WiN	Freedom and Independence – Wolność i Niezawisłość
WO	War Office
ZPP	Union of Polish Patriots – Związek Patriotów Polskich
ZZP	Polish Trade Union – Zjednoczenie Zawodowe Polskie

1 Introduction

The history of the last year of the Second World War and the immediate post-war period has remained a salient issue for historians of the communist takeover of Poland, scholars working on the emergence of the Cold War and those interested in the population transfers/expulsions and border changes in east-central Europe following the defeat of Nazi Germany. Debates on the events of this period also continue to excite passion amongst those who lived in exile following the 'Yalta' agreement and the ascendancy of the Moscow-backed communists.

Today in Poland this period is the subject of criminal investigations as well as renewed scholarly interest, as the Institute for National Remembrance documents 'crimes against the Polish nation' and prosecutes those responsible for such crimes. The combined effect of these interventions has fixed a particular view of the period, which highlights coercion, violence and state-backed criminality at the expense of understandings relating to consent, acquiescence and social approval. This book attempts to redress the balance, not by dismissing the crucial role played by coercion in the establishment of communism in Poland nor through some quixotic attempt to suggest that communist domination was welcome throughout society, but by demonstrating how sufficient consent to the emerging communist hegemony was constructed by the Polish Workers' Party (PPR) and the Polish United Workers' Party (PZPR) through the manipulation of nationality policy, national myths and tropes, and the linking of land reform to the new national and territorial configuration. As Rothwell (1990: 161) points out, '[t]he Soviet Union and the Polish Communists did not rely exclusively on terror in establishing their autocracy over Poland'.[1] In short, the main contention of the book is that nationality policy was a crucial nexus through which population groups were both coerced and able to consent to the unfolding new social order.

Three distinct strands of scholarship that analyse the period 1944–50 are engaged with. The first considers the emergence of communist hegemony and includes works by Polonsky and Drukier (1980), Kersten (1991), Kenney (1997) and more recently by Mevius (2005).[2] These texts examine the establishment of communist rule at various levels – political, diplomatic

and in the world of work. The second strand, exemplified by the publications of Mironowicz (1993, 2000), Tomaszewski (1991, 2000) and Madajczyk
(1998), considers the history of national minorities and isolates turning
points in communist policy.[3] The third strand considers the role played by
nationalism, well exemplified by the work of Zaremba (2001).[4] This study
charts new territory by bringing together concerns regarding the establishment of communist rule, the function of nationalism (and nationality policy
more specifically) and the role played by national minorities.

It is argued that through the drive to national homogeneity, and nationality policy more generally, the communists were able to secure sufficient
acquiescence from Polish society to enable them to move forward with their
social, political and economic programmes. Prażmowska's (2004: 168) assertion that 'the party which was most constrained in its attempt to formulate a
nationality policy . . . was the PPR' is shown to require significant qualification.[5] Indeed, a key mechanism by which the PPR secured a modicum
of consent was the managing of antipathy towards national minority population groups.

By adopting the view that the PPR/PZPR and their leading cadres
were mere Soviet stooges, established assumptions regarding society/party
antagonism are endorsed.[6] This perspective presumes conflict and fails to
acknowledge that for many Poles upward social mobility and national
homogeneity were very attractive following several years of brutal war. In
reality, as work by Kenney (1997) and Mironowicz (2000) has shown, identities within society and party were more fluid, ambiguous and flexible than
popularly imagined, though this is not to deny that strong, sustained anti-
Party sentiment existed. The precise form of We/They antagonisms did not
neatly demarcate society from the party. One of the key arguments made in
this book is that the PPR and later the PZPR worked very hard to manipu-
late the We/They antagonism into a form beneficial to themselves. As I will
demonstrate later, this project shifted resistance from the PPR and PZPR
to minority communities. Communist nationality policy was fundamental in
shaping the social anger regime and securing for the PPR and PZPR some
legitimacy in the eyes of Polish society. The 'social anger regime' refers to
the way in which anger/frustration in a society is managed, channelled or
orchestrated within that society.[7] The drive to national homogeneity provided space for social (and individual) tensions to be legitimately expressed
and, together with the lack of space for the expression of alternative views
of how society should be, sanctioned the unleashing of various forms of
violence against minority community members.

This argument is informed by David Ost's (2005) recent work on the
post-communist period and Chantal Mouffe's (2004) contentions in her
book '*On the Political.*' Both these authors highlight, within contemporary
politics, attempts to suppress the politicization of socio-economic cleavages.
Ost documents that Solidarity activists failed to safeguard the material
interests of rank and file workers, and supported the redirection of social

anger at the decline in living conditions to symbolic and mythical figures such as 'communists, crypto-communists, liberals, non-believers, "foreigners" (often defined as Poles who did not fit "Polish Catholic" norms), criminals, and other assorted "aliens"'(Ost 2005: 180).

Mouffe, who refers to developments in the West, locates the rise of right-wing popularism in the ascendancy of a post-political consensus, which similarly attempts to depoliticize socio-economic cleavages. While Mouffe and Ost come from different scholarly traditions and have somewhat different political sympathies, what brings them together is the contention that it is possible to displace social anger from its original source onto something/ someone else. The cost of doing so is to foster illiberality in the political culture and ultimately fail to resolve the tensions in society. The hinge of both their arguments, and mine, is that social anger is generated in all societies and that one function of the political class is to articulate a narrative that can make sense of reality to broad swathes of the polity.

It is maintained here that the PPR/PZPR worked continuously to shape the social anger regime to their advantage through the exploitation of national(ist) discourses. And while Soviet-backed ethno-nationalism in Poland is well documented, it is no longer sufficient to understand the phenomenon as a 'gift from Stalin' or as an inevitable consequence of the Second World War. Rather, it is crucial to acknowledge that ethno-nationalism was also the only model available to restructure the social anger regime to the advantage of the PPR/PZPR. Strong instrumental reasons existed to pursue national homogeneity and exploit the traditions of the National Democrats, and post-war nationality policy was crucial in shaping the fundamental We/They antagonism through the course of the Polish People's Republic (PRL). It is worth highlighting that the illiberality of post-war communist nationality policy was very similar to that advocated by the non-communist Polish Right before, during and after the Second World War: some social groups were to be excluded from society on the basis of their (essentialized) ethnic background.

There is considerable merit therefore in differentiating between the centripetal and centrifugal aspects of the PPR's ethno-nationalist nationality policy in the immediate aftermath of the Second World War. Although the centripetal and centrifugal aspects of ethno-nationalism are closely connected (overvaluing the in-group implies an undervaluing of the out-group), it is heuristically useful to analyse the two forms as distinct. Centripetal aspects of nationality policy tend to unify (parts of) society, while centrifugal aspects tend to exacerbate social cleavages.

To date, scholars have focused on how communists, not just in Poland but across east-central Europe, tried to link themselves with the population through nationalist rhetoric and symbols. In other words, research has examined how communists mobilized centripetal ethno-nationalism to secure legitimacy. Mevius (2005), for example, has concluded that since communists continued to be seen as 'agents of Moscow', nationality policy was largely a failure. This conclusion can only be drawn if the centripetal aspect of the communist ethno-nationalist nationality policy is emphasized and its centrifugal aspect is marginalized.

In contrast, if the centrifugal aspect of communist nationality policy – which sought to divide society along ethnic and national cleavages while privileging the national core population – is considered primary, then communist nationality policy looks somewhat more successful. The key goal of adopting a centrifugal ethno-nationalism was to provide 'legitimate' targets on which people could vent their frustrations and negative emotions about the state of society. In other words, this aspect of nationality policy aimed to provide a safe outlet (safe, that is, for the PPR) for the release of social anger. However, by over-valuing 'Polishness' and endorsing the view that non-Poles had no place in the country, the PPR risked being outflanked by oppositionists who attempted to portray the PPR as 'Stalin's Polish puppets' (Torańska 1987) and agents of Moscow – that is, insufficiently Polish. In part, then, the PPR's acceptance of the expression of dissent through national symbols and sentiment, encouraged a sizeable proportion of the population to view the communists as foreign representatives, regardless of how close to or far from the truth such an assertion may have been during the course of the PRL.

The ongoing debate about whether the communists were seen as foreign therefore needs not only to acknowledge the lengths to which the PPR and PZPR went to establish their 'Polish' credentials, but also to explore how this centripetal aspect of policy related to the centrifugal aspect. Exclusive focus on the attempt by the communists to be identified as part of the nation or as the defender of the nation's interests misses the precise way that nationality policy functioned as a mechanism to secure hegemony. By reifying Polish nationality, the PPR and PZPR created a situation in which antipathy, whether the result of class or political tensions, could only be legitimately expressed through the lexicon of nationality. This engendered an escalating conflict in which the PPR, and later the PZPR (or factions within it), attempted to demonstrate their Polishness, and redirected social anger towards minority communities (as in 1956 and 1968), while oppositionists frequently claimed to be the repository of the 'true' Poland.[8]

The widespread view that the communists gained and held power in Poland as a result of the Soviet Army's presence in the period 1944 to 1950 is true. Yet the contention that it was *only* because of this presence that communism was established in Poland is a simplification. This study explores the ground between these assertions, and attempts to provide a more nuanced and detailed understanding of how the communists achieved hegemony. Thus, although the role played by coercion must remain in view, and subsequent chapters provide an analysis of communist coercion, it remains particularly important in the current era of lustration and restitution claims to highlight consent and explain how some degree of acquiescence to the new socio-political configuration was achieved. So while the

British Ambassador to Poland, Victor Cavendish-Bentinck, was absolutely correct in a September 1945 despatch to London in which he contended that 'Messrs Bierut, Gomułka, Minc and Radkiewicz are not people who will hand over power without a struggle', the form of their struggle was more complex than narratives focusing on just coercion and repression would suggest.[9]

Furthermore, the idea that it was 'the betrayal at Yalta' that cast Poland into the Soviet sphere, while not holding credence among scholars of the period, continues to guide the popular imagination. This perception is slowly changing, but not radically so. For example, the commercial success of Norman Davies' 2003 publication, *Rising '44: The Battle for Warsaw*, may have altered the imagined timeframe of when Poland was let down by her erstwhile allies, but not the general narrative, which maintains that a heroic nation and people were hobbled by her friends.

This narrative often functions to differentiate good Poles from bad, and those who are idealized as fighters for a free Poland from those who co-operated with or were communists. The history of the period has yet to become the exclusive purview of historians, and remains the battleground of political and 'academic' polemicists as they attempt to use the past to justify current policies and shape contemporary reality. It is in this context that a deeper understanding of the role played by the Western Allies in supporting, consenting to and later contesting the post-war settlement needs to be fostered. The main contention made here is that the alliance was flawed from the beginning: Poland was never treated as an equal ally, and in this sense Davies is correct in identifying the failure of the Grand Alliance as contributing to the tragedy of Warsaw in 1944 and later.[10]

Recognition of the unequal nature of the alliance between Britain and Poland, and later between Britain, the USA, USSR and Poland, brings into focus its pragmatic aspects and helps to highlight how the short- to mid-term rational policies of the British and American Governments ultimately led to the long-term estrangement of Poland from the West. These policies, including military strategy, were sensible from the British and American perspectives, though not from the point of view of their Polish allies.

As early as 30 September 1939, British officials sought to sustain relations with the Soviet Union while meeting Britain's treaty obligations to Poland. The solution advanced by Sir William Seeds, the British ambassador in Moscow, and endorsed by senior Foreign Office official Sir Ivone Kirkpatrick, was to be flexible on Polish territorial integrity and to view Soviet aggression against Poland as being unproblematic so long as the Soviet occupation followed 'ethnographical and cultural lines'.[11] Throughout the autumn of 1939, the Soviet Union justified the occupation of eastern Poland by claiming that the area was inhabited by seven million Ukrainians, three million Belarusians and only one million Poles.[12] This claim was untrue. The actual population of the region, according to analysis of updated 1931 census data, included four and a half to just over five million

Poles, a similar number of Ukrainians, two and a half million Belarusians, a million Jews and a small number of other nationalities.

The Soviet Union also held elections in occupied eastern Poland on 22 October 1939, to further substantiate the claim that the USSR was assisting Ukrainians and Belarusians in achieving national self-determination. Following this rigged election, 'elected' delegates to the Assemblies of West Ukraine and West Belarus called for incorporation into the USSR. Soviet policy in occupied eastern Poland proceeded to restrict and destroy Polish political, social and cultural influence in the region. This policy saw co-ordination between the Nazis' Gestapo and the Soviets' NKVD, such as the simultaneous arrests of professors at the universities of Kraków and Lwów in November 1939.

British officials clearly differentiated Soviet aggression from German aggression. In the perceived British national interest, officials were very keen not to be drawn into a hostile relationship with the Soviet Union, regardless of the fact that in the autumn of 1939 the Soviet occupation of eastern Poland was very similar in practice to the Nazi occupation in the western parts of the country.[13] The British were very aware of the cost of sustaining Anglo–Soviet relations. Sir William Seeds on 30 September 1939 cautioned that,

> It must be borne in mind that, if war continues any considerable time, the Soviet part of Poland will, at its close, have been purged of any non-Soviet population or classes whatever, and that it may well be consequently impossible, in practice, to separate it from the rest of Russia.[14]

Despite the brutality of the Soviet occupation of eastern Poland and the acknowledged longer-term problems that the occupation would create for the re-emergence of a sovereign Poland, Richard A. Butler, the British Under-Secretary of State for Foreign Affairs, maintained – in a statement to the House of Commons on 19 October 1939 – that the Anglo–Polish Treaty of 25 August 1939, in which Britain agreed to defend Poland from aggression, was understood as meaning aggression from Germany alone.

The difficulties and failure of the Polish Government in Exile (based in London following the fall of France in 1940) in articulating its view and in influencing its Western Allies require further scholarly attention. It is sufficient here to note that by mid-1943 – almost two years after the Soviet Union had been invaded by Germany – the Polish Government in Exile was losing influence fast with its Western Allies. The Soviets broke off relations with the Poles in May 1943, ostensibly as a result of Polish demands for an independent investigation into the Katyń graves, and the British and Americans clearly understood the fundamental need to stay on good terms with the USSR.[15]

A concrete example of the lack of impact that the Polish Government in Exile had upon her Western Allies was its failure to communicate successfully the importance of the Balkans theatre. In 1942 the Poles favoured future offensives through the Balkans. As General Anders pointed out to General Sikorski on 27 April 1942: 'From the Polish point of view this would certainly be best, because, after Germany has been defeated, it would enable troops of the Western Powers and Poland to enter Polish territory' (Anders 1949: 109). This was crucial for Polish aspirations because, as Anders noted in a letter to Sikorski on 2 February 1943, 'victory of Soviet Russia would mean deadly danger for Poland' (Anders 1949: 136). It is therefore a matter of historical conjecture that, had the views of the Poles in 1942 and 1943 been treated more seriously, the possibilities of a Balkan offensive may have been explored more fully both militarily and in relation to the future shape of Europe.[16] Indeed, as late as 19 October 1943, Churchill, in conference with the Combined Chief of Staff, decided to reopen the relative priorities of Overlord (invasion of France), and the Mediterranean, and ended the meeting by stating, 'if we were in a position to decide the future strategy of the war we should agree' amongst other objectives, 'to reinforce the Italian theatre to the full . . . and to enter the Balkans'. The following day Churchill instructed British Foreign Secretary, Anthony Eden, to find out where the Soviets favoured Western allied action. Eden replied that the Soviets 'were completely and blindly set on our invasion of France'. The Soviets, thinking long term, knew exactly what was at stake.[17]

Indeed, mid-1943 is when fundamental wartime assumptions regarding the position of Poland changed. Up until that point Poland was, at least in Britain and in the West more generally, taken to be part of the British sphere of influence. As Norman Davies (2003a) reminds us, Poland was Britain's 'First Ally'. After this point, Poland was increasingly treated as part of the Soviet sphere of influence. Indicative of this switch is the way in which the June 1943 request for weapons, made by the underground Polish Army to the Combined Chief of Staff, was handled and ultimately treated. The Soviets protested against the 'arming of Poles in Poland' and the request was denied in September 1943.[18] As Prażmowska (1995: 170) argues, a contributing factor 'permitting Soviet primacy over decisions concerning the future of Central and South-Eastern Europe, was the deliberate British and American decision to concentrate on consolidating their own slender victories'.

Thus, any account of the immediate post-war period in Poland has to deal with Western policy and practice both during and immediately after the Second World War. This is especially the case here, where the focus of inquiry is on Polish nationality policy and all it entailed in terms of population expulsions, transfers and border changes, which the West supported. Indeed, in 1946, British army personnel were stationed in Szczecin and Kaławsk to oversee and ensure that the broad requirements of the Potsdam Agreement of August 1945 were being carried out. This book, therefore, includes an analysis of the role played by the West, especially the British, in this crucial period, and how the PPR, and later the PZPR, exploited its relationship with the USA and UK to its own benefit as it attempted to secure some support from the wider Polish society.

In recent years several important books have explored Polish–British relations during the immediate post-war period. For example, Marek Kamiński's (2005) engaging text analyses British and American policy towards Czechoslovakia and Poland, and provides an account of how the USA and UK tried to influence events in east-central Europe. However, Kamiński concentrates on high politics and diplomacy, leaving considerable areas of relevance unexplored. This includes 'Operation Swallow' of 1946 and the 'Westphalian incident' of 1947, which put additional strain on Polish–British relations.

Hans Persson (2001) examines the British role in the expulsion of the Germans from Poland, focusing on the relationships between the various departments of the British administration. Persson foregoes discussing the wider issue of Polish–British relations during this period, as well as the unfolding situation in Poland itself. Similarly, Matthew Frank's (2007) study overlooks how the arrival of transferees from former Polish lands to the East influenced the urgency of expelling the Germans. Nor does it fully account for how British concern for the German transfers to be 'orderly and humane' was able to provoke a great deal of resentment from the Polish population, other than by alluding to German wartime actions and communist manipulation. So, while the transfers from the East are briefly mentioned, the importance of the relationship between the two population transfer programmes is marginalized. This focus sustains the general Western view of the expulsion of the Germans, that disconnects or, at the very least, parenthesizes their fate from the wider population reconfiguration in Eastern Europe, which took place under Soviet leadership and, frequently, control.

Frank (2007) examines British opinion on the post-1945 population transfers and argues that, though widespread agreement existed on the principle of population transfer, there was considerable disagreement over its practicality. Frank's study describes sentiment in Britain that was critical of the process of expelling Germans from lands assumed by Poland. It also provides an account of the work of the Foreign Research and Press Service based at Balliol College, Oxford University, which was asked by the Foreign Office in 1940 to investigate population transfer on a case-by-case basis.

Three reports were prepared on population transfers in 1940, 1942 and 1944 respectively. The first report provided three scenarios for the future Polish–German border, one of which (the most radical, seen by the report's author John Mabbott, a Fellow of St John's College, Oxford University, as 'a desperate measure') gave Poland Prussia, Danzig/Gdańsk, and Upper Silesia up to the Oder, requiring the transfer of four and a half million Germans (Frank 2007: 48). This report was then discussed by academic specialists, none of whom could be said to be enthusiastic about population transfers. Frank (2007: 51) contends that although Mabbott's 1940 report probably 'never reached the in-tray of the most junior Foreign Office official', it 'is not without significance when considering wartime discussions on population transfer, especially since it was the first major British study on the subject carried out under official auspices'. However, this contention needs qualification. As is examined in Chapter 2, population transfer and the redrawing of Poland's borders had been discussed earlier among senior officials in the Foreign Office. In March 1940, Sir William Strang of the Northern department provided detailed comments on Fred Savery's 27 January 1940 memorandum, which redrew the map of Poland and advocated the removal of Germans. Indeed, the British Ambassador to Poland sent the memorandum to the British Foreign Secretary, Lord Halifax. It is therefore likely that Savery's memorandum was a significant contributing factor encouraging the Foreign Office to commission work on population transfers from the FRPS in the first place. This book aims to fill some of the gaps and oversights outlined above.

Revolutions in Poland

Kenney (1997: 4) and Łepkowski (1984) have noted that in the period 1945–50 Poland experienced two revolutions – the first, from 1945 to 1947, saw the transformation of economic and social relations, as assets were transferred to the state and workers were celebrated as the new hegemonic class; the second, from 1948 to 1950, saw the ascendancy of the Communist Party over the state and society, and the mass recruitment of the lower classes to the heights of the economy and state. In addition to this, the period also witnessed a national revolution whereby a country, the population of which prior to the Second World War was just two-thirds ethnically Polish, became, in a few years, more-or-less nationally homogeneous.

The revolutions of 1945–47 and 1948–50 should be seen as intimately connected with the national revolution that was unfolding through population expulsions, transfers, assimilation and verification programmes, which were underway during this period. The workers were not just celebrated as workers, but as Polish workers; the new people staffing the higher levels of industry and bureaucratic positions were not just from the working class, but from the Polish working class. In addition, scholars recognize that, 'in the communist era, "national" conflicts often concealed class antagonisms and vice versa' (Kenney 1997: 21, Naimark 1992: 68).

It is important to note that the 1948–50 'revolution' was associated with the new Soviet policy line which was articulated in autumn 1947. At Szklarska Poręba in September 1947, Cominform – an agency formed to co-ordinate activities and communications between communist parties in Europe – was launched. On 25 September 1947 Andrei Zhdanov, a leading Soviet communist, delivered his 'two camps' speech, which signalled the end of the Soviet policy of different routes to Socialism, and demanded a

uniform approach across the states of east-central Europe.[19] Jakub Berman,
a key figure in the PPR's politburo, was apparently told by Zhdanov, 'Don't
start throwing your weight around. In Moscow we know better how to apply
Marxism-Leninism.'[20]

The commitment of the Soviets to a single road (i.e. Soviet) to Socialism
hardened with the increased tension and ultimate split between the USSR
and Tito's Yugoslavia in 1948, and the East–West battle of nerves in Berlin.
In Poland, PPR leader Władysław Gomułka's examination of the traditions
of the workers' movement at the 3 June 1948 plenum of the PPR's Central
Committee, in which he expanded on the theme of Polish independence and
the need to defend that independence, provoked, or rather revealed, the
tensions within the Party which had developed because of the new line
coming from Moscow. He was strongly criticized by other members of the
Politburo on 4 June and retreated into a period of relative inactivity.[21] At its
second meeting, which took place in June in Bucharest, Cominform was
effectively transformed into a supervisory organ dominated by the USSR.
The path was now open to discipline advocates of 'national roads to
Socialism' and to force through the policy of deepening Soviet hegemony
across east-central Europe.

Gomułka was replaced as General Secretary of the PPR in August 1948
by Bolesław Bierut, who until that point presented himself as belonging to
no party. The summer of 1948 saw the emergence of Stalinism in Poland,
and the closer integration of the economies of east-central Europe and the
USSR. In 1949 Poland became a member of the Council of Mutual
Economic Aid (COMECON), but, unlike the Marshall Plan, which pumped
a significant amount of funds into the economies of Western Europe to
stimulate economic growth, COMECON did not provide such assistance.[22]

The increased tensions between West and East as well as the PPR/
PZPR's close co-ordination with the Soviet Union in the period 1948–50
reconfigured the practice of nationality policy in Poland. Bloc geopolitical
concerns played an important role, as was illustrated by the PZPR's treatment of political refugees from Greece (see Chapter 6).

The changes in communist post-war nationality practice and the wider
national revolution are now contextualized by an examination of Polish
communist nationality policy in the pre-war period.

Communist nationality policy in the pre-Second World War period

The historical evolution of the PPR's nationality policy can be traced from
the creation of the Communist Workers' Party of Poland (KPRP) in 1918.
During the 1920 war with the Soviet Union, the KPRP agitated for workers
to express solidarity with the Red Army, viewing Poland as a bridge to revolution in Germany.[23] Piłsudski's victory, sealed with the Treaty of Riga in
1921, ended such hopes. Since the anticipated European revolution failed to

materialize, the Communist Workers' Party of Poland at its 1923 congress in Moscow overhauled its policies, including setting up autonomous sections of the organization in the Polish eastern borderlands, thereby giving the Belarusian and Ukrainian communists their voice within the Party. In 1925 the Party changed its name to the Communist Party of Poland (KPP).[24]

In 1926, the Party opposed the Witos Government and supported Piłsudski's coup. Stalin subsequently condemned the leadership of the Party for their error in not seeing Piłsudski as a representative of the bourgeoisie and a threat to the USSR. It is worth noting that the USSR, and most probably Stalin himself, as he took responsibility for Polish affairs in the Communist International (Comintern),[25] had instructed the Polish party to support Piłsudski on the grounds that a communist revolution could be advanced in the wake of Marshal Piłsudski taking power. As this became unlikely, Stalin distanced the USSR from the policy and blamed the Polish communists for an error of judgement (Snyder 2005: 29; Dziewanowski, 1959: 115). The 'May Error' was ultimately used by Stalin to purge the Party and saw two representatives of Comintern placed on the Central Committee of the Communist Party of Poland at the Fourth Congress in Moscow in 1927.

With Hitler's accession to power and Germany's increasing aggressive nationalism, the Comintern's policy changed from condemning social democratic parties to supporting alliances with all those opposed to fascism. In Poland, the death of Piłsudski in 1935 and the consolidation of the Sanacja regime prefaced a shift in the Communist Party's nationality policy to a position less supportive of some minorities and the promulgation of a more nationalistic language, as Zaremba (2001: 77) indicates. This shift can be understood as an attempt to distance the Party from secessionist demands in the west and north of Poland that could only be to the advantage of German nationalists and to Adolf Hitler's regime, as well as the Party's need to embrace as wide a spectrum of public opinion as possible in the fight against fascism, as demanded by the Comintern and, ultimately, Stalin. As Jakub Berman pointed out in 1984, the Comintern's Seventh Congress in 1935 endorsed a people's front (Berman in Torańska 1987: 283). It must be noted, however, that most of the Polish Communist Party leadership were in the USSR and were later killed in the Great Terror – many of them falsely accused of being agents of the Polish Government. The Communist Party in Poland launched a series of purges of the membership from 1935. Ultimately, the Party itself was wound up in 1938 as most of its leaders had been killed by Stalin's regime and Stalin himself felt that it could not be trusted.

In short, the nationality policy of the Polish Communist Party moved from a position tolerant and supportive of national differences under the rubric of worker solidarity to a more restrictive position by 1935. This development was accompanied by greater control exercized by the Comintern on the Polish party and, crucially, a change in the international political climate, from the limited optimism of the early 1920s to the emergence of totalitarian fascism in the 1930s. In addition, the Polish Communist Party's policy of the early 1920s was aligned with the USSR's foreign policy of trying to destabilize Poland's polity by highlighting its repressive policy towards its minorities. Following Piłsudski's coup and the adoption of more liberal policies towards minorities, at least in Volhynia under the governorship of Henryk Józewski, the geopolitical and domestic political value of liberal communist nationality policy was undermined in Poland, as Snyder (2005) makes clear. The ascendancy of fascism in Europe, with the apparently successful linkage of nation, soil and polity, together with increased intolerance of 'aliens', made appeals to respect difference, whether from Communists or Liberals, less attractive. Thus, as much as shaping the political contours of the mid- and late 1930s, the Polish Communist Party was responding to less tolerant social sentiment on the basis that wider support for Communism and the policy of the Popular Front, without the burden of providing substantive equality for all minorities, could be achieved, thereby allowing some pertinent social and political issues to be articulated, if not resolved. However, the reframing of policy was inspired and directed by the Comintern, and derived from the USSR's assessment of the wider international situation.

The 1935 policy modification, informed by the imperatives of the Comintern, influenced the strategy followed by the PPR after 1942. Indeed, if the mid-1930s witnessed a growing intolerance of minority populations and growing adherence to the notion of a one-nation state among broad swathes of the Polish population, the impact of the Nazi occupation intensified these sentiments. This was certainly the view in Moscow, where, in autumn 1941, Stalin authorized the creation of an 'initiative' group, which was ultimately to form the basis of a new Polish Communist Party. According to the minutes of this group, the emerging new party (PPR) did not call itself communist because of, amongst other reasons, the imperative 'that the masses see in our party an organization linked with the Polish nation and its most vital interests and that our enemies will not be able to refer to us as agents of a foreign power'.[27] From the very beginning, the PPR recognized the fundamental need to identify itself with the *Polish* nation.[28] Indeed, speaking in 1984, Jakub Berman argued that the communists' 'aim always remained the same: to create a different Poland, homogeneous as to nationality'.[29]

The PPR was founded in January 1942. During that month, two former members of the Communist Party of Poland, Marceli Nowotko and Paweł Finder, were parachuted into Poland by the Soviets and proceeded to organize and agitate. As Dziewanowski (1976: 163) points out, 'practically no PPR article or proclamation failed to stress the urgent necessity of waging an unrelenting struggle against Germany and of helping the Soviet Union in its life and death struggle'. However, attracting adherents proved difficult. By June, Nowotko reported to Georgi Dimitrov, secretary general of

Comintern, that party membership stood at 4,000 and its military wing – the People's Guard – had 3,000 members. These figures must be treated with caution as they cannot be verified.

Later, on 31 July 1942, Nowotko advised Dimitrov that contacts with the masses were improving and that, unlike the KPP, which he characterized as '80 per cent Ukrainian, Belarusian and Jewish', the PPR would not become a sectarian organization (Prażmowska 2004: 42).[30] During this period the PPR attempted to develop contacts with other political parties, most notably with the Polish Socialist Party (PPS) and the People's (Peasant) Movement (SL).

However, internal problems were spectacularly revealed when Nowotko was assassinated on 28 November 1942. Nowotko had gone to meet another member of the party's leadership, Bolesław Mołojec, near the Western railway station in Warsaw. What happened next is still unclear. According to Mołojec, who reported back to other PPR members, unknown assailants shot at Nowotko and at himself. Mołojec was able to escape, while Nowotko was killed. Other members of the PPR leadership (Paweł Finder, Aleksander Kowalski, Małgorzata Fornalska, Władysław Gomułka, Franciszek Jóźwiak) considered Mołojec responsible for the murder of Nowotko, either directly or indirectly, and believed that Mołojec's brother Zygmunt had played a role. No doubt they were also concerned by the fact that despatches from Moscow were addressed to Mołojec as the *de facto* leading personality within the PPR. A special commission was established to look into the murder of Nowotko, which concluded that Mołojec was responsible and passed a death sentence upon him. Mołojec was killed soon after. His brother was also executed.[31]

Finder assumed the post of First Secretary and continued the effort to build a broad anti-fascist grouping. A year later, on 14 November 1943, Finder, along with Małgorzata Fornalska, a member of the central committee, were arrested in unclear circumstances by the Gestapo. At the same time, radio contact with Moscow was temporarily lost due to the fact that the Gestapo seized the PPR radio (Prażmowska 2004: 54). Consequently, Władysław Gomułka became the *de facto* leader of the PPR, assuming the role of Secretary without Moscow's prior approval.

In November 1943 the PPR published *What are we fighting for?* which outlined the Party's aims and objectives. These included the nationalization of large industry, mines and banks and the breaking up of large estates to benefit the landless and peasants. It offered national self-determination to inhabitants in the eastern border areas – in line with Soviet plans, and congruent with the desire to create a homogeneous nation-state. The document is also of note for what it did not include – for example, it did not mention workers' control of the means of production and the nationalization of land. *What are we fighting for?* went through several drafts. The first two were written by Gomułka and the final November 1943 declaration included contributions from Gomułka and Finder.[32] Those earlier versions were vetted by Dimitrov who emphasized the Popular Front policy and forbade the use of the phrase 'the establishment of the authority of workers and peasants', preferring the phrase 'the establishment of genuine national democratic authority'.[33]

Stalin also maintained indirect control over the PPR by establishing another Polish grouping in Moscow on 1 March 1943 – the Union of Polish Patriots (ZPP) headed by Wanda Wasilewska. Though officially designed to help Poles in the USSR, Wasilewska's radio broadcast of 28 April 1943, in which she stated that the Polish Government in Exile based in London had no right to claim that it represented the Polish people, revealed broader political aspirations. The raising of Berling's Army in the USSR further challenged the London-based government, but the emergence of the ZPP showed communists in Poland, and specifically PPR members, that the status of the PPR after the war remained to be defined.

The PPR maintained close contact with Dimitrov through 1942 and 1943, and adhered to his instructions, but differences between the ZPP and PPR emerged. This was clearly the case following the publication of *What are we fighting for?* and the loss of radio contact with Moscow. Gomułka, following an independent line, supported the establishment of the KRN (Homeland National Council), which aimed to unite 'progressives' within Poland under PPR hegemony. This organization was founded during the night of 31 December 1944, without instructions from Stalin (Dziewanowski 1976: 170). It declared itself to be the supreme legislative authority and to have authority over Polish formations in Poland, Russia and in the West. Around the same time, in the USSR, the ZPP advanced a proposal for the Polish National Committee (PKN), which would form the first administration once Poland was liberated.

The communists based in Poland were, in theory, willing to compromise with non-communist parties, but were hindered by practical difficulties and the suspicions of the Polish underground. Those based in Moscow (i.e. those affiliated to the ZPP) were open to cross-party co-operation. However, 'co-operation' with other parties rested on the assumption that the communists would be the senior partner.[34] The PPR resumed close contact with the Soviet Union in early 1944, with a delegation from the KRN going to Moscow to meet Stalin in March. Those received by Stalin on 22 May included Edward Osóbka-Morawski, General Rola-Żymierski and Marian Spychalski, and they were advised to continue the policy of the Popular Front. On 23 June 1944 the ZPP recognized the KRN as the representative of the nation.

In July 1944, with the Soviet Army advancing into what it agreed to be Polish territory, the 'independent' line of the PPR was reined in with the formation of the Polish Committee of National Liberation (PKWN) and the movement of Polish communists from Moscow to take up key positions in the new administration, initially based in Lublin. It is at this point that the interests of the PPR, PKWN and the Soviets achieved a high degree of synthesis and growing control over 'liberated' Poland. By September 1944 the evocation of national traditions formed an important part of propaganda within the Soviet-sponsored Polish army. Historical figures such as Bolesław Chrobry, Henryk Dąbrowski, Tadeusz Kościuszko and military battles such as that at Grunwald against the Teutonic knights were referred to in army publications to affirm the Polishness and patriotism of the army and its political masters.[35]

Nationality policy in context

While it remains important not to conflate nationality policy with the innovations of theoreticians of nationalism, a brief digression to consider various theories of nationalism can help in understanding the transformation of communist nationality policy from the 1920s to the late 1940s. For, whereas in the early 1920s nationality was seen as being less important than class, and understood as a contingent identity resulting from varied historical experiences, by the late 1930s and early 1940s this view had changed to one which emphasized an essentialized and largely ahistoric notion of nationality. Theoretically, these contrasting positions resonate with different conceptions of nationality and national identity: a modernist conception and a perennialist conception on the one hand, and a civic identity and an ethnic-based identity on the other.

Modernist conceptions of nationality highlight the recent development of nations, linking their evolution to the rise of modernity, industrialization and capitalism. For Marxists such as Rosa Luxemburg, nations are merely a contingent historical phenomenon, which will be surpassed with the emergence of a classless society. It is from this perspective that Luxemburg's animosity to an independent Poland during the First World War should be understood. Luxemburg considered that striving for Polish independence would divert energy from the more fundamental task of a class revolution and the establishment of an expansive worker state. Modernist approaches have led in different directions. Luxemburg argued her position with Lenin, who, while recognizing the contingent historical nature of nations, also framed class revolution in national terms. Lenin, of course, also had practical considerations in mind, seeing Polish aspirations to independence as an additional challenge to the common foe, the Russian Tsar. Lenin's use of nationality was highly instrumental. For him, the key determining factor as to whether a national movement should be supported was the degree to which it would aid the socialist cause. In 1920, Polish independence was a barrier to exporting revolution to Western Europe. Hence, the Red Army invaded and was defeated at the gates of Warsaw, ending the Bolshevik hope of inspiring a proletarian uprising in the West.[36]

This instrumental use of nationality by communists can be traced back to Marx and Engels. In the *Communist Manifesto*, first published in 1848, they equated the nation with the hegemonic political class. As such, they famously declared that '[t]he working men have no country' and went on to contend that 'the proletariat must first of all acquire political supremacy, must rise to be the national class, must constitute itself *the* nation' (Marx and Engels 1992: 23). Thus, Marx backed national movements through the mid-nineteenth century that seemed to open up the possibility of proletarian emancipation, even if these were bourgeois movements. Such national movements were seen to prepare the ground for the historic shift to working-class rule. In addition, Marx operated with a notion of viable nation-states. Such states had to be large enough to function in the modern world. The aspirations of small and numerically inferior nationalities were, for Marx, to be consigned to the dustbin of history. Indeed, it is the notion of viable nation-states which led to communists in Poland being unable to respond effectively to the socio-cultural demands of regional or ethnic minorities in Poland, such as Silesians, Kashubians and Mazurians, for instance. These populations were characterized as caught between Polish and German identities, and the possibility that these groups could be described as national groups themselves was not seriously considered.[37] Instead, they were conceptualized as lagging in the historic process of becoming part of the German or Polish nations. This was most clearly seen in the Polonization campaigns of the late 1940s, which viewed Silesian, Kashubian and Mazurian differences from Polish national identity as a result of German cultural imperialism.

For communist theorists, including Marx and Lenin, class remained the most important social identity. Nationality, on the other hand, was conceived as a secondary marker to be supported or not depending on tactical considerations in the ongoing class war. Consequently, in the 1920s and early 1930s communist nationality policy in Poland sought to accommodate national differences in an attempt to secure support from Poland's numerically significant minority populations by offering substantive equality for members of minorities, who, outside the Party, often suffered discrimination or 'semi-forced' assimilation to Polish norms. Furthermore, since class was of primary importance for communists, during the early 1920s affiliation to a particular nationality was a matter of choice rather than an ascribed condition. Throughout this period the Communist Party advocated a civic notion of nationality that could accommodate people from a wide range of ethnic and religious backgrounds.

Contemporary theorists of nationalism within the modernist camp include such diverse writers as Ernest Gellner (1983), Benedict Anderson (1991) and Eric Hobsbawm (1992) amongst others, who, while differing in specifics, frame the nation and nationalism (the effort to form a nation-state) as historical innovations linked to the processes defining modernity. Gellner (1983), for instance, highlights the importance of the radical social changes concomitant to industrialization, during which the state fosters homogenization through compulsory education, language uniformity and the ideology of nationalism. Montserrat Guibernau's (1996: 47–48, 2004:

132) notion of the nation as 'a human group conscious of forming a community, sharing a common culture, attached to a clearly demarcated territory, having a common past and a common project for the future and claiming the right to rule itself' is a useful and fairly expansive way to understand what the nation may be.

Modernist approaches contrast with perennialist approaches, exemplified most recently by Steven Grosby (2005), and earlier by writers such as Pierre van den Berghe (1978) and Cifford Geertz (1973), who view the nation as existing prior to the rise of modernity. While perennialist perspectives do not necessarily lead to the oppression of minority populations, they are more likely to emphasize the uniform ethnic background of members of a particular nation. Perennialist understandings of nationality can be seen as less plural on two counts: first, they tend to project the nation back to a prehistory, and foster a tendentious historical narrative which may suppress diverse identities, in their attempt to ground a unified 'national' story; and, second, they tend to emphasize ethnic homogeneity.

A third approach, most closely associated with the work of Antony Smith (1986, 1991), highlights symbolic resources mobilized in grounding the nation, and charts the evolution of national consciousness through earlier ethnies. Though, as Kaufman and Zimmer (2004: 66) indicate, 'Smith's work is often cited as representative of a perennialist or primordialist theoretical pole', it is sufficiently distinctive to be considered a separate model. Unlike some primordialists, such as van den Berghe (1978), who highlight biology, Smith's notion of ethnicity is fairly flexible, as he conceives it as emerging from cultural-historical resources, experience and social interaction. The ethno-symbolic approach focuses on cultural characteristics which constitute nations and nationalism. As Smith (1991: 33) puts it,

> there is a felt filiation, as well as a cultural affinity, with a remote past in which a community was formed, a community that, despite all the changes it has undergone, is still in some sense recognised as the 'same' community.

The major drawback of this approach is its delinking of the cultural field from the political. As Guibernau (2004) has shown in relation to Antony Smith's work, this leads to an obscuring of the distinction between nation and state. This is problematic, as those with a minority national or ethnic identity are faced with state power which mobilizes majoritarian national identity as a source of legitimacy. In other words, by effacing the fundamental difference between state and nation, ethno-symbolic approaches can conceal some social processes which configure communities within the polity. Nevertheless, in the context of post-war Poland, an awareness of the claims of ethno-symbolism helps to sharpen understanding of policy towards autochthonic population groups in particular, and of the thinking of academic workers at the Poznań-based Western Institute who sought to promote 'folk' culture to encourage integration and assimilation (see Chapter 3).

Recent theorization on nationalism therefore helps to uncover the significance of the 1935 shift in Polish communist nationality policy. The new line broke with policy up to that date and transformed thinking on national identity.[38] Previously, class was the prime identity indicator; now nationality assumed an unprecedented importance. National identity had been seen as an accident of history: flexible, changeable and of minor consequence; it now became a crucial social marker. And, perhaps more significantly, whereas the understanding of nationality had been firmly entrenched within a modernist framework that emphasized historical development and the civic nature of national identity, it was now transformed radically to a perennialist understanding that placed emphasis on the ethnic nature of national identity. This new understanding of nationality, while facilitating co-operation in the mid-1940s with recognized figures from the Polish Right, compromised the liberationary tenets of the Party's Marxism as it reconfigured the We/They antagonism from contingent class identities to essentialized national identities.[39]

The new direction, as discussed above, was first felt by Germans and groups such as Silesians, Mazurians and Kashubians. And although the Lwów Congress of Cultural Workers in 1936 sought to subordinate nationality to class, the reification of national identity was directly encouraged through nationalist rhetoric propagated by the Polish Communist Party. In the new, tense geopolitical situation, nationality increasingly trumped class. One consequence of this change was that the content of national identity became more significant. The political Left slowly adopted the Right's practice of viewing religion as a cipher for nationality. This process was interrupted by the Second World War, but was later to play a crucial role in the post-war period and in framing the relationship between the PPR and various ecclesiastical institutions (see Chapter 5).

Note on sources

This book makes use of several archival sources in the UK and in Poland. Most of the primary material comes from the New Documents Archive in Warsaw. The key collections consulted include files of the Central Committee of the PPR and PZPR, the State Repatriation Office (PUR), the Ministry of the Recovered Territories and the files of representatives of the Polish Government involved in the 'evacuation' of Poles from former Polish lands in the East. Other collections consulted include the files of the Ministry of Culture and Art and the files of the Polish Committee in Berlin. In addition, reports of the United Nations Relief and Rehabilitation Administration (UNRRA) and the correspondence of UNRRA officials with Polish officials, collected at the New Documents Archive, were examined. The files of the Polish Socialist Party were consulted. Documents relating to the population exchanges and to the 'Westphalian incident' of 1947 were examined in the archives of the Ministry of Foreign Affairs in Warsaw. Documents relating to the Łódź Voivodship Committee of the PPR and the Polish Red Cross collected at the State Archive in Łódź were analysed. Most of this material has been available for several decades, though it is only recently that Western scholars have begun to make full use of these sources.

Further material was collected at the Polish Institute and General Sikorski Museum, London, the Polish Underground Movement (1939–45) Study Trust, London and the National Archives in Kew, London, allowing the source material in Poland to be compared and contrasted with data sources in Western archives. This was important in order to understand the changing relationships between the principal agents – the British Government, Polish Government in Exile (based in London), the PPR, PPS and PZPR, as well as to verify and check varied factual claims, compare propaganda strategies of the various protagonists, and to understand the interpersonal relationships of the main actors. The British Library's newspaper archive at Collindale, London, facilitated an analysis of how events in Poland were reported to the British and American general public. Over the past decade, the Institute of National Remembrance (IPN) and other institutions have published many collections of PPR and PZPR documents. Those collections consulted are listed in the bibliography, including those sourced from regional archives, such as the State Archive in Białystok.

An array of secondary sources was consulted, including recent Polish, British and American publications on the period analysed in this study, which provide both useful insights and checks to the argument made. In particular, it is worth noting the texts of Polish scholars, amongst others, who have explored in some detail the documentary evidence to be found in the regional archives. Their work has formed a very important sounding board for many of the arguments developed in this book.

Terminology

There has been a debate on the correct terminology to employ when discussing the population transfers of the immediate post-war period. 'Transfer' has been seen to be an inaccurate term as it is contended that what actually happened amounted to 'expulsion'. 'Transfer' belongs to an apparently neutral technical and administrative register, while 'expulsion' immediately highlights the forced and coercive nature of the post-war project. Both words are problematic, given the actual history of the population transfers and the way that history has been narrated and memorialized in subsequent decades. Any language employed to describe and explain the shifting of millions of people in east-central Europe in the aftermath of the Second World War is not neutral and is weighted with assumptions and ideological baggage. Furthermore, the terminology utilized is often delimited as to the population in question. Thus, almost immediately, the notion of 'German expellees' was accepted into Western thinking, whereas the history of expellees from Belarus and the Ukraine barely registered in the Western imagination. This asymmetry continues to be important, as the debates and conflicts over the Centre for Expellees in Germany indicate.

In this book both 'transfer' and 'expulsion', 'transferee' and 'expellee' are used to describe the population movements to both the east and the west as, admittedly, an inadequate response to the ongoing terminological debate. By doing so, it is hoped that the difficulty in describing the post-war population programmes will be highlighted and that a substantial part of the varied value judgements that each word carries will be neutralized.

Organization of the book

Chapter 2 analyses the international consensus and support for the programme of national homogenization in Poland. It discusses the transfer agreements that the Lublin Committee made with the bordering Soviet Republics, the practicalities of shifting people and the experience of transfer from the east of Poles and to the east of Belarusians and Ukrainians. It also analyses the agreements with the British, particularly the functioning of 'Operation Swallow' and the role played by British service personnel in Szczecin and Kaławsk in 1946.

Chapter 3 elaborates how the Polish Workers' Party manipulated social anger to its advantage. The main argument is that the PPR was able to redirect society's anger, resulting from the actions of the People's Commissariat for Internal Affairs (NKVD), Soviet Army and the communists, towards more 'realistic' targets such as minority communities, and that this displacement of anger helped the PPR to connect with a broad constituency, as it claimed to be the only party able to protect 'Polish' interests. The chapter shows that through nationality policy the PPR was able to fend off the challenge from the Right, co-opting senior National Democrats, and from the Left through land reform and frontier policies in the 'Recovered Territories'. The chapter also discusses assimilation programmes and verification processes, especially in relation to so-called 'autochthonic' populations.

Chapter 4 explores the difference between structural and subjective violence and contends that subjective violence ('unnecessary' violence) was tolerated as an outlet for social anger up until late 1947, early 1948. After this point, the structural violence of the state dominated. The chapter analyses the violence against minority communities in some detail, and shows that the Polish *gulag* served several functions in the immediate aftermath of war that can be productively understood under the rubric of nationality policy.

Chapter 5 explores the relationship between the Catholic Church and nationality policy. It emphasizes how Catholicism was understood as being part of the substance of Polishness. It argues that the PPR and PZPR treated the Church relatively liberally up until late 1947, as the Church played a significant role in identifying who was Polish and who was not. After late 1947 a much harder state policy was imposed. The 'totalitarian' model which dominates discussion of Church–state relations during the immediate post-war period is challenged. The chapter highlights how the Church in Poland was able to benefit from the state's sustained hostility to the Vatican, and analyses how the Church in Poland made use of its freedom from close Vatican supervision. The chapter also includes an analysis of the state's relationship with other churches and religions. This examination helps to highlight the special, distinctive and, indeed, privileged position of the Roman Catholic Church in Poland.

Chapter 6 analyses two events which disrupted the drive to achieve a one-nation state, and which have an important bearing on the emergence of the Cold War: the 'Westphalian incident' of 1947–48, when the Polish Government attempted to persuade the British to allow 'Poles' in Westphalia to 'return' to Poland, and the arrival of refugees from Greece in 1948, 1949 and 1950. The argument made is that Polish nationality policy transmuted from a *hard* ethno-nationalism that focused on population removal and exclusion to a *soft* ethno-nationalism focused on integration and inclusion. It is noted that, throughout, nationality policy was closely aligned with the assumed imperatives of building socialism. From 1947 this was expressed in the effort to import human capital and in accumulating moral and political capital *vis-à-vis* the West.

Chapter 7 brings the various empirical threads together with the theoretical arguments regarding social anger, violence and nationalism. It highlights the main contentions made in the book, emphasizing the role played by nationality policy in securing acquiescence to communist rule, the role played by the West in population transfers and how the PPR's perennialist understanding of nationality was sufficiently flexible to accommodate 'communist goals', such as international solidarity with Greek refugees. It also outlines why the immediate post-war period in Poland remains an important issue both within academia and for the wider public.

2 Ethnicity and nation

The international consensus

By the early 1940s the notion that national homogeneity would provide stability to the states of east-central Europe once the war was won was in the ascendant. In 1942, the writer Ralph Bieschoff articulated the view that members of the German minority in several east-central European states had acted as a fifth column, easing the Nazi conquest. This was certainly the view of the Premier of the Polish Government in Exile and commander-in-chief of the Polish forces, General Władysław Sikorski, who, in a memorandum of December 1942 to the Western Allied governments, wrote:

> In connection with the problem of population it will be important to reach definite conclusions on the problem of the transfer of the German population as a means of protecting the State against fifth column activities and of eliminating from international relations the source of recurring friction due to the activities of German minorities.[1]

Furthermore, the asymmetry in the League of Nations' minority rights scheme, which allowed the League to receive complaints from members of German minorities in countries such as Poland and Czechoslovakia, but not from Polish and Czechoslovak minorities in Germany, undermined the legitimacy of the League and seriously disturbed the larger geopolitical landscape within Europe.[2] Indeed, Polish withdrawal from its 1919 Versailles Treaty obligations in 1934 was influenced by this asymmetry.[3] Increasingly, policymakers on both sides of the Atlantic began to argue that only a significant reconfiguration of populations could inhibit future problems and avert war. This was the opposite of the view taken at Versailles just over two decades earlier.

In the USA, population transfers had been considered as early as 1942. Hoover and Gibson (1942: 315) maintained that:

> Bitter experience for a hundred years shows that these European irredentas are a constant source of war. Consideration should be given even to the heroic remedy of transfer of population. The hardship of moving

is great, but it is less than the constant suffering of minorities and the
constant recurrence of war.

In Britain, the future borders and ethnographic make-up of Poland were
discussed in the Foreign Office as early as January 1940.[4] Fred Savery, an
attaché to the British Embassy to Poland, based in Angers, France, composed a memorandum entitled *The problem of reconstruction of Poland*,
which redrew the map of Poland to take in most of East Prussia and modified the Curzon line to draw the eastern border.[5] It also proposed the expulsion of Germans, assimilation of 'white Russians' and population exchanges
in Galicia.[6] Savery did not make any suggestions in relation to the Jewish
population, but did comment on the potentially varying degree of loyalty
Jews would demonstrate to Poland.[7]

Savery framed his argument by pointing out that 'smaller, or less developed States are inevitably at the mercy of their larger neighbours' and that
some form of federation would help such nations to resist bigger and more
powerful states such as Germany and Russia.[8] He proceeded to argue that,
for such federations to be successful, some degree of parity and cultural
connection between the states involved was required. On the one hand,
Savery contended that a Polish–Lithuanian federation would have the best
chance of success, if Lithuania were reconstructed 'on the scale of the
historic Grand Duchy'.[9] Thus, Vilnius and Nowogródek would be incorporated into the new Lithuania. He then highlighted the fact that the loss of
Vilnius would be a tragic one for the Poles and asserted that it would 'mean
the withdrawal of the north-eastern frontier of western Christendom and
European civilisation from the historic stronghold of Wilno [Vilnius] to the
mushroom manufacturing town of Białystok'.[10] On the other hand, Savery
expressed deep scepticism in relation to a possible Polish–Ukrainian federation, suggesting that religious differences and Ukrainian 'instinctive hatred
for everything Polish' effectively prevented such a union. Lwów, except in
the exceptional circumstance of it becoming the capital of a pro-Polish
Ukrainian state or main city in a more or less autonomous province in a
Ukrainian state, would remain in a future Poland.[11]

Savery then briefly considered the possibility of a Czech–Polish union,
pointing to a significant degree of distrust between Poles and Czechs, largely
due to the Czechs' sympathy for Russia, before arguing that in order to
resist Russian influence, 'Poland must become a state with a larger percentage of Poles in the total population'. Savery maintained that an 'ethnographic' Poland would be more 'western' and European in its character than
the Poland of 1921–39. He was of the view that there could be no permanent
settlement in Eastern Europe, 'unless the Germans are forced . . . to cede
[East Prussia] and . . . to agree to a removal of Germans from it and also
from the rest of Poland'.[12] Thus, the future Poland which Savery sketched
was to be more ethnographically Polish, within compact geographical

frontiers, expanded slightly in Silesia, more substantially in the north, and contracted in the east. Map 2.1 shows the Poland that Savery proposed.

Savery's memorandum is important because it marks the first attempt of the British to think in detail about a new ethnographic Poland. British Ambassador Howard Kennard made it clear in his covering note to the Foreign Secretary Lord Halifax on 29 January 1940 that he considered the memorandum to be more of 'a preliminary attempt to bring out salient features than a final expression of view as to the future composition of the Polish state'.[13] The memorandum received high level attention during the first part of 1940. William Strang of the Northern Department of the Foreign Office sent his review of Savery's memorandum to Ambassador Kennard in March 1940. He expressed his sympathy for the assertion that Poland must have Lwów, but was doubtful about the proposed Greater Lithuania. Strang was also sceptical about the ejection of Germans from

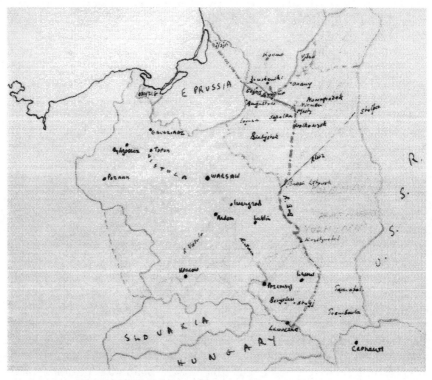

Key to hand-coloured original:
Red dash and blue dots – Polish frontier proposed by Fred Savery.
Area shaded in pencil to be allocated to Lithuania.
Area shaded in blue to be the new Poland.
Orange/reddish lines – 1939 borders.

Map 2.1 Polish frontiers proposed by Fred Savery, January 1940.
   Source: NA.FO 371/24470/355.

East Prussia, stating that 'revenge may be sweet, but in this case it would be terrible'.[14] He proceeded to contend that 'Polish hatred of the Germans at the end of the last war was a traditional and national hatred – now it is personal'. Presciently, Strang suggested that 'the Poles will simply take the law into their own hands in accordance *with their ability to do so*'[15] (my italics), but asserted that it was too early to look at the issue of a future Poland. Nevertheless, the British Embassy to Poland requested funds from the Foreign Office to facilitate the collection of ethnographic data about Poland from the Bibliothèque Polonaise in Paris, in April 1940.[16]

Despite the different signals coming from the various branches of the Foreign Office, it is worth noting that the main points of Savery's memorandum were seriously considered by senior officials, and that the redrawing of borders the better to fit an ethnographic geography and expulsions/ population transfers became official policy once it looked like the war would be won. In 1940, however, the deliberations about the future Polish state were kept secret from Polish politicians and officials.[17] And, as indicated in the introduction, the Oxford University scholar John Mabbott, as part of the Foreign Research and Press Service, based at Balliol College, was asked to look into the feasibility of population transfer in May 1940 on a case-by-case basis.

The idea of removing the German population had been circulating within Polish nationalist circles throughout 1941 and 1942. Intimately connected with the idea of removing Germans from the future Poland was the hope of expanding Poland in the west.[18] The first mention of moving the Polish border west to the Oder was published in the Polish underground press as early as 29 August 1940 (Strauchold 2001: 200). This was followed in 1941 and 1942 by a number of publications that suggested the possibility of expanding the Polish borders west into Germany and the removal of Prussia from the map of Europe, such as Lech Neyman's 1941 text, '*Szaniec Bolesławów*' (Stronghold Bolesławów).[19] Neyman viewed both German and Soviet expansionary tendencies as worrying. In 1942, Henryk Jeżewski, an activist in the Polish Underground (not to be confused with Henryk Józewski, former Voivod of Volhynia, also active in the Polish Underground at that time), produced '*Granice Wielkiej Polski*' (Borders of Greater Poland), in which he argued for a western border on the Oder-Neisse, the assumption of the Prussian lands and an eastern border on the Dmowski line, leaving within the Polish borders Połock, Mińsk, Płoskirów and Kamieniec Podolski.[20]

The vision of Poland articulated throughout 1941–42 rested on a belief that Soviet Russia would be contained following an Allied victory. The course of the Second World War followed a different trajectory, a trajectory at odds with the hopes and ambitions of most of those loyal to the Polish Government in Exile. At this point, the removal of the Germans and the acquisition of German territory dominated thinking. Underpinning these views was the notion that minorities such as Belarusians and even

Ukrainians within the new Polish state could be assimilated and integrated into the Polish mainstream. By 1943, however, the true complexity of the national makeup of the territory was beginning to be acknowledged.

In August of that year, Roman Knoll, the Director of the Commission for Foreign Affairs of the Government Delegation in Poland, wrote what was supposed to be a private letter to the Polish Government in Exile's Foreign Minister, Tadeusz Romer, in which he outlined Poland's international position. In this 12-page secret document Knoll argued that it would be necessary, when the war was won, to claim Gdańsk, Prussia and Opole Silesia, and that the new Polish state would not be able to tolerate a German minority, requiring the expulsion of between 3–4 million Germans.[21] Knoll contended that Poland's pre-war mixture of national and ethnic groups had been detrimental, as it stimulated neighbouring states to make ethnographically-based territorial claims. Knoll gave the example of the Soviet Union breaking the Treaty of Riga.[22] The general policy outlined by Knoll was one that advocated the coincidence of the borders of the state with those of the nation. To achieve such a coincidence, voluntary migration, comprehensive education and military service were to be promoted. In other words, population movement and programmes of assimilation to mainstream Polish norms would make the Polish nation-state a reality. In this vision, tolerance of minority communities as minority communities had no place. Domestic nationality policy was viewed as a crucial part of Poland's foreign policy, especially its eastern policy – a perspective long recognized by many officials in the Polish Ministry of Foreign Affairs and important practitioners such as Henryk Józewski. The policy to be followed in relation to minority communities was seen to be dependent on those minorities' relationships with the USSR. Overall, Knoll supported the *independent* nationalist aspirations of Belarusians and Ukrainians, but worried that nationalist stirrings were a front for Soviet imperial ambitions on Polish eastern lands.

Knoll's document therefore analysed the situation of minorities in Poland and suggested future policy directions. In relation to the Belarusian minority, Knoll argued that Polish policy could take one of two courses. Should a Belarusian sentiment of separateness manifest itself, then Polish policy could support it to provide a buffer between Poland and Russia. However, caution was necessary because Belarusian independence might well give rise to an all-Russian feeling, and thereby compromise Poland in relation to Russia. Knoll claimed that these feelings among the Belarusians were not noticeable, although data on the matter were insufficient. If the lack of any sentiment of separateness persisted, then eastern Poland should be treated as just a borderland area and should be incorporated fully into the Polish mainstream – that is, people of the borderland ('proto'-Belarusians) should be treated as Poles.

Knoll contended that Poland should fully support an *independent* Ukrainian nationalist movement within the Ukraine proper – defined as central and eastern Ukraine. He was of the view that a Ukrainian revival would drain Poland of Ukrainian militants and the issue of mixed areas could be negotiated at a later date. However, there was to be no ceding of territory. Lwów was certainly to be Polish after the war was won. In relation to the Ukrainian minority within Poland itself, Knoll argued that tolerance and conformity to the law should be promoted. The underlying assumption was that those who felt Ukrainian would leave for the Ukraine proper and those who remained would be assimilated. Such a vision of the future was at best hopeful, especially given the inter-community tensions and violence in Galicia during the 1930s.

Embarrassingly for the Polish Government in Exile, the document was leaked and found its way to Bundists in the USA, who were appalled at Knoll's proposals for the Jewish population, which suggested that Jews should not be allowed to return to Poland, but should have their own territory in Eastern Europe.[23] The Polish Government in Exile issued denials that this was government policy and also denied knowledge of Knoll's proposals.[24] It is clear, however, that Poles whose loyalty was orientated towards the Polish Government in Exile in London were arguing for, and generally expected to create, a more nationally homogeneous state than that which existed prior to the Second World War. They did not expect that this increasing homogeneity would be paid for, in part, by the loss of the eastern borderlands.

The Government in Exile had limited influence on decisions relating to the future Polish borders, especially from 25 April 1943, when the Soviets broke off diplomatic relations, ostensibly as a result of Polish support for an independent investigation into the Katyń massacre. A further source of tension was the Polish National Council's statement of 17 April 1943 regarding the Soviet execution of the two Jewish Polish citizens and leaders of the Bund – Wiktor Alter and Henryk Erlich.

The Polish–Soviet break also tested Polish–British relations. As Prażmowska (1995: 168) has argued, 'the Polish–Soviet estrangement alienated Poland from Britain. Churchill was now even less willing to see the Polish issue intrude upon the course of British–Soviet relations'. The lack of a Second Front sorely tested relations between Britain, the USA and the USSR. Churchill was determined that Poland would not compromise his efforts to reassure the Soviets about Britain's war effort. By the end of 1943 the British, as Rothwell (1982: 160) points out, saw their relations with Poland as 'exclusively ones of moral obligation to an ally', which allowed political pragmatism to dominate policy.

With the failure of the Warsaw Uprising of 1944, the impact of the Government in Exile's views on events remained marginal, as Poland's borders were shifted, populations expelled and 'repatriated' under the rubric of Soviet hegemony. The hopes for the eastern borderlands had been crushed by the successes of the Soviet Army and the failure of the Western Allies to resolve the Polish issue satisfactorily prior to the Soviet push beyond her 1939 borders in 1944.

By the time of the Tehran Conference in late 1943 (28 November to 1 December 1943) which advocated the Curzon Line as Poland's eastern border, the underpinning rationale of nation-state convergence in east-central Europe was not seriously questioned by any of the three main Allies. And while the policy of increased national homogeneity was aligned with that of the Polish Government in Exile, the Polish Government in Exile had no input into how it was to be realized. The Poles were unaware of Churchill's late-night proposal to Stalin at Tehran on 28 November 1943, in which he suggested that Poland should move westward, 'like soldiers taking two steps left close'.[25] The Poles were also not advised of Roosevelt's private conversation with Stalin on 1 December 1943, in which Roosevelt agreed that the Soviets could keep the Polish territory that they had acquired in September 1939.[26] Indeed, it was only on 20 January 1944 that British Prime Minister Winston Churchill met with Polish Prime Minister Stanisław Mikołajczyk, Foreign Minister Tadeusz Romer and Polish National Council Chairman Stanisław Grabski to advise them what had been agreed at Tehran. The loss of the eastern borderlands, despite their nationality diversity, was never going to be easy, especially given the role they played in Polish national myths.[27]

On 22 February 1944 Churchill spoke to the House of Commons, endorsing Soviet border demands on the Curzon line. The response from Poland itself was swift. The Polish Socialist Party despatched a message to the British Labour Party, via Deputy Prime Minister Clement Attlee, in which it raised the spectre of appeasement: 'Shocked by the statement of Prime Minister Churchill we are delivering a protest to you. We see in this the old spirit of Munich and the contradiction of the Atlantic Charter'.[28]

However, the Curzon line itself was extremely problematic. The line was proposed by the British Government as a frontier between Poland and the USSR during the Polish–Soviet War of 1919–20. On 4 February 1944 Anthony Eden pointed out to the British War Cabinet that there was a significant disjuncture between the line agreed with the Polish Government on 10 July 1920 and the proposed line sent to the Soviet Government via telegram on 11 July 1920. They were supposed to be the same line. It is worth quoting Eden at length:

> This telegram contained a strange anomaly. It proposed that the Polish Army should withdraw to the line 'provisionally laid down last year by the peace conference' and in describing this line it referred to it as extending southwards 'east of Przemyl [sic] to the Carpathians' ... A little further on it proposed that in Eastern Galicia each army should stand on the line it occupied at the date of the armistice. The document signed by the Polish delegate at Spa had merely referred to the line defined in the Supreme Council Declaration of 8 December 1919, and had not mentioned any southward extension through Eastern Galicia.[29]

The Soviet rejection of the British proposals in late July 1920, and the subsequent defeat of the Red Army at the gates of Warsaw later that year, did not reduce the Curzon line to an historical curiosity. It enjoyed a strange half-life in the Western imagination, being mentioned in the British press and encyclopaedias, and virtually always being drawn in accordance with the telegram sent to Moscow, rather than in accordance with the line agreed by Poland. This left Lwów outside Poland. For the USSR, the July 1920 telegram provided a further pretext to advance its claim for Eastern Galicia in 1943 and 1944.[30]

As late as 29 August 1944, in an attempt to keep hold of Poland's eastern lands, especially the oil fields of Galicia and cities such as Lwów and Vilnius, the Polish Council of Ministers issued a memorandum declaring that, 'in the East the main centres of Polish cultural life and the sources of raw material indispensable to the economic life of the country shall remain within Polish boundaries'. The memorandum also declared that 'all Germans will be removed from the territories incorporated into Poland in the North and West by mutual Soviet–Polish cooperation' and that 'a voluntary exchange of the Polish, White Russian and Ukrainian population will be carried out'.[31] The three main powers were sympathetic towards the last two points.

The tensions created by Soviet intransigence, together with the USA and UK's conciliatory stance in relation to Soviet demands, put the Polish Government in Exile under tremendous pressure. On one side were those who refused to accept Soviet *faits accomplis* and held out for the complete restoration of Polish eastern borders, together with the incorporation of Prussian lands into Poland. On the other side were politicians such as Stanisław Mikołajczyk, who, squeezed by British and American political demands to accept the Curzon line and Soviet effective control of eastern Poland, slowly came to accept the reality defined by the main wartime Allies. The new reality was spelled out by Churchill in his 28 September 1944 speech to the House of Commons:

> Territorial changes on the frontiers of Poland there will have to be. Russia has a right to our support in this matter, because it is the Russian Armies which alone can deliver Poland from the German talons; and after all the Russian people have suffered at the hands of Germany they are entitled to safe frontiers and to have a friendly neighbour on their Western flank.[32]

Stalin could take comfort from this declaration and subsequently maintained an uncompromising position on the issue of the Curzon line at the Moscow Conference on Polish affairs, which took place two weeks later on 13 October 1944. He informed the Polish delegation that 'if you want to have relations with the Soviet Government you can only do it by recognising the Curzon line as the principle'.[33] The following day Churchill kept up the pressure on the Polish delegation, advising them 'to settle upon the frontier question. . . . It means compensation in the west and the disentanglement of populations'.[34]

The price of compromise for the Polish Government in Exile was high, as Mikołajczyk's acceptance of the eastern territorial settlement, as advanced by the three main Allies, led to his exit from Prime Ministerial Office and the fall of the government coalition in November 1944.[35] On 28 November 1944 he wrote to the government delegate in Poland and to the Council of National Unity, and argued that, although the decision to agree to the Curzon line was tragic, 'the possibility of compensation along the Oder and economic assistance, and such a Poland could be non-Communist' would be 'better than a Communist Poland cropped in the east and not enlarged in the west'. Mikołajczyk continued:

> Such a Poland would undoubtedly have a hard existence, but the national substance preserved, with its demographic and great economic potential, nationally homogeneous, without minorities, is a foundation for a strong Poland in the future and a fairly acceptable place for the development of the nation.[36]

Thus Mikołajczyk rationalized the Allied *fait accompli* by maintaining hope of an independent and democratic Poland subsequent to the cessation of hostilities with Nazi Germany. Mikołajczyk and others in the Polish Government in Exile maintained trust in the Western Allies. Indeed, at the 14 October 1944 meeting in Moscow with British officials, including Winston Churchill and Foreign Secretary Anthony Eden, the Polish delegation was advised by Eden that, 'Supposing we get an understanding on the Curzon line, on all the other things we will get an agreement from the Russians. You will get a guarantee from us'.[37] At this point the Polish delegation resisted Allied pressure, but only until November when it was clearly understood that, without agreement on the Curzon line, London-based Poles would not be able to contribute to the future shape of Poland.

Western leaders lent their support to the contention that countries must be 'national' rather than multinational. To achieve this objective, redrawing borders and shifting populations were part of a legitimate policy mix. Furthermore, the Western Allies affirmed the Soviet Union's primacy in relation to Poland, and cajoled and bullied key politicians of the Polish Government in Exile to accept the Curzon line and abandon the eastern borderlands.

On 15 December 1944, in a speech to the House of Commons, Churchill encapsulated Western support for population transfers.

> Expulsion is the method which, so far as we have been able to see, will be the most satisfactory and lasting. There will be no mixture of populations to cause endless trouble . . . A clean sweep will be made.[38]

Three days after Churchill's speech, the US Secretary of State, Edward Stettinius, articulated US support for population transfers on the basis of nationality in a memorandum on the Polish situation.[39] Later, on his return from the Yalta conference (4–11 February 1945), Churchill told the House of Commons that the new frontiers were 'an essential condition of the establishment and future welfare and security of a strong, independent, *homogeneous* Polish state' (my italics).[40] Maps 2.2 and 2.3 (pp. 32–33) show the borders of pre-1939 and post-1945 Poland respectively. Poland was moved 150 miles west and was reduced in size by 20 per cent. Only 54 per cent of pre-war Poland passed into post-war Poland's borders (Davies 1981: 489).

While US and UK support for population transfers and redrawing of borders has to be considered in the context of sustaining the Grand Alliance in the final push for victory over Nazism, it remains a theme of historical conjecture that the Western Allies were far too accommodating to Stalin (Davies, 2006). Kamiński (2005), for example, argues that the Americans, in particular, were too amenable to Stalin's wishes, pointing to the American failure to support British efforts to link the issue of the western border with free and unfettered elections in Poland at the Potsdam Conference in July–August 1945 (Kamiński 2005: 126–8). And while Churchill canvassed support in parliament for population expulsions in late 1944 and early 1945, the USSR's programme of population reconfiguration was well underway in eastern Poland, as was NKVD repression of the Polish Home Army. It is to this that we now turn.

Population 'transfer' in the East

The Lublin-based PKWN, founded in July 1944, maintained the objective of nation-state convergence high on its agenda. It also claimed to be the legitimate Polish authority and, as such, it had, by September 1944, signed population transfer agreements with the Soviet Socialist Republics of Ukraine, Belarus and later with the Soviet Union itself.

Although the Polish Government in Exile supported the ideal of national homogeneity, it was extremely troubled by the population exchanges being carried out under the agreements signed by the Committee of National Liberation. Polish Foreign Minister Tadeusz Romer, in a letter to the British Government on 7 October 1944, argued that those agreements 'do not cover the repatriation of Polish citizens deported into the interior of Russia in 1939–41 which seem to indicate that in this case the Soviet Government had a purely political effect in view'.[41] He also expressed concern at the 'unilateral decision to change the traditional ethnographical face of these territories by arbitrarily moving masses of millions of people'. Given the limited authority which the Government in Exile possessed, Romer had to highlight every issue in an attempt to influence British policy,

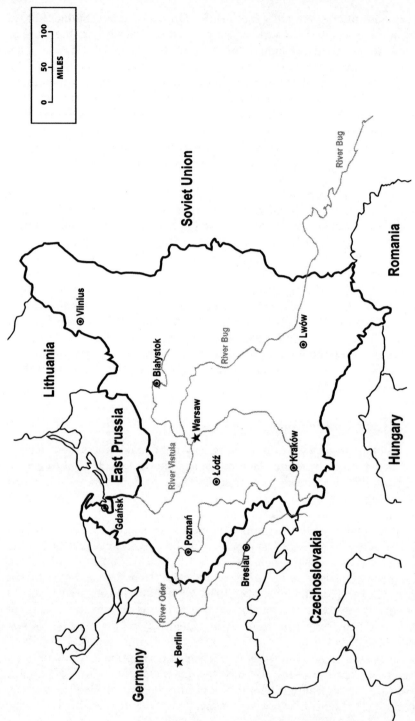

Map 2.2 Poland's frontiers 1921–39.

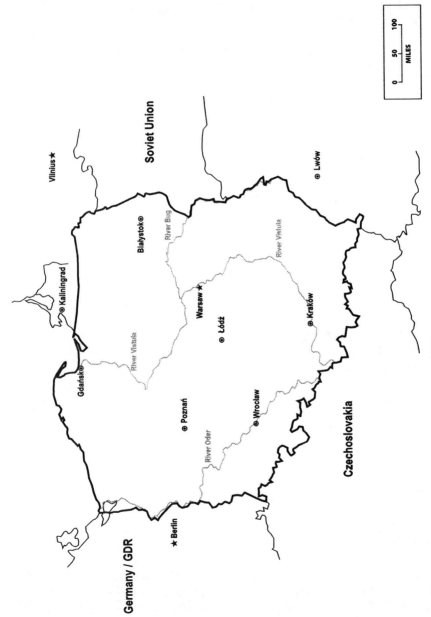

Map 2.3 Poland's frontiers after the Second World War.

especially in the period prior to the Moscow Conference. Indeed, he considered it 'an indisputable fact . . . that the Soviet Government have carried out a new partition of Poland and consequent upon it are creating facts, on the strength of their own decisions' – and he appealed directly to the Western Allies for an 'effective reaction'.[42] As indicated above, he was to be disappointed.

The transfer agreements between Poland, Belarus and the Ukraine were signed on 9 September 1944 by Edward Osóbka-Morawski, head of the department of Foreign Affairs representing the PKWN, Panteleimon Ponomarenko, representing the Belarusian Soviet Socialist Republic and Nikita Krushchev representing the Ukrainian Soviet Socialist Republic. The Polish–Belarusian agreement sought to transfer Belarusians to Belarus from Poland and Poles to Poland from Belarus, and envisaged a transfer operation lasting from 15 October 1944 to 15 February 1945. However, this was not achieved, and a subsequent supplementary protocol was signed on 25 November 1945. Similarly, the tight timeframe envisaged in the Polish–Ukrainian agreement was revised by the supplementary protocol of 14 December 1945, which extended the registration period for 'evacuees' until 15 January 1946 and the resettlement deadline until 15 June 1946.

The agreement between the PKWN and the Lithuanian SSR was signed on 22 September 1944 by Osóbka-Morawski and Mečislovas Gedvilas, head of the Council of People's Commissars of the Lithuanian SSR. This agreement was also modified on 10 December 1945 to extend the period of resettlement to 15 June 1946. The agreement with the Soviet Union itself was signed by Zygmunt Modzelewski and Andrei Wyszynski in Moscow on 6 July 1945, nine months after the other agreements, and served to regulate the movement of Poles from the USSR to Poland.

The transfer policy put enormous strain on the emerging state apparatus in Poland. Expellees, repatriants and transferees had to pass through several administrative stages: registration of person and property, movement to collection points, transportation across the relevant border, resettlement. In addition, tens of thousands of German expellees endured periods of time within holding and labour camps – many of which had previously been run by the Nazi authorities.[43]

In order to co-ordinate the mass movement of populations, the PKWN established the State Repatriation Office (PUR) on 7 October 1944.[44] It was given six key responsibilities: to organize repatriation; to regulate the planned arrival of repatriants; to ensure sanitary and nutritional care during repatriants' relocation; to allocate destinations to repatriants and organize their resettlement in Poland; to help repatriants in the rebuilding of workplaces; and to support associations and social institutions in Poland and abroad, provided that their objective was to assist and care for repatriants.

From 7 April 1945 until 13 November 1945, PUR was accountable to the Ministry of Public Administration (MAP), and then to the Board of the 'Recovered Territories'. Throughout its existence, co-operation between

PUR and the Ministry of Public Administration was close, especially at the highest levels, with the Director of PUR, Michał Sapieha, sustaining good relations with Władysław Wolski of MAP, who maintained oversight of the process. By 7 June 1946, PUR had 7,785 employees distributed across the country, with a significant presence in the 'Recovered Territories', as Table 2.1 shows.

The transfers were ostensibly 'voluntary'. The transfer agreements declared that 'resettlement is voluntary and no duress must be applied either directly or indirectly. The wish to be resettled may be registered either verbally or in writing'. In practice, coercion frequently provided the motivation to leave.[45]

In the north-east around Białystok, for example, Soviet officials enumerated people of Orthodox faith in preparation for removal to Belarus – outside the control of the Polish Voivod. Indeed, the Voivod requested advice from Warsaw on how to handle the situation. As none was forthcoming, he did not assist in the removal of Belarusians during the first half of 1945.[46] Nevertheless, only around 36,000 Belarusians were transferred to Belarus from the Białystok voivodship between 1944 and 1946, a mere quarter of the number originally envisaged (Mironowicz 1993: 111). This was largely due to the Polish belief that Belarusians could easily be assimilated and the strong resistance of the population. By 1948, in some areas near Białystok, the local mayors simply declared that there were 'no national minorities' (Mironowicz 1993: 153).

From the Soviet Republics, and the depths of Russia itself, the transfer of Poles and Jews to Poland was, in the most part, extremely unpleasant for the 'repatriants' and, for an unknown number, lethal. In the final three months of 1945 201,330 people were transported into Poland from the east,

Table 2.1 Distribution of PUR employees 7 June 1946

Voivodship	*Number of employees*
Białystok	260
Bydgoszcz	474
Gdańsk	517
Kraków	278
Kielce	148
Lublin	254
Katowice	818
Łódź	425
Olsztyn	407
Poznań	1,052
Rzeszów	264
Szczecin	1,020
Warsaw	245
Wrocław	1,623
Total	7,785

Source: AAN 522/II/46/21.

and 144,703 in the following three months (Czerniakiewicz 1987: 56). The very poor weather conditions badly affected the health of the repatriants. Even when they arrived in Poland their ordeal was not over. Roman Modrzejewski, the head of the social welfare office in Wrocław, filed a complaint against PUR on 20 December 1945. He described the situation of a convoy which originated in Lwów and was stalled between Katowice and Wrocław. He reported that trains 'were kept at small stations for 2–3 days for no reason. As a result there were three casualties in the carriages. . . . Many children had frost bite, bad colds, and everyone was exhausted and on their last legs'.[47] Problems such as these were often put down to sabotage, but in reality often resulted simply from very poor management. Even so, PUR personnel resented Modrzejewski's intervention and a critical response to his complaint was sent to the Director of PUR by Ludwik Sowiński. In addition, a co-worker of Modrzejewski described him as 'unbalanced'.[48] The venom directed against Modrzejewski was largely the result of an unpalatable truth being revealed, which could only bode ill for those PUR employees who were systematically failing to fulfil the tasks assigned to them.[49]

In addition, the settling of repatriants was often marked by gross incompetence. For example, a convoy of oil workers from Bitków-Nadworna was supposed to be taken to Międzyleś, but was instead taken to Międzybór. There, the workers requested assistance from PUR's office in Wrocław, which sent them to Jasień with the promise of work in a synthetic benzene factory. Arriving in Jasień, they discovered there was no such factory.[50]

Compounding PUR's difficulties was the poor state of inter-departmental communication, which often adversely affected repatriants. Throughout the second half of 1945 PUR settled repatriants on land earmarked for industrial development in Poznań. This provoked a response from the legal office of the Ministry of Industry, which requested that the Ministry of Public Administration ensure that PUR cease 'mishandling' the disposition of industrial land.[51]

However, given the scale of the repatriation movement, it should be no surprise that there were many problems, both in the actual transportation of hundreds of thousands of people, in the resettlement of these people, and in the process of compensating them for their losses in the east. Reports of poor treatment of the repatriants flowed steadily to the authorities responsible for repatriation, and both the Director of PUR Sapieha and Undersecretary of State, Władysław Wolski, were advised of the difficulties.

In addition, through the end of 1945 into early 1946, PUR faced logistical problems due to other branches of the administration commandeering PUR resources. Director Sapieha wrote to Wolski on 29 October 1945 to complain that PUR's fleet of cars (150 were allocated and intended to assist PUR in its repatriation mission) was being appropriated by local authorities to fulfil various unrelated tasks, and that the allocation of fuel was consequently insufficient to meet repatriation-related needs.[52] This, in part, helps to explain why PUR teams frequently failed to meet repatriants at various train stations and disembarkation points in Poland. Furthermore, PUR employees and the repatriants themselves had to deal with varying levels of insecurity. Repatriant trains coming from both the west and east were often attacked by Soviet soldiers and 'bandits'.[53] Officials involved in the population transfer programme were also targeted, especially in the Polish–Ukrainian borderlands. Many were killed, others were threatened with execution by partisan groups.[54]

The problems of the repatriation from the east are illustrated by the example of Transport number 282 from the USSR, which entered Poland at Medyka on 17 April 1946. It was not serviced by PUR personnel at Przemyśl, Rzeszów or Tarnów, as scheduled, resulting in considerable hardship (including hunger) of the repatriants on board. A subsequent investigation found several PUR employees to be at fault, including the transport manager. Similarly, Transport number 4 from Szumsk, which entered Poland at Kiercz, generated a considerable number of complaints.[55]

Criticism of the transportation was voiced by the repatriants themselves. Jerzy Borecki, a repatriant from the depths of Russia and a member of the PPR, was one of many who wrote to the repatriation authorities complaining about the manner in which the transportation was carried out, describing it as 'unacceptable neglect'. He outlined the four-week journey which he and his co-repatriants endured on Transport number 282, and proceeded to describe tensions on the train, highlighting the development of nationalistic sentiment.[56] On the outside of one carriage, carrying ethnic Poles, the repatriants stuck a religious picture and wrote 'Here travel only Poles'. He also detailed how Jewish agitators boarded the train and advised Jewish repatriants that there was only terror and murder in Poland, and persuaded young Jews to leave the train for new lives abroad, while Polish agitators whipped up anti-Semitism, which occasionally led to fights between ethnic Poles and Jews. A further point of complaint raised by Borecki was the announcement by a PUR official in Mikulczyce that Jews were to be sent to Lower Silesia, while Poles were to be sent to Pomerania.[57] He argued that the problems of the transfer process could easily be rectified if PUR officials acted correctly. And, to an extent, Władysław Wolski agreed. He wrote to PUR director Sapieha requesting an investigation, and demanded that appropriate action be taken.[58]

The Ukrainian transfers were dogged by violence, as wartime hostility between Ukrainian and Polish nationalists continued. In addition, the new Polish state attempted to impose its authority within its newly defined borders. An unpublished attachment to the supplementary protocol of the 14 December 1945 Polish–Ukrainian agreement reported 'an increase in terrorist acts against people coming under the agreement, as well as against workers of the apparatus of the Chief Representative of the Government of the Ukrainian SSR . . . In November 1945 alone 6 responsible co-workers of the Chief Representative were killed'.[59]

Some 482,000 Ukrainians were removed from Poland in the period 1945–46 (Ther 2001: 56). Though much of the initial movement in late 1944 and early 1945 was voluntary, poor reception facilities, poor transport and the low standard of living in the Ukraine persuaded many to return to Poland and inhibited others from volunteering. Indeed, Transport number 42 from Tarnopol to Zegan caused repatriation officials a serious problem as the people on board refused to disembark. The army was called in, but failed to persuade the 'repatriants' to leave the train. After seven days and under threat of arrest, the passengers finally disembarked.[60]

By mid-1945 the movement of Ukrainians out of Poland became increasingly forced by state agencies. The 'transferees' frequently fell victim to Polish underground violence as well as robbery – the soldiers of the Soviet Army also preyed upon them. By spring 1945 the Ukrainian Insurgent Army was operating on the Polish side of the border and the violence had escalated to such an extent that, in September 1945, the Polish Government dispatched three infantry divisions to Ukrainian-inhabited regions. The UPA directed armed action against both Poles and Soviets. But, by August 1946, the Polish and Ukrainian Soviet Governments announced the completion of the operation. As research conducted by Subtelny (2001: 164) points out, it had been a costly operation, with 4,670 Ukrainians killed and 305 villages burned.

The complex rules governing what could and what could not be taken to new places of residence on the other side of the border also inhibited voluntary movement. Precious metals, antiques, money in excess of 1,000 roubles/złoty equivalent, automobiles and furniture were forbidden, while clothes, farm tools, home appliances, farm animals and, in the case of professionals, tools necessary for their professional duties, were allowed. However, the quantity of possessions permitted to be taken was limited to a weight total of two tonnes per family. Possessions that could not be taken were valued by Government representatives, and the 'evacuees' were given forms entitling them to goods of the same value on the other side of the border.[61] Clearly, there was plenty of scope to undervalue evacuees' possessions, and in reality the like-for-like principle was poorly enacted, due to the general material shortages throughout the Ukraine and Poland during this period.

Following the completion of the transfers, 200,000 Ukrainians remained in Poland. These were ultimately 'resettled' in the 'Action Vistula' of 1947 to the 'Recovered Territories'. The objective was to divorce the Ukrainians from their traditional lands, and to prevent proximity to and contact with the border and each other in order to facilitate rapid assimilation. To achieve this goal, 20,000 soldiers were placed at the service of the director of the operation, General Stefan Mossor. Villages were surrounded and the inhabitants given a couple of hours to prepare their belongings and leave. Around 140,000 people were evicted from their homes during Action Vistula.

In contrast, transfers between the Lithuanian SSR and Poland were substantially less violent, though some transports were targeted by 'bandits' and Soviet soldiers.[62] By the end of 1945, 73,050 people had left Lithuania for Poland, over two-thirds from Vilnius. In 1946, a further 123,000 people were transferred from Lithuania to Poland.[63] The movement of Lithuanians from Poland to Lithuania had a more voluntary and individualistic character. There were relatively few Lithuanians within the new borders of Poland. Tarka (1998: 38) estimates that at most there were only 8,000–10,000 Lithuanians in post-war Poland, most of them concentrated in the extreme north-east of the country. This population was not put under strong pressure to leave, though the teaching of the Lithuanian language was restricted. Given that the Lithuanians were Catholic and considered loyal to the Polish state, it was assumed that they would quickly assimilate into the Polish mainstream (Mironowicz 2000: 37).

Jews who were Polish citizens in 1939 were, through the transfer agreements signed by the Committee of National Liberation and the various Soviet governments, allowed to return to Poland. The Polish Government policy towards them was ambiguous. On the one hand, the Government championed Zionist demands for Jews to leave Poland and set up their own state in Palestine, and, on the other, acceded to demands mainly made by Bundists to rebuild Jewish communities in Poland. The policy towards Jews is elaborated more fully below.

The settling of the financial costs of the transfer programme was finally concluded in Moscow on 21 July 1952. It included claims regarding evacuees' moveable and immoveable property, costs of maintaining the transfer infrastructure, loans granted to people transferred from the Belarusian SSR, and the costs of transporting people. Poland was obliged to pay the Soviet Union 76 million roubles.[64] For both the Polish state and the transferees themselves, the economic cost of the transfer policy was high.

Outside the framework provided by the various transfer agreements signed by the PKWN with the Soviet Republics and the USSR, there existed a programme of deportations conducted by the NKVD and the Soviet Army. These actions included the deportation to the USSR of several thousand former Home Army soldiers.[65]

Population 'transfer' in the West

While the transfer of population in eastern Poland was orchestrated by the USSR, the situation in the West was more complex, and depended not only on Western political support, but also on Western practical assistance. After all, the Germans scheduled for expulsion from the new Poland had to be settled both in the Soviet zone of occupation in Germany and in the British zone. In addition, the programme of national homogeneity pursued by the PKWN, and later the Provisional Government of National Unity, also aimed to bring Poles to Poland. This included those deported to Germany during the course of the war as slave labour and prisoners of war, as well as members of Polish Armed Forces in the West, who had been loyal to the Polish Government in Exile based in London. In addition, the Polish Government (in Warsaw) also sought to persuade Poles and people of Polish background, who had settled in Western Europe prior to the Second World War to resettle in Poland. Western co-operation was therefore crucial to the success of Polish nationality policy.

UNRRA's planning document for repatriation in 1947 makes this collaborative imperative clear. Entitled 'Spring campaign for repatriation of Polish displaced persons', it was worked out by UNRRA in co-operation with military representatives in the US zone of Germany, senior Polish officials including Minister Władysław Wolski, representatives from the Ministry of the Recovered Territories and the Ministry of Labour and Social Welfare, as well as the Polish media. It sought to capitalize on the 1947 'amnesty' declared by the Polish Government, which UNRRA hoped to use as an 'indication of the general settlement in the country and the freedom of the individual, even those who have committed offences against the state'.[66]

UNRRA sought to 'present the plans of the new government insofar as they affect future social and economic developments within the country'.[67] It publicized the parliamentary resolution of 22 February 1947, which affirmed the equality of rights irrespective of nationality, race, religion, sex or social status.[68] A key part of the campaign was the use of propaganda material in the US zone of occupation, such as showing the repatriation film, *The Way Home* and distribution of informational pamphlets, posters, radio broadcasts and newsreels.[69] Even earlier, on 28 January 1946, a note from Brigadier Kenchington, head of the British Prisoner of War and Displaced Persons Division in occupied Germany, to the Polish Repatriation Mission in Berlin, clearly outlined the British priority of sending Poles to Poland, even if this meant tolerating unjust criticism of the occupational authorities in Germany. He stated that in 'regards to newspapers from Warsaw it is known that they frequently contain statements which are not favourable to the occupational forces or the London Polish officers. They will NOT however be held back on this account'.[70] This was followed up by the marginalization of liaison officers loyal to the London-based Government in Exile operating in the various Displaced Persons camps in Germany, and the privileging of liaison officers from Warsaw, who were attempting to persuade Poles to return to Poland.[71]

The leadership of the PPR (and others) echoed the integral nationalist position of the interwar period advocated by Roman Dmowski, the leading figure of the various national movements collectively known as the *Endecja* or National Democracy, which argued for the coincidence of nation (ethnically conceived) with the state's borders. Indeed, this vision of the state helped to promote co-operation between the PPR and the nationalist camp led by Stanisław Grabski (formerly a member of the Polish Government in Exile and veteran of the National Democratic circles, who accepted the post of Vice-President of the Homeland National Council (KRN)). In a letter dated July 1945 to London, Grabski called for honest people to participate in the rebuilding of the country, arguing that, 'If honest people delay, the rabble will take over public life and we will lose the right to the western borderlands in the opinion of the world'.[72] Grabski's co-operation within the Provisional Government was grounded on the belief that a homogeneous, compact nation-state was in the best interest of Poland – a view shared by the PPR leadership.

By 31 August 1948, 865,637 people from the Western zones of occupation in Germany had been repatriated to Poland and, by 1950, the number of people from the whole of Germany was 1,642,599. In addition to this, the Warsaw Government managed to persuade around 200,000 'old' emigrants, that is people who left Poland prior to the Second World War, to return, including approximately 78,000 from France, 60,000 from Germany, 15,000 from Yugoslavia and 4,000 from Romania and Belgium (Eberhardt 2000: 56). But, for many, a return to Poland was out of the question, mainly on the grounds that they anticipated discrimination by the Government and feared political repression. For others, it was fear of social marginalization which inhibited a return to Poland. In a letter dated 10 February 1947, UNRRA official Carl Martins advised Mrs Palmowska of the Polish Red Cross that:

> There are other cases of young Polish unmarried mothers who still have their babies with them in the camps but they are refusing to be repatriated with the babies because of the fear of condemnation in Poland and the very real concern over how they will be able to take care of themselves and their babies after they are back in Poland.[73]

And while many 'repatriants' from the east perceived that 'repatriants' from the west were initially better treated by PUR, with well-equipped barracks awaiting them at reception points while Easterners endured nights in the open air, arrivals from the West were frequently less than impressed.[74] Kazimiera Ostrowska, a PUR official in Gdańsk, reported on 21 May 1946 that repatriants from the United Kingdom and Italy being housed in a PUR camp prior to relocation to Silesia, Warsaw, Poznań and Łódź were not being fed properly and were trading cigarettes for bread, and pointed to the troubled relations with local government.[75]

The principle of expelling the German population had commanded the support of the main three Allies since the Tehran conference of 1943. But it was the advance of the Soviet Army that initiated the process of removing Germans from Prussia. Soviet atrocities at Nemmersdorf on 21 October 1944 were widely publicized by Goebbels' propaganda ministry, and encouraged Germans living near the front to flee west. By the time the war finished it is estimated that there were 500,000 people in East Prussia, including those parts that were to become Poland.[76] However, this figure must be treated with caution, as people continued to leave while others returned to their homes after the firing stopped. In May 1945 the new Polish authorities estimated that there were 125,000 Germans in the Allenstein/ Olsztyn area, which rose to 142,312 by August of that year.[77]

The period following the USSR's announcement of victory on 9 May 1945, through to the Potsdam Conference of late July to early August of that year, was marked by a period of unregulated 'wild' expulsions of the German population from the area that the Polish Government sought to claim as the territory of the new Polish State. The influence of the Western Allies on the course of events during this period was limited, though on the general policy level the expulsion of the German population was accepted. It was only after the Potsdam Conference, which called for the expulsion process to be conducted in a 'humane and orderly manner', that Western humanitarian concerns were able to be expressed frankly.

As early as 10 June 1945 the Polish Army was ordered to remove all Germans located east of the Oder, near the 'borderline'. The order was implemented by the 2nd Polish Army by surrounding a village or part of a town and instructing the Germans to leave, allowing them to take a minimal quantity of possessions. The expellees were given anything from a couple of minutes to a couple of hours to gather their things up to the weight of 20 kilos. Precious items were generally 'confiscated' (Jankowiak 2005: 91).

They were escorted to the 'border' on the Oder and left there. In the Szczecin area the expulsion process affected people living in the Choszczno, Chojna, Szczecin and Wolin districts, amongst others.[78] Jankowiak (2005: 100) argues that the Polish Army's frequently brutal expulsion of Germans only ended because of the forthcoming Potsdam Conference and antici-pated international concern. Indeed, in early July the Russians had objected to the expulsion as it was putting pressure on its administrative zone in Germany, but the expulsions continued (Jankowiak 2005: 92). The actions of June and July 1945 allowed the emerging Polish state to claim that the key western border areas were German-free, strengthening their claims that the Polish western border should run along the Oder.

The Potsdam Conference outlined the framework for a more orderly removal of the German population from these territories. This framework was given more detail in the Allied Council agreement of 20 November 1945. However, at times the process of the expulsions fell short of the 'humane and orderly manner' outlined at the Potsdam Conference. As early as 27 August 1945, British Foreign Secretary Ernest Bevin wrote to the British Ambassador to Poland Victor Cavendish-Bentinck, reporting that he had spoken to the Polish Ambassador to Britain about 'arrests, con-centration camps and other matters which seemed to be contrary to the assurance given . . . at Potsdam'. Cavendish-Bentinck had previously raised these issues with President Bierut and had received a fairly hostile response. Bevin's letter to Cavendish-Bentinck continued: 'I had, on behalf of His Majesty's Government, acquiesced in extending the zone under Polish administration up to the Oder-Neisse' only after assurances from Bierut and colleagues.[79]

The British had hoped that their co-operation in acknowledging Polish administration as far west as the Oder would assist in the creation of a plural democracy and give the British some sway with the Soviets. However, by 18 July 1946, Bevin confided to the Prime Minister:

> In fact, looking back I think we made a mistake in accepting the Oder-Neisse line at Potsdam. It would have been better and given us greater pull on Russia if we had stuck our ground . . . The only hold I have is to leave them in some doubt (and I admit this is a slender one) as to whether we shall ever agree to the Oder-Neisse line.[80]

It is estimated that over 7.4 million Germans fled or were expelled from former German territory in the east and from Poland (Nitschke 2004: 60). The Soviets agreed to accept 2 million Germans into their zone and the British were committed to accept 1.5 million Germans into their zone of occupation in Germany. By February 1946, the technicalities of shifting 1.5 million people to the British zone had been finalized and by late February 1946 'Operation Swallow' was in progress, as trains rolled west filled with Germans.[81] These trains frequently returned to Poland carrying Poles who had been either prisoners of war or slave labour in the Reich.

'Operation Swallow' envisaged the movement of Germans from Poland to the British zone of occupation in Germany by four routes: one by sea and three by rail.[82] It was also hoped that Poles in displaced persons (DP) camps in Germany would return to Poland using the same transport. However, it was not long before difficulties emerged, with British concerns that the agreements reached at Potsdam in the summer of 1945 and the subsequent Allied Council Agreement of November were being breached, both to the disadvantage of the expellees and to British interests in Germany. By March 1946, the British had advised the Polish Military Mission in Berlin of their dissatisfaction. The main issues which required resolution included insufficient food given to the expellees, the short eviction notice and the consequent dearth of belongings held by the expellees and the fact that pregnant women, sick people and the very old and unfit were being expelled contrary to the agreement. The British liaison team stationed at Kaławsk was then 'directed to inform Polish authorities in Breslau . . . to ensure that the Berlin Agreement is fulfilled'.[83]

The British therefore gathered evidence regarding violence directed at the expellees, many of whom had had property confiscated at collection points, or had been robbed earlier on the journey from their homes to the collection point, beaten or raped. However, an effective response was only possible at the collection points where the Polish authorities were monitored by the British. Indeed, according to some expellees, in March 1946 'it was conspicuous that at Stettin when the British team arrived the Poles changed their ruthless and cruel methods to a more humane way of treatment'.[84]

Yet neither the British liaison teams nor the Polish authorities were always in control of the situation on the ground. During May 1946 an unofficial influx of people, at a rate of 700 people a day, caused a serious overcrowding problem at the departure point at Kaławsk.[85] By 5 June posters were put up to forbid unofficial entry to the town and to restore order to the transfer process. The British liaison team allowed trains to be filled to capacity to clear the area.[86]However, the issue of overcrowding was to reoccur and with far more serious consequences in the winter.

In May 1946 a series of notes was sent through the British section of the Control Commission reporting a slight improvement in the conduct of the expulsions, though the violence against expellees was also highlighted.[87] The third report on 'Operation Swallow' advised its readers in the Control Commission and the Foreign Office 'that responsibility for the lawlessness attributed to the Poles can be placed to the Polish youth of between 16 and 18 who now form part of what is known as the Militia'.[88]

By 6 July 1946 some 765,063 Germans had been moved to the British zone. By the end of the month, the arrival of destitute Germans in the British zone was causing such severe problems that there were calls for 'Operation Swallow' to 'cease immediately'.[89] Overcrowding was compounded by the fact that the expellees could 'not make any contribution to their own upkeep, or to any reconstruction of Germany by reason of their deplorable physical and economic condition and the extremely low percentage of potential workers amongst them'.[90]A further issue which was discussed by the British at this point was the fact that Jews from Poland were using forged papers to board 'Swallow' trains west to the British zone, so that by early August 1946 some 2,000 had arrived at the Hohne camp. Major General Erskine maintained the view that 'the only way to stop this Jewish movement, which is becoming large in scale is to close down "Operation Swallow"'.[91] The movement of Polish Jews west via 'Operation Swallow' was a continuous issue for the British. On the one hand they were committed to accept German expellees and on the other they wished to inhibit the movement of Jews to decrease pressure on the DP camps in Germany and to avoid complications in Palestine. Screenings at the collection points in Szczecin and Kaławsk frequently failed to identify Polish Jews attempting to leave Poland via 'Operation Swallow'. Indeed, train number 165, which arrived at Marienthal in the British zone on 19 May 1946, caused such concern that a full investigation was launched. Of the '2,028 people on board only 56 were genuine swallows', the rest were Jews.[92] The British were of the view that the 'illegal' movement of Jews was well organized and supported by Zionist organizations and a number of functionaries in UNRRA, though they did not fully appreciate the extent of the *Brichah*'s activity or the unofficial assistance lent to the movement of Jews out of Poland by members of the Ministry of Defence under Marian Spychalski.[93]

At the same time, the Polish authorities maintained pressure on the British to ensure the return of Poles from Germany – and Poles of the right quality. In a report of 13 April 1946, Brigadier Kenchington noted that the head of the Polish Military Mission in Berlin, Colonel Prawin, had complained about the high proportion of ex-Wehrmacht and ex-Polish Armed Forces personnel sent to Poland proving to be Volksdeutsch. Kenchington was moved to opine that 'he prefers, of course, to have racial Poles'.[94]

In addition, a newspaper report in *Trybuna Dolnośląska* from 24 March 1946 highlighted the 'scandalous British methods' used in transporting Poles from Germany to Poland, noting insufficient rations given to the Poles and very poor organization. The article finished with the sarcastic suggestion:

> It would be a good idea if British papers which publish so incredibly many stories on Polish brutality against German repatriates would convince themselves on the spot what the completely humane repatriation of Poles by the British HQs looks like in reality.[95]

This strategy of comparing the condition of transports of Polish repatriants and German expellees was used recurrently through 1946. But the sentiment that the British viewed German interests as more deserving of attention than Polish interests was popularized by the PPR to discredit oppositional groupings and those loyal to the Polish Government in Exile, as well as to maintain pressure on the British.

The British, for their part, generally dismissed criticism directed against them, largely because the trains used were the same ones that the Poles had provided for Germans.[96] And while Polish repatriants were vocal about the lack of heating stoves within carriages and blamed the British authorities for this deficiency, the British worked to redirect their complaints to those whom they held responsible – the Polish authorities.[97] In actuality, most carriages originally carried stoves, but many went missing as the trains passed through the Soviet zone of occupation in Germany and were not replaced.[98] Thus, both German expellees and Polish repatriants suffered in winter from the cold.

In Britain, throughout the second half of 1946, there was growing concern for the fate of the German expellees, generally organized through the 'Save Europe Now' group, though there was also parliamentary interest. The severe weather of December 1946, coupled with the lack of heating in most train carriages, resulted in a number of deaths and cases of frostbite. On train number 513 which arrived at Marienthal on 15 December 1946, with 1,885 passengers, four had died (two on board, two later), 106 were suffering from frostbite and 15 amputations were later performed. The next train (number 514) had only 8 stoves for 55 wagons. A total of 16 deaths and 57 cases of frostbite were recorded, provoking a British internal memo which advised readers that 'sending people in virtually unheated trains in this way in such conditions is a gross case of inhumanity'. Yet, the British liaison team in Kaławsk had approved the train's departure on the grounds that there was 'nowhere for the Germans to go', and that 'at least the train provided some shelter'.[99] The condition in which people arrived from Poland in the British zone scandalized British public opinion.[100] By late December 1946 'Operation Swallow' was suspended until 15 January 1947, initially on account of the bad weather, and was later cancelled as the British tallied the number of people received in the British zone.[101]

The British authorities recognized that they might be seen as complicit in the poor transportation of the expellees. On 8 February 1947 the deputy chief of the Political division at the Control Commission Headquarters wrote to the PoW/DP division, stating that:

> experience has shown that they [liaison teams] are powerless to prevent Germans from being transferred under inhumane conditions and their presence only serves as an excuse for the Poles to claim that the British authorities have approved the conditions under which the Germans have been expelled. [102]

In April 1947 Jakub Prawin requested the resumption of 'Operation Swallow', and by May he was attempting to cajole Brigadier Kenchington to accept more Germans into the British zone with the promise of a high percentage of able-bodied people. But, in June 1947, the British affirmed that the agreed 1.5 million people had been accepted – 1.4 million from Polish-administered territories and 100,000 via the American zone.[103]

The difficulties involved in transferring Germans out of Poland have to be placed in context. The British were well aware that the Polish authorities were under tremendous time pressure to resettle Poles from the east in the areas to be vacated by the Germans. This was spelled out as early as 19 December 1945 at a meeting attended by senior officials to be involved in the transfer process. Not only had the Polish–Soviet Treaty agreed that the transfer of Poles from the east would be completed by 15 June 1946, but the British representatives were also advised that the arrival of Poles in the 'Recovered Territories' was crucial 'to carry out the vital spring sowing', as without the 'resultant crops there will certainly be famine'.[104] As Kochanowski (2001: 138) points out, 'the forced migrations of Germans and Poles were contingent upon each other: The former had to vacate land for the other'. And, as the Germans frequently had to endure poor transport to new Germany, so too did Poles en route to new Poland. As early as September 1945, Stanisław Grabski highlighted the problems in a report to the Presidium of the KRN: the repatriants were 'unable to find shelter from rain or wind, and exposed to robbery at night. They could not go back to their homes because they had sold their flats and furniture'.[105] On a train delayed at the border between the Ukraine and Poland, 'repatriating' Poles in December 1945, four people froze to death (Kochanowski 2001: 143).

British public opinion was being managed to secure support for the Curzon line and the creation of a Polish nation-state, and was not informed of the conditions of the transfer of people from the USSR to Poland. The fate of the people of Britain's first wartime ally generally faded from view. But the impact of British and American acquiescence to Soviet territorial demands had consequences similar to those of the expulsion of Germans from Poland a year later, with a significant difference. The 'inhumane' treatment of Germans became a focus of British civil society campaigns and parliamentary questions in 1946 and 1947, yet there was more or less silence about the experience of those deported to new Poland.[106]

The postwar population transfers of the mid- to late 1940s in central and eastern Europe shifted several million people across borders, most of whom were forced to endure considerable hardship, loss of property, poor health and, for some, loss of life. Figure 2.1 illustrates the scale of the population movements.

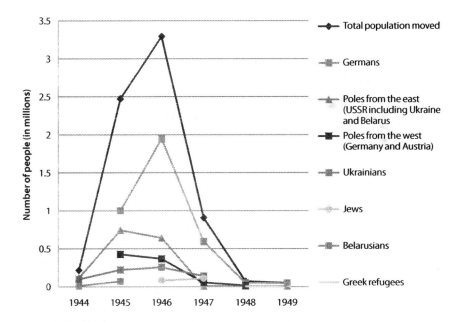

Figure 2.1 Population movements to and from Poland 1944–49.

Source: derived from data in Mironowicz (1993), Ther and Siljak (2001) and Eberhardt (2000).[107]

The movement of Jews

The experience of Polish Jews during this period is sufficiently different from that of the wider Polish population to warrant further discussion. Although the movement back to Poland of Jews who held Polish citizenship in 1939 was sanctioned by the various agreements that the PKWN signed with the Soviet republics in September 1944, their arrival in Poland was problematic. It is estimated that around 200,000 Jews in total returned from the USSR during 1944–48. Furthermore, the State Repatriation Office reported that, by 2 June 1945, 16,900 Jews had returned to Poland from Germany.[108] On the one hand the Provisional Government faced Zionist demands to facilitate Jewish movement out of Poland and, on the other, demands made by Bundists, members of the Jewish faction of the PPR, and PPS members that the Government assist in the rebuilding of Jewish life within the country. The Provisional Government also had to respond to the fairly widespread hostile social sentiment directed against the returning Jews. However, it soon became clear that, while the Government would support efforts to re-establish Jewish life, the form of this life would be strongly inflected by majoritarian norms. British officials monitoring the situation of Jews in Poland in August 1945 were of the view that 'the Polish government evidently continues to favour the Zionists'.[109] The British Ambassador in Warsaw considered that the Polish Government's policy was 'to encourage emigration of Jews and prevent emigration of Poles except in exceptional cases'.[110]

By January 1946 the position of the Polish Government in Warsaw regarding Polish Jews remained in tension. The bulletin of the Central Committee of Polish Jews of 26 January, quoted Prime Minister Osóbka-Morawski reiterating the Government position of helping Jews to rebuild their workplaces in Poland and assisting legal voluntary emigration.[111] This was followed on 29 April at the plenary session of the KRN, where Osóbka-Morawski defined the Polish Government position, which affirmed the 'full equality of all citizens regardless of race, nationality and creed' and which demanded that 'all citizens without prejudice are entitled to full care from the state and equal rights'. The Prime Minister also stated that

> the government will not, however, stop the emigration of those Jews who will wish to leave Poland. In the face of the tragedy suffered by the Jewish nation, Jews who wish it should have their national aspirations in Palestine facilitated.[112]

Organizations to help Polish Jews rebuild their lives in Poland were created, such as the 'Office of the Government Commissar relating to the Productivisation of the Jewish populace', and fora to allow Jewish perspectives to emerge, such as the Central Committee of Jews in Poland, were set up. There was a policy to redirect Jews away from occupations viewed by society as being 'Jewish' and retrain them so they could work in mainstream manufacturing and agriculture, and thus aid assimilation. Jews returning to Poland from the USSR were mainly resettled in the lands claimed from Germany, such as Lower Silesia.[113]

A leading figure among the re-establishing Jewish community in Lower Silesia was Jacob Egit. In his memoirs, published in 1991, he recalls that in June 1945 the Regional Central Committee in Lower Silesia wrote to the Minister of Public Administration, with several requests to facilitate the rebirth of the Jewish community there. Minister Edward Ochab replied positively to the request and, according to Egit (1991: 48), declared that 'we shall support you with your endeavours and with all the forces at our disposal'.

However, the movement of Jews out of Poland continued and, as indicated above, the commencement of 'Operation Swallow' provided the transport for many thousands to leave. So, while two trains arrived at Marienthal (late May and early June 1946) almost completely full of Jews, it has been contended that Swallow trains leaving Stettin (Szczecin) included an average of 200 Jews (Bauer 1970: 234). The scale of this illegal movement was not fully recognized by the British. Indeed, by June 1946 large numbers of Polish Jews had arrived in Szczecin from Łódź. The *Brichah* leaders in Szczecin claimed that these Jews were German Jews returning to Germany to reclaim property lost during the Nazi period. Łódź *Brichah* produced documents with false stamps affirming that their bearers were German, and *Brichah* people held talks with PUR representatives to prioritize the return of 'German' Jews to Germany. The degree to which actual German Jews who had survived returned to Germany in this way, and the extent to which the 'Swallow' trains provided an exit for Polish Jews cannot be conclusively ascertained. However, the *Brichah* had three representatives working for PUR in Szczecin, including Dolek Landau, who was manager of the registration division of section IV of PUR (Stankowski 1997: 117). Polish Jews were advised by PUR to claim that 'they are German Jews, that they are not to speak Polish, but only and exclusively in German or in a German dialect. Each such group had its elder who knew German' (Stankowski 1997: 117). In August 1946, a commission from PUR Warsaw inspected PUR Szczecin and, although they suspected that departing 'Swallow' trains included Polish Jews, they eventually allowed them to leave after checking the authenticity of the passengers' documents. Stankowski (1997: 118) contends that

> it is difficult to believe that the Polish authorities did not realise that the refugees' documents were false . . . and that the verbal agreement made in July 1946 between the Polish authorities and the Zionist Co-ordination regarding permission for emigration through Poland's southern border covered also the Szczecin section.

The movement of Jews out of Poland via the so-called 'Operation PUR' was closed down at the end of November 1946 after the British increased checks and an alternative route through the Russian zone into the French zone proved too difficult. It is estimated that, from June to October 1946, about 8,000–10,000 Jews left from Szczecin (Stankowski 1997: 119). Prior to this, during 1945, Jews crossed into Czechoslovakia en route to DP camps in the American zones of Austria and Germany.

After the Kielce pogrom of 1946 the rate of exit from Poland increased as the fear of becoming a victim of violence escalated, despite efforts by Bundists to convince Poland's Jewish population to remain. Indeed, by June 1946, the Bundist newspaper *Unsere Stimme* was concerned by the movement of Jews out of Poland and accused 'the Zionists of spreading and sowing despair and weakness among the Jewish masses purposely'.[114] The view that Poland was a graveyard in the aftermath of the Holocaust, the fact that the country was seen as unsafe for Jews and the promise of a better life in Palestine or elsewhere persuaded many to leave. In total, between July 1945 and December 1947, an estimated 126,000 Jews left Poland illegally (Stankowski 2000: 110, Bauer 1970: 287, 289).

The movement of Jews out of Poland from 1945 onwards remained a sore point with the British. By October 1946 the Americans were also concerned, given the pressure that arrivals from Poland were placing on US-run DP camps in Germany. Indeed, Theatre Commander General McNarney's speech from a press conference, in which he outlined the difficulties in the American zone created by the unregulated arrival of Jews, was forwarded to Władysław Wolski, Undersecretary of State responsible for repatriation affairs on 8 November 1946.[115]

Changing loyalties, continuation of policy, new complications

On 31 December 1944, the USSR unilaterally recognized the PKWN as the Provisional Government of Poland, while the USA and the United Kingdom continued to recognize the Polish Government in Exile based in London. This discrepancy was increasingly embarrassing during the first half of 1945 and was only resolved on 5 July 1945 when the USA and the United Kingdom formally recognized the Warsaw Government. This long-expected shift became politically possible when assurances were given that the basis of the Provisional Government would be broadened, and several prominent personalities returned to Poland to take up positions. The new Government of National Unity continued the nationality policy of the PKWN and, with the presence of well-known 'London' Poles amongst its ranks, such as Stanisław Grabski and Stanisław Mikołajczyk among others, was able to persuade tens of thousands of Poles in Western Europe to return to Poland.[116]

However, not all governments withdrew recognition of the London-based Polish Government, and it continued to function. Through its emissaries in DP camps in Germany and Italy, it played an important role in reducing the number of Poles returning to Poland and in facilitating the mass settlement of Poles in the United Kingdom after 1946.[117] For the British, the presence of the Government in Exile in London, and General Anders' Second Corps in Italy, as well as tens of thousands of Polish DPs in Germany and Austria who refused to return to Poland, became increasingly problematic. Indeed, Anders' antipathy towards the Warsaw Government was well-known, and the British twice reprimanded him for his outspoken comments about the international situation. Furthermore, Captain Zdzisław Stahl, director of press relations for the Polish Second Corps, justified the taking of Polish children from DP camps in Germany to Polish military camps in Italy by arguing that

> if a Polish child of ten is allowed to go back to Poland, he will be Sovietized and will grow up in a different culture and way of thinking, nationalist in form and Soviet in substance. We want to save as many of these as possible.[118]

The notion that the political situation in Poland, with the communists hegemonic under Soviet tutelage, would change, probably as a result of a third global conflagration, guided the thinking of many senior officers loyal not only to Anders, but to the Polish Government in Exile.

Thus, despite the recognition of the Warsaw Government, British–Polish relations remained tense due to the continued existence of a Polish government in London claiming legitimacy, the declarations of a well-respected military leader and the fact that over a hundred thousand Polish military personnel refused to return to Poland. By the time the British decided to allow those Poles who would not go back to Poland to come to Britain in 1947, East–West dissonance was on the rise. Before examining that issue we now turn to how the PPR managed to secure a degree of acquiescence through its management of the social anger regime.

3   Manipulating social anger

Over the past decade there has been renewed scholarly interest in the work of the German political and legal theorist Carl Schmitt. This may seem surprising to many, given Schmitt's compromise with Nazism, yet his work has provided the basis for several leftist critiques of contemporary democratic practice.[1] These include David Ost's (2005) examination of Solidarity in the post-communist period in Poland, Chantal Mouffe's (2005) discussion of what constitutes 'the political' and the Italian philosopher Giorgio Agamben's (1998) examination of sovereign power and the Nazi concentration camps.

For Mouffe and Ost, Schmitt's insistence that societies are structured around an adversarial We/They dichotomy reflects reality more truthfully than the notions of theorists who contend that such a dichotomy has been overcome. For Agamben (1998), the idea of the exception, or rather she/he who decides the exception, has been a productive way to analyse the meaning of sovereignty and bio-politics. Agamben's exploration of the status and functionality of the figure of *homo sacer* offers insight into the condition of minorities in postwar Poland.[2]

Here, the strand of Schmitt's thought which is taken up is the same as that considered by Mouffe and Ost: the centrality of the We/They dichotomy to the political. Pursuing this line overcomes some of the perceived inadequacies of liberal political theory in dealing with collective identities, and allows a fuller investigation of the state/society/social anger matrix. For, as Chantal Mouffe (2005: 14) argues: 'despite what many liberals want us to believe, the specificity of democratic politics is not the overcoming of the We/They opposition but the different way in which it is established'. Schmitt's contention that *the political* 'can be understood only in the context of the friend/enemy grouping, regardless of the aspects which this possibility implies for morality, aesthetics and economics' (Schmitt 1976: 35) invites us to think in terms of collectivities which constitute the polity, to explore how each specific collectivity engages with others and to seek out the borderlines between friend and enemy. Where liberal theory frequently collapses non-resolvable positions to points of compromise and sustained dialogue, as in deliberative models and aggregative models, an adversarial understanding of the political singularly fails to do so. The merit of this approach is that exclusions are clear and apparent, rather than opaque and frequently denied. It also mirrors the understanding of practitioners in the mid-1940s, for whom exclusion of some from the polity was an objective. Thus, the discussion below is guided by an understanding of politics that is adversarial in substance, and presents PPR policy as the attempt to construct hegemony within a frequently hostile polity, without prematurely polarizing the relationship between Party and Society. The 'We/They' division was drawn through both the Party and Society, and the key co-ordinate to locate the shifting borderline was the PPR's, and later the PZPR's, nationality policy.

So, while the language of class was emphasized in the building of socialism in the aftermath of war, so too was the language of nation.[3] The task facing the PPR was how these two languages could be reconciled in a way that would solicit social support for itself and its programme. This issue was complicated by the way in which social anger (discussed below) had been structured by the experience of several years of brutal war, memories of Soviet/Nazi collaboration between 1939–41, and Soviet Army and NKVD actions on Polish territory during the 'liberation' and immediately afterwards.

The notion of social anger elaborated here echoes David Ost's (2005: 21) view of the connection between anger and structure: 'all social systems generate popular anger, but they do so in different ways and with different results'. Thus, within social system A, the development of popular anger will be different from that generated by system B. However, the way in which the sentiment of social anger is manifested is inflected by the way it is politically elaborated. What this means is that anger can be guided and organized by political actors to achieve various political objectives. Ost's main argument that 'the structural nature of the political and economic system shapes how and against whom we are able to express our anger' is thus expanded to include systems in flux. In addition to the structure of the political and economic system and the guidance provided by political elites, social anger is also constituted by a series of sedimented social practices formed under previous social relations and events. As an example, consider the anti-Semitism expressed in the textile mills and factories of Łódź and the dearth of such expressions in Wrocław during the period 1945 to early 1946. Kenney (1997: 111) maintains that, 'in 1945, anti-Semitic incidents or statements appeared to express memories of pre-war antagonisms' in Łódź, while in Lower Silesia 'there were no examples of anti-Jewish demonstrations like those in central Poland' (Kenney 1997: 156). In Łódź, historical stereotypes were resurrected as Poles attempted to re-establish pre-war labour traditions, where Jews were conceptualized as being either managers or shop owners – that is, part of the exploitative strata, while in Lower Silesia the lack of such narratives, a consequence, in part, of the widespread anomie concomitant to population displacement, inhibited anti-Semitic expressions. In addition, while in central Poland, including Łódź, the issue of property restitution often played a role in fostering anti-Jewish senti-ment, in former German lands in Silesia property claims could not be similarly used.

The way in which social anger is actually expressed is conditional, as the relation between the social and the political remains unstable and requires continuous intervention. The triangular model of social anger outlined above – the fundamental role of the political and economic system, elite guidance/management and social sedimentation/memory – indicates that the expression of social anger can take many forms, but not any form. There are clear limits imposed by the political and economic system and social sedimentation, but also considerable flexibility, allowing political elites to choose from a variety of possible narratives to describe particular con-junctures.

This model of social anger highlights the material basis of anger, but recognizes that the relationship with the 'ideal' – that is, elite guidance/ management – and the 'cognitive' (social sedimentation/memory) is not linear or simply derivative. At best, political actors are engaged in a contin-uous project of shaping the anger regime, which, once hegemonic, leaves traces (social sedimentation/memory) even as an alternative narrative supersedes it.

Conceptualized in this way, the task of the PPR, and later the PZPR, was to shape the anger regime to its advantage, drawing on those resources embedded in society which could be mobilized and rejecting those hostile to its project. In this, nationality policy was to be fundamental, for it was through nationality policy and practice that those to be included and excluded constituted the new polity, while at the same time it helped to collapse the languages of nation and class to a unitary We/They dichotomy.

Thus, despite proclamations of equality and assertions that chauvinism would not be tolerated, the PPR and PZPR incorporated rather than challenged in any meaningful way the anti-minority discourses latent within society. As Michlic (2006: 208) has pointed out:

> The increasing intolerance of minorities, manifested in open hostilities towards Jews and also Slavic groups, was one of the chief features of early post-war life. Despite its various political and ideological declara-tions, the PPR not only failed to alleviate interethnic tensions but in fact contributed to sustaining ethnic tensions.

This insight raises questions about the relative strengths of the political and economic system (in formation), social sedimentation and the role played by elite guidance on the expression of social anger in the immediate after-math of the Second World War. The degree of freedom the PPR and PZPR had in developing nationality policy in the context of internationally agreed population transfers/expulsions and Stalin's 'ethno-nationalist' vision also has to be assessed. These issues are discussed below.

Grounding social anger

The notion of social anger articulated by Ost (2005) rests on the assumption of fairly stable social relations embedded within a specific political and economic system. It is persuasive, as such systems can be recognized and cleavages within societies that are structured in particular and defined ways can be easily identified. The problems of communist systems, such as a shortage economy, lack of democratic participation and the proclaimed totality of Party hegemony, helped to structure protest though not to determine the form it took. In *established* communist systems political power is transparent – that is, everyone knows who is responsible for decisions – and the Party and the system it defends are the natural recipients of negative emotions produced in society. However, Ost's (2005: 21) assertion that 'power transparency means that social anger is naturally directed at a common target; the anger requires no organisation', needs to be qualified. *Because* of power transparency and the relatively automatic organizing of social anger against the Party, it is absolutely essential that the common target (the Party) finds or creates alternative targets for the expression of negative emotions and passions in order to sustain a modicum of legitimacy. In communist Poland these targets were often minority communities.

Complications emerge when societies in systemic flux are considered. Although the communists maintained authority in Poland more or less from the foundation of the Lublin Committee in July 1944, this was contested both within and without Poland by the Polish Government in Exile, even after July 1945 when the Western Allies recognized the Provisional Government (Government of National Unity). At the very least, until July 1945, the political system in Poland was unsettled, notwithstanding the disciplining impact of the Soviet Army and NKVD on both communists and non-communists. Indeed, intelligence reports reaching Britain from Poland in the period from March to July 1945 highlighted the actions of the NKVD, including mass arrests and deportations to Soviet Russia. Analysts in London felt that the reports were exaggerated and, on 17 March 1945, restricted reports to a limited readership within the Foreign Office, despite news that the NKVD was 'arresting people for their political views'.[4]

Even after July 1945 the political system remained, to some degree, in a state of flux; 1946 saw the harassment and intimidation of the Polish People's (Peasant) Movement (PSL) by the PPR; 1947 saw the rigged election and the flight of Mikołajczyk from Poland, fearing for his life, in November of that year. Following the crushing of the opposition, the PPR merged with a rump PPS to form the PZPR in December 1948 and affirmed its monopoly on power.

The economic system was also in considerable turmoil in the aftermath of war. The basis of the economy had to be refounded: first, in accordance with the new territorial configuration, and, second, with regard to the greater control of the state over the means of production. The land reform decrees of 6 September 1944 and 17 January 1945 aimed to increase the size of farms of less than 5 hectares, create new farms for land tenants, farm workers and craftsmen, provide plots for town residents, reserve plots for agricultural schools and increase medium land holdings to between 5–10 hectares. It also transferred holdings of more than 50 hectares to the state, allowing previous owners to apply for holdings outside the district of their former farms or obtain a monthly allowance. Those people who 'took a conspicuous part in the fight against the German invaders' were awarded a larger allowance, though this was largely restricted to those in communist organizations and did not include those in the main Polish resistance groups associated with the Polish Government in Exile such as the Home Army (AK). There was no compensation for German citizens or their allies, those sentenced for treason, those who assisted the German invasion, those who acted against the state or local populace, deserted or evaded military service.[5] In addition to depriving Germans of their land, the land reform decrees gave the PPR considerable latitude in favouring some social groups at the expense of others, especially since, through the September 1944 decrees, the district land office was given responsibility for executing the land reform, which was subordinated to the PKWN's department of agriculture.[6] The land decrees linked the social and national revolutions. It is worth noting that, while the decree of 6 September 1944 earmarked all rural real estate belonging to citizens of German ethnic status for agrarian reform purposes, the amending decree of 17 January 1945 expanded the reform by using the expression 'non-Poles' in its introduction.[7] In 1945, three-quarters of the population were involved in agriculture, meaning that most of the population had some interest in the land reform. Furthermore, the Catholic Church's holdings were excluded from the land reform decrees, as Korbonski (1965: 70) points out, due to their relatively small size and to avoid offending the sensibilities of the population.

There is evidence that the second question of the 1946 referendum relating to the economy: 'Do you want the new constitution to safeguard the economic system introduced by the land reform and nationalisation of the basic branches of the national economy while preserving the rights of private initiative?' was rejected. Dudek and Zblewski (2008: 46) summarize the results, which show that 42% of the population endorsed the proposition, while 58% were against.[8] However, the result had its own geography, with major cities such as Warsaw and Łódź, and voivodships in the 'Recovered Territories' such as Wrocław, Olsztyn and Szczecin, being in favour.[9] Other places, for example Wielkopolska, rejected the proposition, which suggested that the land reforms were not as popular in some locations as the PPR had hoped.[10] Even the opposition PSL endorsed a positive answer to the second question. The reasons for the locally-specific negative response to the second question are multiple, but most salient were peasants' suspicion of the PPR and of change more generally, as well as the varied intensity of PPR propaganda. The actions of the Soviet Army, which confiscated crops and seeds, no doubt undermined belief that the reforms would be beneficial for those earning their living by working small patches of land. Since the PPR 'fixed' the results of the referendum, what should have been a setback for its reform agenda had no effect and the Party proceeded to implement its policies. It nevertheless faced formidable problems, given the crisis of agriculture in the country.

The problems facing farming in Poland were summed up in the United Nations Relief and Rehabilitation (UNRRA) report entitled *Agriculture and Food in Poland* (July 1946), which advised its readers that Poland's production of and stock of food goods were substantially below pre-war figures: wheat 62 per cent, rye 57 per cent, potatoes 51 per cent, livestock 33 per cent, horses 50 per cent and sheep 33 per cent of the pre-war levels.[11] These figures had not significantly improved from nine months earlier when Hilary Minc, the head of the Economic Planning Commission and architect of the three-year plan, advised colleagues at a plenary session of the PPR Central Committee in October 1945 that production was 50 per cent of its pre-war level, and endorsed efforts to obtain grain from UNRRA to provide foodstuffs to the Recovered Territories.[12]

The chaos and instability in the 'Recovered Territories' continued until late 1947 and early 1948, when the Warsaw Government was able to exert greater control. Up to that point, the Soviet military authorities failed to control their soldiers' excesses, which included robbery, rape and murder.[13] This clearly had an adverse impact on the image of the PPR, which could neither control its ally nor publicly criticize the conduct of her troops.

The period up to late 1947 has been characterized by Kenney (1997: 4) as a time of social and economic revolution. Workers were celebrated and economic assets transferred to the state. After that point, the PZPR proceeded to claim increasing control over the state and society. Thus, identifying the main sources of social anger consequent on a political and economic system in flux is considerably more complex than in societies with established political and economic systems, and requires a sensitive reading of the historical record. But there can be little doubt that with the ascendancy of the PZPR in 1948 the structural basis of the social anger which was to be manifested over the next several decades was laid. Prior to 1948 there were many sources of tension, allowing considerable space for different narratives to be mooted, propagated and reformulated by elites from the different parties. Neither the economic nor political system was stablized, though the general form and direction was fairly clear as early as late 1945, and opposition to communist rule was of such intensity that many authors describe the period up to late 1947 as one of civil war (Prażmowska 2004).[14]

As a result, the assumption that, in the final analysis, the economic system is primary has to be qualified by the fact that the economic system had yet to be settled, with UNRRA aid playing a key role in preventing famine during the harsh winter of 1946. The fact that the PPR dominated government and was able to manage (and claim credit for) the distribution of this aid throughout the country was not only a propaganda coup, but also gave credibility to its claims of economic competence, while problems could still be explained away by reference to wartime damage and those opposed to the PPR. The fact that the PPR could not *fully* exploit its role in the distribution of aid and, more importantly, the distribution of land in the 'Recovered Territories' owes much to the lack of control that the PPR was able to exercise over the Soviet Army. In November 1945, for example, Leon Dąbrowski of the PPR district committee in Wielun in the Łódź voivodship reported how Soviet soldiers committed various outrages and then killed a 19-year-old youth.[15] As late as January 1946 Władysław Gomułka complained to Soviet commanders about the appalling conduct of Soviet soldiers. This was compounded by the shifting of plant and other materials out of Poland to the Soviet Union, as well as the deportation of up to 200,000 people, mainly from Silesia, to the USSR for slave labour, 10 per cent of whom are thought to have been of Polish origin (Kulczycki 2001: 213).

In short, during the immediate aftermath of the Second World War, the serious shortages, general confusion about the real economic situation in the country and large-scale theft by Soviet soldiers and administrators, coupled with the fact that the population itself was in flux as people returned home or were settled in new places, complicated the relationship between the economic system and the articulation of social anger, but its general outline was decipherable. For, as Hilary Minc argued at the February 1945 plenum of the PPR, Lublin Poland was capitalist but '[i]t was a capitalist system different from all the others without historical precedent ... a capitalist system without the capitalists in political command'.[16]

The geography of the anger generated by the emerging economic system varied across the country. In places where the population had not been displaced by war, the replacement of capitalist owners by the state was not understood as a qualitative change – hence striking to improve wages remained a legitimate strategy. The real weakness of the economy could not be explained away in places with established bonds of solidarity. Strikes did indeed break out in Łódź in the summer of 1945. The Łódź voivodship PPR committee, analysing the strikes in August 1945, noted their political and anti-Semitic character.[17] And, as Kenney (1997: 109) points out, strikes at the Kindler mill, Pabiance, in October 1945, and in various mills and factories in Łódź during 1945 and 1946, also expressed strong anti-minority sentiments and justifications (anti-German and anti-Jewish respectively). In contrast, in frontier zones such as Lower Silesia, anger took some years to become structured, while, in the east of the country, established myths linking minorities, especially Jews and Belarusians, to communism helped many to account for the difficult living conditions.

Before considering how social anger was guided, it is necessary to outline briefly the impact which the traditional understandings of social relations had on shaping social anger.

Social sedimentation/memory/tradition

Taking late 1947 and early 1948 as a dividing line in the establishment of communism is useful for several reasons, one of which is to allow detailed examination of how society in Poland understood what was happening prior to the consolidation of power by the PZPR. Furthermore, the PPR took great interest in people's perceptions and monitored rumours, myths and storytelling throughout Poland in the immediate aftermath of the Second World War. The PPR was attempting to assess the mood in the country and, given its claim to represent the working class, it undertook the task with some diligence.[18] As with all projects assessing social opinion, a dialectic exists between what is *out there* and what is expected, whether consciously or subconsciously; no translation of reality captures that reality in its full complexity. Communists, too, remained part of history, and their prejudices and attitudes influenced what was deemed important enough to record and report. Thus, given the 1935 switch in communist nationality policy, the PPR's commitment to be a 'Polish' party and the ongoing transfer/expulsion programmes, a tendency to record anti-minority sentiments was to be expected. Such sentiments were fairly widespread.

On 11 August 1945, the same day as the Kraków pogrom, at a meeting of the Central Committee of the PPR, it was noted that PSL activists had protested against the inclusion of Jews in the Peasant Self-Help Union and had expressed anti-Semitic sentiments (Michlic 2006: 204). In Łódź anti-Semitic sentiments frequently framed workers' discontent. Indeed, in 1946 Jewish leaders in the city received reports of a planned pogrom in the Bałuty area and were able to prevent it (Kenney 1997: 115).

In the Białystok region sentiment against the Belarusian minority was expressed through negative stereotypes, which depicted Belarusians as communists. Like the Jews, Belarusians were alleged to have co-operated with the Soviets during the occupation period of 1939–41. There also existed some suspicion that, as Orthodox Christians, they represented a fifth column, aiming to Russify the border region. In the south-east of the country, anti-Ukrainian feeling often broke out into violence.

Overall, one can conclude that anti-minority sentiment was fairly high in Poland in the aftermath of war. Belarusian and Jewish minorities were identified with communism, with the wider society drawing on pre-war stereotypes promulgated by factions linked to National Democracy. For, although the demographic situation in Poland had changed considerably, and 90 percent of Poland's pre-war Jewish community had been murdered in the Holocaust – over three million people – pre-war imagining of inter-community relations continued to guide action. Indeed, the British Ambassador to Poland wrote to the Foreign Office in London on 18 December 1945, advising that:

The Jewish population has decreased from 3,250,000 in 1939 to 80,000. This has not lessened anti-Semitic feeling, and the determination of the Poles to monopolize trade will make the position of the 180,000 Jews expected to return from Russia very hard.

He continued that, '[b]efore the war the Poles had on the whole been strongly anti-Semitic . . . The Poles appear to me to be as anti-Semitic as they were 25 years ago'.[19] Though Cavendish-Bentinck's appraisal is not unproblematic in its generalizations and unqualified use of the Pole-anti-Semite stereotype, it does give a clear indication that in late 1945 the situation for Jews was particularly uninviting.

Michlic (2006) examines the image of the Jew from 1880 to the present. She argues that the Polish ethno-nationalists on the Right – from National Democracy, National Armed Forces (NSZ), and right-wing segments of Freedom and Independence (WiN) – 'categorized the Communist takeover of power as a takeover with a "Semitic face" – the rule of Judeo-Communism' (Michlic 2006: 200). The linkage of Jews with communism was a long-standing stereotype repeatedly promulgated both by the Right and the Catholic Church in Poland. Yet that is all it ever was – a stereotype. Research conducted by Andrzej Paczkowski (2001) has shown the limited number of Jews in the communist security apparatus.[20] However, this stereotype is still being promoted, most recently by Chodakiewicz (2003).[21] Excluding Chodakiewicz's argument, two different positions explaining anti-Jewish sentiment in the aftermath of war have been advanced recently. On the one hand, it is understood as the continuation of pre-war animosity expressed by the various factions linked to National Democracy and also the Catholic Church (Michlic 2006). On the other hand, Jan Gross (2006) sees Polish conduct during the war as being particularly important. Gross (2006: 256) has contended that 'Jews were so frightening and dangerous . . . not because of what they had done or could do to the Poles, but because of what Poles had done to the Jews'.[22] Animosity directed towards Jews was the consequence.

Though not mutually exclusive, the relative weighting of the time frames differentiates the two positions. Gross's argument rests on a contestable view of Polish conduct during the Second World War, and, while anti-Jewish activities ranging from informing Nazi occupation authorities of hiding places to mass murder, as happened around Łomża in the summer of 1941, suggest widespread anti-Jewish sentiment, there is also evidence of Polish assistance to Jews.[23] As Gunnar Paulsson (2002: 230) argues in relation to the situation in Warsaw, 'but for the Hotel Polski and the Warsaw Uprising, the survival rate among Jews in hiding in Warsaw would have been about the same as that in Western Europe, contrary to all expectations and contemporary perceptions'.[24]

Paulsson (2002: 111) highlights the fact that, 'though the number of "hooligans" who were prepared to betray Jews was small, Jews in hiding had so many encounters with them that their overall chances of survival were significantly diminished', and agrees with Helen Fein's (1979) view that progressive elements of Polish society regarded the Jews as outside their 'universe of obligation'.[25] This, he notes, was not

> the result of some Polish policy of apartheid, but as agreed by mutual consent for centuries... it protected Jews from assimilation... [but]... when they desperately needed their neighbours' help... [they]... found them, even when friendly, preoccupied with their own affairs (Paulsson 2002: 42).

Furthermore, given that members of other minority groups were victims of violence and marginalization at the hands of the wider society in the immediate postwar period, exclusive focus on Polish wartime conduct is extremely problematic. Certainly, Gross's thesis with regard to Polish fear of Jews as motivating violence against them in the postwar period is not as persuasive if placed in a comparative perspective with the violence perpetuated against other minority groups and with the insights of the research conducted by Paulsson.

This suggests that the longer time frame is key to understanding attitudes to minority communities in the postwar period. For it was through various *idées fixes* created and propagated by the different factions of National Democracy during the interwar period, and by its nationalist precursors, that caricatures of minority collaboration with occupying forces could assume the status of social truth. And it is worth noting that stereotypes of minorities' sympathy for communism were not just confined to large sections of the Polish population. Even British analysts in the Foreign Office (FO) failed to question widespread (negative) stereotypes about Polish Jews, for example. Indeed, during the internal Foreign Office discussion in July 1944 about Roman Knoll's secret letter to Tadeusz Romer, segments of which had found their way into the public domain, a Mr Walker, commenting on an extensive analysis by the FO's Poland expert, Fred Savery, claimed that 'the Jewish population of Poland will tend to look towards the USSR – Jews always do, and that may cause difficulties with the native Poles . . . There is no remedy'.[26]

Although anti-minority sentiment had its roots in the pre-war and pre-independence period, and such sentiments were 'legitimated' to some degree by the internationally sanctioned programme of national homogeneity, it was by no means inevitable that social anger would be so forcefully directed against minorities. Even if the view is taken that the experience of the Second World War increased the social distance between the varied national groups within Poland, a believable narrative needed to be created to motivate action. Alternatives could have been promulgated which would have eased, though probably not eradicated, anti-minority feeling. As Knoll reported in the summer of 1943, 'the prevalent mood amongst the peasant population is that a post-war Poland has to be purely ethnically Polish'.[27]

Ethno-nationalism – guiding social anger

As shown in Chapter 2, there was widespread consensus at both the international level and within the Polish political elite (whether based in London or in Moscow or, later, in Lublin), that the future Polish state would be nationally homogeneous. The presence of minorities was deemed antithetical to state stability. Yet, while such consensus existed at the level of high policy, the practicalities of achieving such a goal were both difficult and complex.

Furthermore, and perhaps more importantly, the underlying view that minorities constituted a danger not only for individual states, but also for the wider European state system, was not contested. The problem with such a perception was that it essentialized minority communities. By nature they were dangerous for the majority. So, while at the international level attention was focused on German minority communities and the problems they caused in the interwar period, justifying mass population transfers and expulsion, other minorities were also seen as problematic.

However, there remained some ambiguity at both the international and national level. For example, there was international outcry when part of Roman Knoll's secret document to Tadeusz Romer was leaked, prompting the Government in Exile to deny knowledge of it through media announcements in New York and Palestine, as well as through detailed discussions with representatives from the British Foreign Office.[28]

The international anti-minority climate, the unquestioned belief that a homogeneous nation state would both be strong and avoid the problems of the interwar period, helped to frame and justify anti-minority sentiment in Poland itself. The PPR's drive to national homogeneity reflected Stalin's geopolitical ambitions in eastern Europe, the PPR's desire to be seen as a Polish party and its need to redirect social anger. The Government in Exile did not face such pressures.[29] Yet a more pluralist conception of the future demographic composition of Poland was not expressed by the Polish Government in London.

The position of the PPR was highly ambivalent. On the one hand, it attempted to define itself as Polish through ethno-nationalist rhetoric and, on the other hand, it guaranteed the equality of all citizens. It confronted an opposition – the PSL until 1947 – which either remained silent on the issue of minorities in Poland (the leadership was playing to both domestic and international audiences), or which mobilized the Jewish-Communist stereotype (low-level activists) to discredit the PPR in the eyes of the wider society. For example, Michlic (2006: 203) quotes a PSL activist at a meeting on 19 August 1945, who claimed that, 'This is a Jewish Poland. Jews are occupying all high positions in the Public Security Office. They should be arresting Jews, not Poles.'

The irony of the PPR's ethno-nationalist agenda was that it had more in common with Roman Dmowski's vision than with traditional communist ideals as Zaremba (2001: 140) points out. The PPR legitimated anti-minority discourses but it was not able completely to control how such discourses were understood, appropriated and remade by the wider population. As Knoll's report of 1943 and Karski's earlier report of 1940 showed, anti-minority and, in particular, anti-Jewish sentiment was fairly widespread.[30] It was one thing for the PPR to align itself with general social sentiment and to mobilize centrifugal ethno-nationalist arguments, quite another to control how society responded. Indeed, in 1945 and later, it was but a small step for the population to reuse (continue to use) the stereotypes of National Democracy to describe the PPR as a Jewish-Communist clique – the very thing the PPR leadership wished to avoid.

It is in this context that Władysław Gomułka's nationalist line has to be understood. Gomułka spent the war years in Poland and was attuned to social sentiment in the country. His earlier efforts to moderate Polish ethno-nationalism, as exemplified in the December 1943 paper, *Our relations with the Germans*, which criticized Nazi efforts to divide Poles from Germans, and reflected established internationalist traditions, had come to nothing.[31] However, Gomułka's discussions with comrades from Moscow clarified to him the nationalist line being promoted, and he soon became its main backer. He was aware that the Communist Party of Poland (KPP) had been seen as being dominated by minority populations, which the 1935 policy modification did little to change.

Georgi Dimitrov, the Comintern official responsible for Polish affairs (and later the official on the international section of the Soviet Party after Comintern was dissolved in 1943), supported a nationalist line. It was considered fundamental that the Party did everything that it could to identify itself as Polish – both to attract adherents in Poland and to deflect criticism that it was a Soviet interloper. Yet there remained tension between the emancipatory rhetoric inherent within its 'Marxist' agenda and the prioritization of part (albeit the majority) of the population on the basis of essentialized criteria.

The political problem facing the PPR had no easy solution. First, the party was small, and, in 1944 and 1945, desperately needed to expand its social base in order to secure at least a modicum of legitimacy within Polish society.[32] Second, it rightly understood that society's toleration of minorities had collapsed during the course of the Second World War, and that an ethnocentric world view which demarcated Polishness in opposition to other national and religious groups had become hegemonic. Third, it also recognized that within society there had been a leftist shift on economic issues and property ownership.

Hilary Minc, a key member of the PPR Central Committee, clearly understood the connection between securing a wider base for the PPR, the war and the promulgation of the PPR social reform programme, arguing at the February 1945 plenum of the PPR that:

> [t]he characteristics of the People's Revolution, therefore, have been its organization from above and its links with the war of national libera- tion. This made possible the neutralisation of part of the bourgeoisie which was threatened with extermination by the occupying authority and which therefore joined the National Front.[33]

Although Minc's reading of the population's war alliances and the form of the 'National Front' bears little connection to reality, his contention does illuminate a deeper truth: that the PPR needed to show that it had played a fundamental role in the 'liberation' of Poland from Nazi occupation, and that it was through national rhetoric that 'class' opposition could be over- come – ('neutralise the bourgeoisie'). Thus 'class' opposition could be iden- tified as 'unpatriotic'; this was a strategy used repeatedly in the immediate aftermath of war and especially in the attacks on the PSL in 1946 and 1947.

The leftist shift on economic and social issues by the population of the country was also noticed by the Government in Exile, whose quasi- parliament in Poland, the Council of National Unity (RJN), advocated a planned economy, the state's right to nationalize industry and far-reaching land reform which would leave the question of compensation to previous owners to be resolved by a future parliament.[34] So, while the RJN main- tained unity out of fear of the PPR, the PPR's initial programme had much in common with that proposed by the opposition. The main differences were related to the issues of foreign policy, in particular the relationship with the Soviet Union and, as became increasingly clear during the course of 1946, the commitment to a plural democratic system.

The PPR and the Government in Exile came to similar conclusions about the mood in the country in 1944 and understood that large swathes of the population were desirous of increased national homogeneity and radical socio-economic reform. The position of the RJN reflected the various strengths of the parties which constituted it, and its manifesto of March 1944 (*What the Polish nation is fighting for*) has to be recognized as an uneasy compromise specific to its time and place. Neither the PPR or the RJN had complete freedom to manoeuvre, but the changing war situation, especially after the failure of the Warsaw Rising of 1944 and the Moscow conference of October of that year, reconfigured the relative balance of power between the RJN and the PPR. The PPR's nationalist line presented opportunities to co-opt National Democrats, while its radical socio-economic policies opened avenues for co-operation with Socialists.

Pursuing an agenda which had an established constituency within the country not only allowed the PPR to claim that it represented 'Polish' inter- ests, but enabled it to shift the entire political discourse on nationality issues to the Right, and effectively to close more pluralist possibilities. No criticism from the Left in relation to the PPR's nationality policy could be successfully articulated.[35] The Labour and Socialist parties, which might have attempted to do so, were neutered by their alliance with National Democrats and their awareness of the sentiment in the country. Given this degree of consensus, the PPR's task was to ensure that the population identified it with the new territorial and socio-economic configurations, to enable it to reap the political benefits and to direct dissent against those groups whose incorporation into the polity was to be circumscribed and parenthesized. This remained particularly important given that the PPR could not criticize the Soviet Union, whose soldiers in 1945 and 1946 were considered a 'universal plague' due to their violence and thieving in the area around Gorzów and in many other places where they were stationed (Curp 2001: 585).

From 1945 the PPR publicized several slogans which sought to affirm the Polishness of the Party and claimed that its primary goal was to defend the interests of the masses. Slogans such as – 'Polish patriots join the ranks of the PPR!' (Patriota polski wstępuje w szeregi PPR) implied that any other political affiliation was unpatriotic, while 'Peasants! Stop the landlords returning, join the ranks of PPR!' (Chłopie! By nigdy już nie powrócił obszarnik, wstąp w szeregi PPR) and 'PPR fights speculators and looters. Join its ranks!' (PPR bije w spekulantów i szabrowników. Wstąp w jej szeregi) spoke to the aspirations of the workers and peasants.[36]

The importance of maintaining an anti-minority stance was clearly understood throughout the structures dominated by the PPR. The slogan 'Man in the right place' was promulgated to justify the expulsions and population transfers in the so-called Recovered Territories.[37] In the interparty Committee of People's Voting Affairs, the slogan '3 × yes = Poland without national minorities' (3 × tak – to Polska bez mniejszości narodowych) was accepted prior to the 1946 referendum.[38]

Gomułka's speech at the plenum of the PPR's Central Committee on 20–21 May 1945 set out the PPR's general position. There was to be zero tolerance for Germans in the west. Gomułka argued that 'the Germans must be expelled and those who stay get the kind of treatment that will not encourage them to stay' – which became reality during the period of wild expulsions a month later. He insisted that 'We should simply clear out the Germans and build a national state'. The objective of building a national state included controlling the type of recruits to the PPR and its structures. Gomułka was clearly displeased that 2,000 people taken in by the director of the personnel department were 'all obviously Jews by their appearance and speaking Polish with a poor accent. This was a cheap trick . . . Our party cannot be like the PPS or SL. The party must be controlled.'[39]

Gomułka had taken the view that the Party should prioritize ethnic Poles in order to align itself with widespread social sentiment and to strengthen its position in the battles which it chose to fight with the opposition. And each of the confrontations over the course of 1945 to late 1947 and early 1948 saw the PPR narrate political differences in a language which unified discourses of class and nation. Oppositionists were described as reactionaries, bourgeois and unpatriotic. The conflict with the PSL clearly illustrates this point.

In September 1946 the US Secretary of State, James Byrnes, delivered a speech in Stuttgart in which he suggested that the question of the Polish–German border should be reconsidered. The response of the PPR was swift. Its Central Committee, together with the PPS's Supreme Executive Committee, published an open letter which asked the population,

> are you ready together with us to defend the western borders of Poland, to oppose the Byrneses and Churchills, and explain to all nations of the world that they are acting against peace, against Poland, and on behalf of the Germans?[40]

This open letter has, rightly, been taken as the beginning of the final chapter of the PPR's fight against the PSL. The difficult co-operation which characterized the Provisional Government of National Unity since its formation in June 1945 was now tested to the limit as the PPR's intentions towards its coalition partners became increasingly transparent.

The subsequent PPR propaganda campaign claimed that the PSL was compromised by its links with the Western powers which, according to the PPR, were prepared to deal with Germany at Poland's expense. The wider point, that only the PPR could be trusted to defend Poland's rightful postwar territorial gains in the west, was clear.[41] Indeed, the PPR publicized a series of slogans from 1945 through to the late 1940s, which brought together the national issue of the western border and the benefits of land reform. These included: 'If you want to make the border on the Neisse, Oder and Baltic last, join the ranks of the PPR!' ('Chcesz utrwalenia granic na Nissie, Odrze i Bałtyku, wstąp w szeregi PPR') and 'Settler! Yours is the land which you have taken over and no force will rip it from you. Join the ranks of the PPR!' ('Osadniku! Twoją jest ziemia którą objąłeś i żadna siła Ci jej nie wydrze, wstąp w szeregi PPR'). The PPR also organized a series of lectures, parades, demonstrations and radio broadcasts to promote its vision of the new Poland. The PPR claimed to be the defender of the working class and of the Polish nation.

The importance of the western border was also clearly articulated by Stanisław Grabski, veteran of the National Democrat camp. In conversation with British Foreign Secretary, Ernest Bevin, in January 1947 he argued that it was

> essential that Great Britain not oppose the new Polish–German frontier on the Oder–Western Neisse. This would shatter the confidence of Poles in the West and immeasurably facilitate the transformation of Poland into a Sovietised State at which the Communists aim.[42]

That same month, Jakub Berman was publicly arguing that 'it is no secret that Mikołajczyk is looking toward those statesmen abroad who are questioning our frontier'. The statesmen Berman had in mind included former British Prime Minister, Winston Churchill, and the US Secretary of State, James Byrnes, and Berman proceeded to condemn what he saw as the West's conciliatory attitude to aggressive German elements.[43]

So, while the PPR attempted to position itself as the defender of territorial gains in the west, and articulated an increasingly hostile attitude to Western intentions and actions, a softer line was taken by seasoned National Democrat politicians like Grabski. Nevertheless, the lack of clear recognition of the western border only served to support PPR propaganda and provide an avenue for some nationalists to connect with the PPR. By late 1948 the Oder–Neisse border had become 'the border of peace', according to PPR propaganda. Those who questioned it were depicted as warmongers.[44]

The amalgamation of traditional communist support for the working and peasant classes, and an uneasy and frequently ambiguous ethnonationalism, framed political discourse within postwar Poland. Those who supported this programme and were of the right background were the 'We'; those who opposed and were of the wrong background the 'They'. And since the We/They dichotomy bifurcated society both along contingent identities (class) and essentialized identities (ethnicity), tensions in society could not be, and were not, resolved but were (re)directed as class antagonisms played out in the register of nationality. In short, the PPR sought to manage social anger in the immediate postwar period through the configuring of a We/They opposition which attempted to disconnect social tensions arising from a changing economic and political system (as manifested by the PPR's hegemony) and redirect them onto essentialized population groups. Established myths and stereotypes, together with real and imagined experiences of the war and wartime conduct, made this task surprisingly easy. The consequence was that an illiberal political culture was accentuated by the PPR, much to its own advantage.

Nevertheless, PPR nationality policy and practice were not National Democrat nationality policy and practice, despite the strong resemblances and political rhetoric. Ambiguities and contradictions existed, and it is to these that we now turn.

Policy tensions

Nationality policy in Poland during the period 1944–50 broadly aimed to secure national homogeneity, and to create 'facts on the ground' to legitimate the acquisition of former German territory in the west and north. The German population was largely expelled from the new Poland, with temporary exemptions made for skilled workers in heavy industry and mining.[45]

In the east and south, Belarusians and Ukrainians were shifted to their 'homelands', and around two million Poles from former Polish territory in the east and the USSR itself were 'returned' to Poland. Like the expulsion of Germans from Poland, the Poles from across the River Bug experienced hardship, illness and death, the scale of which is only now becoming known to Western audiences (Kochanowski 2001). In the west, Polish liaison missions loyal to the Provisional Government in Warsaw attempted to persuade Home Army men and women, former prisoners of war and former slave labourers, to return to Poland.

Throughout 1945, the colonization of former German land and the concomitant promise of national homogenization was promoted both as a means of making the Polish state viable and strong, and as way to secure support for the PPR. The PPR's general secretary Władysław Gomułka, at the PPR's plenum of the Central Committee on 20–21 May 1945, explained the policy.

> Polonisation is important because the acquisition of the western territories is one of the arguments we are using in seeking the support of society. If there is no Polish population there the administration will be in the hands of the Red Army. We must expel all Germans because *countries are built on national lines and not on multinational ones*[46] (my italics).

In August 1945, Bolesław Bierut, President of the Polish Provisional Government, highlighted the merit in moving Poland west of the Curzon line, during a press conference held at the Belvedere Palace, Warsaw.

> As a rule the lands that leave Poland are those inhabited by populace of a foreign nationality. Poland gets rid of the source of constant unrests, constant internal discord. In this way the issue has been solved in the spirit of mutual interest, in the spirit of the idea of a one nation state.[47]

In addition, the Provisional Government issued a decree in November instituting Polish as the language of state and state administration, which indicated that a criterion of Polishness was the ability to speak Polish.[48] The result was to exclude those who did not speak this language and to marginalize those who were deemed to speak it poorly. Later, in 1946, with the founding of the Commission for the Determination of the Names of Places and Physiographical Objects (Komisja Ustalania Nazw Miejscowości i Obiektów Fizjograficznych), geographical space was progressively Polonized.[49] Thus, the scope for minority self-expression was compromised in order to aid the building of a Polish nation-state – minority languages were not only marginalized, but became suspect to various degrees. By 1950 Poland was more or less ethnically homogeneous, as a result of population transfers, verification programmes, and legal and illegal migration to and from the country, as Table 3.1 illustrates.

Table 3.1 Nationalities in Poland 1931–50.

Nationality	1931[a]	1931[b]	1946	1950
Polish	21,993,000 68.9%	20,644,000 64.7%	20,520,700 85.7%	24,448,000 97.8%
German	741,000 2.3%	780,000 2.4%	2,288,300 9.6%	170,000 0.7%
Jewish	2,733,000 8.6%	3,114,000 9.8%	70,000 0.3%	50,000 0.2%
Ukrainian	4,442,000 15.0%	5,114,000 16.0%	220,200 0.9%	150,000 0.6%
Belarusian	990,000 3.1%	1,954,000 6.1%	116,500 0.5%	160,000 0.6%
Other	978,000 0.3%	271,000 0.13%	107,000 0.1%	30,000 0.1%
In process of verification	na	na	417,400	na
Total	31,916,000	31,916,000	23,929,800	25,008,000

Source: Tomaszewski (1985b: 35) and Eberhardt (2000: 76).[50]

Notes
a Recorded figures based on response to the census language question, and for 39,000 people there is no data.
b Adjusted estimate taking into account other measures.

Despite the ethnocentric rhetoric, anti-minority sentiments within the PPR, discriminatory laws and the commitment to creating a homogeneous Polish state, the PPR also paradoxically attempted to guarantee the rights of minorities. The PPR Declaration of November 1943 affirmed the equal rights of all citizens, as did the PKWN manifesto of 22 July 1944, which adhered to the Polish constitution of 1921. The manifesto also specifically guaranteed equal legal rights to Jews 'who were subjected to inhuman tortures by the Nazi occupiers'. These promises should not be seen as completely empty, but rather as a glimpse of the ideals of internationalism and fraternity which formed part of communist ideology. However, such idealism was always secondary to practical consideration and political strategy. Michlic (2006: 214) argues that the ethno-nationalist image which the PPR presented was directed at the ethnic Polish population, while its declared promises of equality to all citizens were directed at the 'Western Allies, who were concerned about the development of democracy and anti-Semitism in post-1945 Poland'. This interpretation has much to recommend it, but requires some qualification.

First, it is true that the PPR's ethnic line was directed at the ethnic Polish population, but, as shown above, it was also the mechanism through which social anger could be managed (with varying degrees of success), rather than merely pandering to prejudice or opportunism. Second, promises of equality were directed at Western audiences,[51] but they also functioned to further undermine the Polish Government in Exile, which had long struggled with accusations of anti-Semitism, and to reassure Polish Jews within Poland.[52]

Clearly, there was significant tension between pursuing national homogeneity through population transfers and expulsion, arguing that 'Piast' Poland was the most desirable territorial and demographic option for the future Polish state and supporting minority communities in a meaningful way.[53] As early as 1945, the Jewish section of the PPR identified links between advocating a homogeneous nation-state, the displacement of minorities and anti-Jewish actions (Michlic 2006: 208). Yet, as the anti-minority rhetoric continued, so did the attempts to reassure the minority that was not scheduled for transfer out of the country, which excited considerable antipathy within the wider society. In addition, some Polish Jews attempted to reassure Jewish community leaders in other countries. As early as September 1945, Dr Emil Sommerstein sent a cable to Rabbi Schenk in Sydney, Australia, advising him that 'Jewish survivors enjoy equal rights'.[54] However, following a visit to Poland in late 1945, Solomon Schonfeld from the British Chief Rabbi's Council reported to Mr Henderson at the British Foreign Office that 'conditions I found there were most disquieting'.[55]

In January 1946 Jewish representatives from Poalei Zion-Left (Adolf Berman) and the Bund (Michał Szuldonfrei) participated in discussions at the ninth session of the KRN in which they declared fidelity to the government line and focused on the problem of anti-Semitism.[56] On 3 January 1946, the bulletin of the Central Committee of Jews in Poland (CKŻP) informed its readers of the CKŻP's policy line which was supported by the Government.[57]

Practical assistance was forthcoming. The 'Office of the Government Commissar relating to the Productivisation of the Jewish populace' and the CKŻP managed efforts to assist, train and integrate the Jewish population. Nevertheless, the limits of these efforts, predicated upon the integration of Jews as Polish citizens rather than as Jews to the majoritarian culture (assimilation), were acutely felt by those Jews hostile to the assimilation model pursued under the rubric of building socialism. This included Rabbi Kahane, whose complaints against the Jewish communists were clearly heard by British officialdom, while his implied protest against assimilation was not.[58]

Thus, the efforts to substantiate equal citizenship rights were also efforts to make Jews 'Poles'. Training institutes were set up to help Jews move into 'Polish' occupations, such as manufacturing and agriculture, in an effort to break the historic ethnic division of labour – itself, in part, the consequence of previous anti-Jewish legislation and practice. In addition, voluntary and legal migration out of Poland was supported. And, as indicated in Chapter 2, 'illegal' exit from Poland was unofficially tolerated.[59] However, despite a policy environment which promoted assimilation, emigration and a more general ethno-nationalist policy, Jewish life from 1944 to 1948, though difficult, re-emerged. The American Jewish Joint Distribution Committee (AJDC) was very active in Poland from the moment it was allowed to operate following the Second World War until 1950 when it was forced by the Polish Government to cease action and leave the country.[60] By April 1946 it had sent goods worth $8.4 million to Poland, assisted 15,000 children and supported 78 Jewish communities and 134 co-operatives in Poland.[61]

Autochthonic populations

As discussed in Chapter 2, the expulsion/transfer of population affected millions of people, and at times conditions were somewhat less than 'humane and orderly'. Germans, Poles, Lithuanians, Russians, Ukrainians and Belarusians were all caught up in the operation to create a Polish nation-state.

In addition there remained the problematic category of Poland's so-called autochthonic populations.[62] Kashubians, Mazurians and Silesians straddled the moving We/They boundary of nationality policy between 1944 and 1950. In the immediate aftermath of war tens of thousands were expelled as Germans, especially if they were not Catholic. Those who remained were subjected to verification and 'Re-Polonization' procedures to, as the Catholic writer Władysław Grabski (1945) argued:

> liberate the Slavic blood flowing in the veins of Germanised Silesians and Pomeranians . . . disinfecting them and returning them to health by teaching them the native tongue in order to incorporate them back into the mother country, not as prodigal sons but as victims rescued from the ultimate outrage.[63]

The verification process sought to claim for Poland those with an uncrystallized national identity, and was a project which witnessed co-operation between the Ministry of Public Administration, Ministry of the Recovered Territories and the Ministry of Public Security. A number of non-governmental organizations also provided support, such as the Polish Western Union (PZZ), the Social Committee of Opole Silesia and the Association of Mazurians. The PZZ was especially active, viewing nationality policy as a key instrument in the long-term struggle against Germanization. This perspective allowed the claiming for Poland of those who had recently been Germanized. The PZZ also contended that mixing autochthonic and settler communities from the east would help to remove German influence among the population, and help to protect the Polish nation from German infiltration.

The verification procedures executed in different places were not uniform, and through 1944 and 1945 local authorities exercised various methods, resulting in some people being expelled from Poland whom the central Government may have wanted to remain. On 20 June 1945 the Ministry of Public Administration issued instructions recommending that certificates giving people temporary Polish nationality for three months be issued, pending verification. The criteria to determine Polish identity were not rigid, and gave functionaries on the ground considerable discretion. Applicants of Polish nationality who had lived in the Recovered Territories on 31 August 1939 and submitted a written declaration of faithfulness to the Polish nation were to be recognized as Polish. Those who had not been members of the National Socialist German Workers' Party (NSDAP), were not to be discriminated against as fascists.

The PPR had a strong interest in the autochthonic populations in the immediate aftermath of the war, as it was important to secure international recognition that the 'Recovered Territories' were Polish. So, in addition to removing the Germans, the native population in former German lands whose national identity was ambiguous was claimed as part of the Polish nation. This is clearly illustrated by the PPR-organized Congress of Autochthones which took place in Warsaw over 9–10 November 1946, as a response to James Byrnes' Stuttgart speech (6 September). It aimed to show the world that the estimated million autochthones were Polish.

As Kulczycki (2001: 209) points out, Polish policy in relation to the autochthonic population groups aimed to achieve what could be understood as opposing objectives: 'Polish *raison d'état* and the social consensus demanded both the widest possible inclusion of German citizens of Polish origin and the strictest exclusion of all Germans'. In July 1945, a special commission, the Council of Experts on the Question of the 'Recovered Territories', advised the Government to grant full citizenship to German citizens of Polish origin. And in early 1946 an important paper by Zygmunt Izdebski, one of the key theorists of verification, was circulated within the Ministry of the Recovered Territories. This paper brought into question the usefulness of both objective criteria (religion, language spoken) and subjective criteria (declared self-identity), and argued that the Polishness of those being verified could only be assessed in a holistic way, that is how the person acted, brought up children and related to others in the community.[64] Clearly, such loose criteria gave verification assessors considerable scope for manoeuvre with regard to who would be included and who excluded from the Polish nation. It also allowed the Ministry of the Recovered Territories to respond pragmatically to the need for labour in order to develop agriculture and industry, and to the loss of manpower suffered during the Second World War. Nevertheless, the Polishness of the autochthones had to be verified and, in April 1946, a comprehensive programme of nationality verification was rolled out in the 'Recovered Territories'.

The tension between the determination to expel all Germans and the desire to retain German citizens of Polish origin proved difficult to resolve. The social anger regime legitimated hostility towards those perceived as not

Polish and, for many Poles, especially those being resettled from beyond the River Bug, autochthonic populations exhibited clear German characteristics.

In Opole Silesia, for example, the passing of verification tests, together with affiliation to Catholicism, as Sitek (1986) indicates, allowed many people to stay in Poland whom the repatriants from the east considered to be German. This perception continued to be a source of poor inter-community relations for several decades. Izdebski's call for a holistic approach was frequently replaced by the affirmation of objective criteria in practice and the discretion of local functionaries. Łodziński (1998: 157), for example, notes that the ability to speak Polish was used as a criterion to grant Polish citizenship to the autochthonic population in the 'Recovered Territories' following the act of 28 April 1948 that regulated citizenship in those areas. A uniform, consistent approach to the issue of verification did not emerge, which proved to be unsettling for autochthonic populations, who tended to retreat into their own communities. As early as 1949 the Polish authorities had noted that even in the context of schooling, auto-chthonic populations were not fully participating in the wider life of society.[65]

Tensions between the policy of the central authorities and local administration often had an adverse impact on the autochthonic populations. Verification committees were often staffed by leading personalities from the local area, including those who had recently arrived from the east. These settlers frequently saw the entire local population as German and demanded their expulsion. And, as Strauchold (2001: 53) observes, there were cases where people were expelled because the new arrivals wanted their property.

In Mazuria and Warmia, the challenge posed by the autochthonous population was the subject of a voivodship conference on 13 June 1949. The PZPR wished to integrate these people into the mainstream of Polish society.[66] Minister Edward Ochab argued that:

> . . . certain specialists proclaimed all Mazurs as Germans. They did not understand and did not want to understand that this Mazurian people, for long centuries remaining under German occupation, kept a Polish heart and soul, national customs in the specific ethnic Mazurian form.[67]

Following the conference, a resolution was passed by the Executive of the Voivodship Committee of the PZPR in Olsztyn on 6 July 1949 outlining concrete measures to integrate the Mazurians and Warmians. Re-Polonization courses were rolled out using as a framework the programme combating illiteracy and as part of worker education. In addition, efforts were made to educate settlers to the region in the history of Warmia and Mazuria – especially the fight against Prussian landowners in the context of class struggle.[68] Autochthonic populations were depicted as resisting both foreign rule and class oppression. Yet, as Strauchold (2001: 60) points out, many Mazurians in the mid- to late 1940s refused to submit to verification procedures and did not view themselves as Polish. Their evangelical Protestant faith was one objective characteristic which differentiated them from the Polish majority, and, for settlers from the east, affirmed the Mazurians' Germanness. Indeed, local Catholic clergy promoted the view that 'a Pole is a Catholic, an Evangelical is a kraut' (Polak to katolik, a ewangelik to szwab).[69] A report from the organization department of the Central Committee of the PZPR noted that many young Mazurians and Kashubians did not know the Polish language.[70] Nevertheless, an administrative decree of 1949 verified the entire population as Polish, resulting in assimilation and integration policies being formulated, and the close monitoring of the autochthonic population groups.

Scholars were also mobilized to assist in the (re)integration of auto-chthones to the Polish mainstream. Throughout the 1940s academic workers at the Western Institute in Poznań produced studies supporting the notion of a 'Piast' Poland, and articulated primordialist arguments about the identity of autochthonic populations. Indeed, in a 1946 contribution to the journal *Przegląd Zachodni*, Bożena Stelmachowska argued that a common Polish folk culture existed and could underpin the drive to integration and national homogeneity.[71] This view influenced government policy. In December 1949 the Ministry of Culture and Art proposed that ten regional artistic groups be set up in the 'Recovered Territories'. The objective was to nurse folk culture.[72]

However, the integration of autochthonic populations to the Polish mainstream proved extremely difficult. This was largely the result of the persisting mistrust of these groups expressed by the incoming settler population in daily life, and their resulting marginalization. The social anger regime orchestrated by the PPR, and later the PZPR, which proved so effective at channelling discontent towards minority populations, could not be fine-tuned to accommodate those who failed to fulfil society's conception of Polishness, despite the state's efforts at 're-Polonization'. The hopes of the PZZ – that the mixing of populations would remove German influence among the autochthonic populations and lead to a homogeneous population – failed to be realized, as discrimination against and suspicion of the autochthonic populations was sustained through the course of the PRL.[73]

Impact of the social anger regime

The manipulation of ethno-nationalism played a crucial role in forging a narrative about the future of Poland in which the majority of society believed. On the one hand, there was social approval for violence against minority communities to achieve national homogeneity. On the other, there was a lack of such approval for violence against the PPR's enemies, such as Home Army personnel and the political opposition. But, by endorsing the creation of non-people – people who were conceived of as having no place in the future Poland – the opposition unwittingly contributed to a form of political storytelling which was used to liquidate them politically at the same time.[74] In other words, contesting the PPR and PZPR became, in the view of the PPR and PZPR, unPolish. Those cast outside the frequently tendentious definition of Polishness were exposed to the full force of violence aimed at non-people or, to be more precise, *homines sacri*. Indeed, it was the regime of structural and subjective violence concomitant to the drive to national homogeneity that played a crucial role in assisting the PPR, and later the PZPR, to achieve hegemony. And it is to the important issue of violence that we turn in the next chapter.

4 Violence

The reconfiguring of the ethnic topography of Poland, together with the institution of its new borders, was accompanied by widespread violence. Prażmowska (2004) has argued that, in the period immediately following the declaration of 'Victory in Europe' on 8 and 9 May 1945, a civil war raged in Poland and assaults, killings and rapes continued.[1] It is in this context that an assessment of the process of the expulsions/transfers should be made. The violence that took place in the aftermath of the Second World War in Poland can be analytically differentiated into two broad types – structural and subjective.

Structural violence is, in certain ways, necessary for the wider goals of society or state to be achieved. Structural violence has three aspects. First, there is the violence which inheres within the dominant social relations, and its precise form is determined by those social relations. In a capitalist society, for example, a reserve army of labour (unemployment) seems to be a necessity for the continuation of profitable accumulation.[2] This aspect is described as *non-intentional structural violence*. Second, there is the violence which inheres within language and in the hegemony of particular notions of common sense, for example, pervasive stereotypes and fixed ideas about gender roles. This form is described as *representational violence*. The third aspect of structural violence is directed and serves to ensure the continuation of the dominant social relations. In the West this has often taken the form of anti-union legislation, outlawing of communist parties and black-listing of individuals, among other measures. This form is usually operationalized by the state and its allies to ensure the continuation of the set of social relations in which the state is embedded. This aspect is described as *intentional structural violence*.[3] Its intensity can be eased, though not eliminated, within the context of a specific set of social relations, by the state.[4] In the period 1944–50, the appropriation of private property was a structural necessity for the building of communism, but so too was the elimination of opposition.[5]

Subjective violence, on the other hand, has identifiable authors and is superfluous and gratuitous as it is not strictly necessary to sustain a particular set of social relations.[6] By definition it is excessive.[7] It has no *direct* bearing on insulating the dominant social relations from dispute. This is not to say that subjective and structural forms of violence are contradictory. Indeed, the two forms may be aligned so that subjective violence aids the achievement of systemic goals, by fostering fear and inhibiting protest, for example. But, analytically, subjective violence is not seen as a *necessary* violence, nor does it inhere within the structure of social relations.[8]

'Violence' here is understood as individual, group or institutional actions, or a consequence of the dominant social relations, which inhibit self-development and the self-expression of individuals and/or communities.[9] The consequence of violence, whatever form it takes, is to restrict the freedom of the victim. Separating subjective from structural forms allows a more nuanced analysis of violence in general, while demonstrating the pervasiveness of violence within the social relations of society. Structural violence may be eased by good policies, but can only be overcome through a radical reframing of social relations – with the risk of new forms of structural violence emerging. Subjective violence can often be combated within the framework of a particular set of social relations.[10] The point is that violence comes in different forms, all of which restrict the self-development and self-expression of the victim.

The notion that violence inheres within a particular set of social relations has been explored in some detail by Pierre Clastres in relation to primitive societies (Clastres 1987, 1994). In an important essay from 1977, Clastres demonstrates the structural imperative of constant war in such societies, if the drift from unity of the community to social and political differentiation in that community is to be avoided.[11] He reverses Hobbes' (1991) argument, by contending that 'war is against the state'; that is, war functions as a means of social dispersion, while the state seeks to unify society (Clastres 1994: 167). Though Clastres speaks of primitive societies, his insights have a bearing on the modern era in that he forces us to examine closely not only the social function of violence in society, but also the way in which violence embedded within society's social relations is articulated. More recently, Slavoj Žižek (2008) has focused attention on the systemic violence (non-intentional structural violence) that characterizes contemporary Western societies. The work of these writers, among others, highlights the limits of arguments that focus on subjective violence. For Arendt (1970), violence is consciously chosen by individuals or groups and the possibility of it emerging from, or inhering within, the social relations of society without conscious action is not considered in her 1970 text.[12] This same criticism can be levelled at Laitin's (2007) work on nations, states and violence as well. Clastres' (1977, 1994) and Žižek's (2008) contribution is to indicate that such voluntary violence is just one specific type. It is therefore crucial that the various forms of violence are identified so that the logic which defines them can be isolated and examined.

The argument made here is that, in the period 1944–47, subjective violence was fairly widespread, whereas in the period 1948–50 subjective violence was less frequent and structural violence was, by some margin, dominant. The scale of subjective violence decreased over time, largely due to the Government's lower level of toleration of society's subjective violence in the second period of 1948–50, the departure from Poland of most of the Soviet troops and, crucially, the transfer/expulsion of virtually all members of minority population groups. The late 1940s witnessed the subjugation of armed opposition groups such as WiN and NSZ, but it was the achievement of more or less complete national homogeneity that dissipated the PPR's toleration of subjective violence and removed 'sanctioned' targets from society. If minority communities were to be harmed, it would be the state rather than thugs on the railway network or elsewhere that would act. With the achievement of political hegemony, clearly expressed by the 'merger' of the PPS and PPR in 1948, the actual scale of (intentional) structural violence was also reduced in the second period, though it remained at a fairly high level (Kemp-Welch 2008: 42).

Notions of violence that conflate subjective and structural violence if applied to the postwar situation in Poland serve to affirm a We/They binary of society versus communists. The main problem with such conceptualizations is that they cannot deal with the specificity of subjective violence against minority communities, and the role it played in structuring social relations and social anger in the period 1944–47. They further *naturalize* the structural violence inhering within the social system, as such violence is reclassified as the expression of power.

This raises an important question. Why did the PPR tolerate widespread subjective violence up until early 1948? The standard response would be that the PPR could do nothing else; it was small and not in full control of the situation. However, such an answer underestimates the potentialities of the PPR at this point and pays no attention to its strategic goals. It also misreads the balance of power within the country. Following Arendt's (1970: 44) contention that 'power corresponds to the human ability not just to act but to act in concert', it is clear that the PPR and its Soviet allies could and did 'act in concert.' In contrast, most of the wider society in the immediate aftermath of war found unified action difficult on account of social and physical dislocation during the war and the immediate postwar period. So, although it is true that the opposition, up until the 1947 election, commanded a great deal of sympathy and support from the Polish population, it would be wrong to underestimate the power of the PPR.[13]

The PPR was able to influence events quite considerably by managing the social anger regime through widespread propaganda. Subjective violence was often indirectly incited against minority communities. This is not to say that all acts of subjective violence were orchestrated by the PPR. They did not have to be. It was often sufficient that the PPR did little to counter widespread representational violence, which characterized some groups, especially minorities, in a negative manner.

The PPR maintained a high level of tolerance of subjective violence to the extent that it was aligned with the PPR's goals of achieving national homogeneity and being seen by the wider society as a Polish party. Activities that threatened the PPR and its bid for hegemony, on the other hand, were ruthlessly suppressed, resulting in a veritable *gulag* being created to incarcerate hostile elements. Arguably, it was the overzealous actions of the security forces that necessitated the amnesty of 1947. This amnesty can be understood as an effort by the communist-dominated Government to endear itself both to the wider Polish public and to international opinion. It should be noted that 'criminals' rather than 'anti-state' prisoners were prioritized for release.[14] By 1948 the leadership of the prison service was in triumphant mood. At the third general briefing of the heads of prisons and prison camps on 21 February 1948 in Warsaw the following statement was read:

> The two years that have passed since the last briefing have witnessed the ultimate victory for the democratic bloc in Poland. A distinguished role in the achievements of the last two years has been played by the apparatus of public security . . . The neutralising of reactionary enemies of the state, of the nation and of democracy will remain an historic achievement of the authorities of public security.[15]

Nevertheless, the process of identifying and isolating 'anti-state' individuals continued in earnest, with specialized prisons at Rawicz and Potulice, amongst others.[16] In 1949 the prison population rose by 32.8 per cent (14,692 people) as a result of 'the strengthening of class war and the increase in the work of the courts from the post-war period regarding common criminals'.[17]

The PPR did not seriously attempt to combat subjective violence during the period 1944–47 as it did not wish to risk jettisoning the support that it had attracted. Tackling subjective violence would have required either allowing social anger to be freely expressed, and thus risking greater direct action against itself and its Soviet Allies, or foregoing the drive to national homogeneity, which would have alienated the PPR from both domestic audiences and its Soviet sponsor. It would also have given the Polish Government in Exile the political initiative. Neither was a real possibility. This situation was recognized by senior Party cadres. Initial attempts by the PPR to encourage workers in Łódź to condemn the pogrom in Kielce on 4 July 1946 backfired badly, and workers saw the PPR and the Government as being 'Jewish' (Kenney 1997: 114). Strikes broke out in a number of factories. And, despite Adolf Berman's entreaties to enhance the legal protection of Jews and to combat anti-Semitism, the view of the KRN's legal expert, Itzhak Klajnerman, that such action would be 'counterproductive, perhaps even harmful, as such a decree would certainly become an excellent pretext for energized agitation against the Jews and against the government', won out.[18] Initial actions which called for society to condemn the pogrom had fallen on deaf ears and the PPR was not about to make the same mistake again. Indeed, the Kielce PPR secretary on the day of the pogrom refused to address the crowd to diffuse its anger as he 'didn't want people saying that the PPR is a defender of the Jews'.[19]

The state controlled by the PPR and later the PZPR is estimated to have devoted 8–11 per cent of its budget to the Ministry of State Security (MBP) in the period 1944–49. This was the third largest element after the armed forces and education (Dudek and Paczkowski 2005: 236), and clearly shows that resources were mobilized to ensure the hegemony of the PPR.[20]

The PPR attempted to manage social anger to its own advantage. However, the *pattern* of postwar ethnic violence was not so much the outcome of a deliberate PPR strategy, but the result of the complex interaction of social anger, social sedimentation and party actions, especially its centrifugal ethno-nationalist rhetoric. A similar situation was to be found elsewhere. In Czechoslovakia, violence against Germans occurred almost three years before the communists consolidated power, but the goal of national homogeneity was widely accepted, and German nationals stood in the way of this objective. Glassheim (2001: 212) points out that 'Czechoslovak leaders, including Beneš, Gottwald and others, continually called for *očištěnί* (cleansing, purification) of the German borderlands in 1945'. Where violence against Germans did not have the imprimatur of sanction, as in the areas occupied by American forces, there was considerably less violence.[21]

In short, the postwar subjective violence which erupted across east-central Europe found guidance and direction through consensus on the need for national homogeneity. So, while *communist* orchestration was not a necessity, some form of guidance was. There is nothing 'natural' about widespread subjective violence. It takes place in environments which sanction it in one form or another. In Poland, the PPR was not prepared to fight energetically against the subjective violence or representational violence that affected minority communities. The opposition, at least at the rank and file level, exploited anti-minority sentiment and, with a handful of exceptions, the Catholic hierarchy attempted to justify and blame the victims for the violence inflicted on them.[22] The use of negative stereotypes played an important role in framing and 'justifying' the eruptions of physical acts of violence. In short, there was no consistent, unambiguous voice condemning subjective violence directed at minority communities. On the contrary, it was legitimated, rationalized or ignored. The widespread discursive acceptance of subjective violence allowed it to flourish.

The differentiation of violence into subjective and structural types allows us to compare and contrast the experience of violence among the various population groups affected. Let us first consider structural violence.

Structural violence

Structural violence is frequently ignored, but it is the most pervasive form of violence. In contrast to liberal capitalist societies, non-intentional structural violence in communist societies is relatively underdeveloped, while intentional and representational violence are relatively overdeveloped. In *established* communist societies power is transparent, but in liberal capitalist societies power is opaque (Ost 2005: 21). Because of power transparency in which everyone recognizes that the communist party is responsible for almost everything and therefore can be blamed for almost everything, it is crucial that the party redirect the social anger of which it is naturally the focus. The main ways in which it can do this are to orchestrate and manage representational violence against Other groups and to sustain the social relations in which it is embedded through intentional structural violence.

The state, as established by the PPR and its allies, had several systemic goals. In 1944–47 it sought to transform social relations in the country through economic and social reform, and to ensure that the population was nationally homogeneous. The use of negative and harmful stereotypes of various minority groups (representational violence) helped to 'legitimate' population transfers and expulsions, and to redirect social anger away from the PPR. Millions of people had to be moved across state borders because of their ethnic origin. Violence inhered within the process of movement, rehousing and resettlement itself, and found physical expression in holding and transit camps, and, for some members of the German population, in labour camps. Without the internationally sanctioned policy of population transfers and expulsions, the hardships and deaths which accompanied transfers/expulsions would not have occurred in the form that they did. In addition, the commitment to national homogeneity denied substantive equality for minority members as it inhibited the expression of minority cultures and encouraged assimilation into majoritarian norms. Each national group was affected by structural violence in different ways but, before considering how minority populations were affected, it is worth highlighting the violence which accompanied the PPR's bid to transform, in a fundamental way, Poland's social and political relations. In this, Poles were both the supposed beneficiaries and the victims of the concomitant structural violence.

Poles

The ethnic Polish population was the target audience for assertions detailing the benefits of national homogeneity and the re-emergence of a glorious 'Piast' Poland. In spring 1945, Polish 'repatriants' from former Polish lands in the East, passing through the repatriation point in Łódź, were greeted at Łódź Kaliska railway station by the sign 'We are returning to the Baltic' (Wracamy na Bałtyk) – a reference to the 'Piast' Polish frontiers.[23] Poles were also the victims of the state's structural violence, as the PPR attempted to link the national and social revolutions. Those from the east were 'forced' to come to Poland, and suffered hardship both in transit and on arrival in Poland, having to create new lives in unfamiliar places. Of those who were channelled through Łódź to resettlement locations in the 'Recovered Territories' in the period up to 1 January 1946, an estimated 25 per cent returned to the Łódź voivodship due to the insecurity and lack of social organization in the places to which they were sent.[24]

However, it was those who either opposed or were thought to oppose the form of state being created that felt the weight of the state's security forces, as well as those of the USSR, such as the NKVD. In 1944 and 1945 Home Army soldiers and members of the civilian underground were arrested. It is estimated that between 12,000 and 13,000 Poles were sent by the NKVD to the depths of Russia in 1944. In Vilnius, following Operation Tempest (Burza), which saw the Home Army fight the Nazis, some 5,000 Home Army soldiers were interned by the Soviets and in the wider Vilnius region some 11,000 Poles were arrested.[25] This violence was (intentional) structural, in the sense that it inhered in the project establishing PPR hegemony.[26] Gomułka was moved to point out at the plenary session of the PPR's Central Committee in October 1945 that, 'We [PPR] are weak in number. We have reached the lowest point. An increase is beginning, but it is too slow'.[27] In short, the low level of social acceptance, together with a political framework which could not easily deal with dissent, necessitated the liquidation of oppositionists through incarceration (and other punishments) if the PPR project were to remain on course, while greater social support was accumulated through nationality policy and land reform.

The number of those imprisoned is difficult to ascertain with accuracy, though a report by the Ministry of Internal Affairs from 1979 states that: in 1944, 11,063 were arrested; 45,148 in 1945; 44,411 in 1946; 30,521 in 1947; 24,443 in 1948; 22,848 in 1949; and 20,727 in 1950. Almost half of the figure for 1945 is made up of arrests for war crimes so, as Dudek and Paczkowski (2005: 272) contend, if Germans and alleged collaborators are excluded, 1946 was the peak year for arrests. However, these figures do not include the 80,000–100,000 who were detained prior to the election in January 1947. It is worth noting that soldiers assigned to remove Ukrainians and pacify areas inhabited by them were temporarily reassigned to assist with the election, ostensibly to protect agitators and later polling stations, but in reality to ensure that people voted in the right way. Harassment and intimidation of PSL members during late 1946 and 1947 was routine. At the end of November 1946 Mikołajczyk estimated that 100,000 PSL members had been arrested (Kersten 1991: 325).[28]

Earlier, in March 1945, the leaders of the Polish Underground were invited to meet with Soviet representatives near Warsaw and were promptly arrested, taken to Moscow and placed on trial in June 1945 – at the same time as Mikołajczyk was in the city in conference with Soviet officials over the future of Poland. The trial sought to 'discredit the non-Communist opposition movement in the eyes of world public opinion and, thus, to weaken the position of the political camp represented by Mikołajczyk' (Kersten 1991: 154).[29] Representational violence (propaganda) played a key role in the PPR's attempts to marginalize the PSL and other opposition groups.

The (intentional) structural violence against Poles was primarily aimed at ensuring that the PPR dominated the state and decided its form. Between 1946 and 1948 some 32,477 people were sentenced for 'crimes against the state' (Dudek and Paczkowski 2005: 273). In addition to imprisonment, summary executions of those in opposition took place, including some carried out on the spot by military firing squads. Between 1944 and 1945 some 8,000 death sentences were passed, of which 3,100 were carried out. To this must be added the casualties of combat, which Dudek and Paczkowski (2005: 273) record as 2,830 in 1945, 3,383 in 1946, 2,149 in 1947 and 306 in 1948.[30] This violence was enhanced by sanctioned subjective violence, which included torture and horrendous conditions in prisons and camps.[31]

Germans

The German population was the main target for of the programme of expulsions from Poland. Unlike the transfer agreements in the east, compensation for property left behind was not part of the project. Thus, the internationally sanctioned programme of transfer had a strong element of collective retribution for Nazi wartime atrocities. For, although transferees from the east were frequently inadequately compensated and were, more often than not, coerced to leave, in principle they were entitled to reparations. The Germans were not. Thus, the expulsion of the Germans fulfilled four crucial functions for the Polish government and its Soviet sponsors. First, it helped to bring the goal of national homogeneity close to realization. Second, it contributed to the substantiation of the idea that the USSR guaranteed Poland's western border and that the PPR acted as an advocate of the historical national interest. Third, it provided space and resources to resettle Poles transferred from former eastern Poland. And, fourth, it provided a safe target on which the population could vent frustration and anger.

For the Germans, the price of expulsion was high. They were deprived of the rights of citizenship (those with Polish citizenship), forced to leave their homes and many were interned or forced to work without compensation or paid significantly less than Poles for the same work. In addition to the loss of property, an unknown number lost their lives. The loss of life, though frequently the consequence of the excesses of soldiers, both Soviet and Polish, as well as civilians, was also a result of the expulsion process itself. For, although the Potsdam Agreement of 1945 provided for 'humane and orderly' conditions, the scale of the movement (1.5 million people to the British zone of Germany, two million to the Soviet zone) provided scope for serious problems to occur. The transfer out of Poland, especially in winter in unheated wagons, was responsible for fatalities and amputations. Even the notification of expulsion precipitated the suicide of an unknown number of Germans. The arrival of Poles from the eastern regions increased the pressure on the Germans to leave, and many set out voluntarily for departure points (such as Kaławsk, see Chapter 2), where they had to wait in the open air for a transport to Germany. In the winter of 1946–47 this disorganization had fatal results for many.[32]

Within Poland, the process of moving people out of their homes, taking them to a concentration point and then on to the departure point, was frequently brutal, for two main reasons: the timeframe of the expulsion process was fairly tight and there was widespread negative sentiment towards Germans. By summer 1945, for example, due to the high level of theft of German property and foodstuffs, the political section of the Soviet Army reported back to Moscow stating that, 'the German population is starving in many places'.[33] Elsewhere, in some towns, the Polish local administrators forced Germans to wear an 'N' for Niemiec (German) on their breast.[34] This occurred as late as October 1945 in Reszel (Rossel). Jacob Egit (1991: 50), a Jewish community leader, recalls a meeting with Stanisław Piaskowski, Voivod of Lower Silesia, who responded favourably to his demand that Germans should wear an identifying armband, amongst other requirements.[35]

Other administrative measures were taken against the German population. From 17 April 1946 the use of the German language in public and at home was forbidden, with the police empowered to arrest people speaking German as 'provocateurs of our national feelings'.[36] Place and street names were changed from German into Polish, and those with German names, both forenames and surnames, coerced to change or Polonize them with the addition of -wicz, or -ski, for example. The objective was to alienate Germans from those areas which they considered their 'Heimat'. Everyday life in the 'Recovered Territories' was to be Polish. This policy also impacted on autochthonic populations, who freely mixed German in their dialects and spoken Polish.

Members of the German population were also exploited as labour, and incarcerated in forced labour camps and penal institutions, mainly during the years 1944–46. As Jerzy Laudański points out in the guide to the records of the Department of Prisons of the Ministry of Public Security, 'the intention was to maximize the productive exploitation of the labour potential of the camps'.[37] Germans made up most of the forced labour in the Polish labour camps, which up to November 1945 had made a gross profit of 14,958,619.41 złoty.[38] In Upper Silesia alone, there were 86 camps and 48 prisons. It has been estimated that 60,000 Germans died in these camps (Borodziej and Lemberg 2000: 11) though, as Kopka (2002: 10) points out, given that tens of thousands of Germans were working outside the camps' boundaries, establishing accurate figures for how many were detained and died is problematic. The main causes of death were typhus and diseases associated with malnutrition. The lack of medicines, such as penicillin, allowed venereal disease to become widespread. Scabies and lice were also prevalent.[39] The Polish prison administration was concerned about the spread of diseases within the camps and prisons. A report from 1945 noted that transfers of prisoners to different prisons had been halted, and that '[a]ll possible methods were employed in fighting insects and in improving the general sanitary state of prisons and camps by sending to them the anti-insect powder DDT and disinfecting agents/sulphur'.[40]

The violence which the Germans in camps endured – or perished from – was a reflection of the labour/incarceration regime itself and the temperament of the camp guards. As Naimark (2001: 130) notes, many camp personnel were not paid a regular salary and attempted to extract payment from the inmates. The harsh regime was made more unbearable by the subjective violence practised by camp guards and directors (see below). As Dudek and Paczkowski (2005: 243) point out, thousands of MBP functionaries, which included personnel at the camps, 'were charged with theft, rape or abuse of power'. They argue that 'the most serious offence, in the eyes of the authorities, a functionary of the security apparatus could commit was not murder, mugging or rape, but collaboration with the anti-communist underground'. Such collaboration was clearly directed against the state, whereas murder, rape and pillage could be aligned with state objectives.

The treatment of Germans varied according to their position on the Nazi 'Volksliste', their geographic location and, to a degree, their age and gender. Those classified as 'Reichsdeutsche' (category one) were either tried as war criminals or expelled immediately, though some exceptions were made for highly skilled workers. 'Volksdeutsche' (category two) were frequently sent to labour camps or tried as traitors. People in categories three and four on the Volksliste, which included most of the autochthonic population, could, starting in 1946, apply for 'verification' as Poles. It is also worth noting that in autumn 1945 the Soviet army deported around 100,000 people, ostensibly from categories one and two, to the USSR for forced labour, often in mines.

The expulsion of skilled labour was delayed until Poles could be found to perform the tasks. Sometimes, skilled Germans were assigned low-skilled work as factories recognized that 'at the moment of beginning production the firm will not get a Polish expert on demand'.[41] Given their crucial position in the economy, such workers received enhanced rations and housing benefits despite their German nationality. Throughout 'Operation Swallow', the British were of the view that the Poles were holding back skilled male labour.[42] This view was partially substantiated by Jakub Prawin, head of the Polish military mission in Berlin, in 1947, when he offered a head-for-head exchange of German miners in Silesia for 'Polish' miners in Westphalia (see Chapter 6). In reports and memos about Operation Swallow throughout 1946, the issue of the quality of expellees was highlighted. The lack of fit men being sent to the British Zone of occupation, together with the over-representation of the old and sick, caused serious concern. The British viewed this as being contrary to the Potsdam Agreement. One report argued that 'what might be accepted as humane conditions for the young and vigorous may well be most inhumane for the sick, aged and pregnant'.[43]

Structural violence varied geographically. In areas claimed by Poland, such as Lower Silesia and East Prussia, the full force of the expulsion process, imprisonment and forced labour regime affected Germans. The area around Opole had the highest number of camps outside the industrial region of Upper Silesia, including the infamous Łambinowice camp.[44] Elsewhere, such as the port cities of Gdańsk (Danzig) and Szczecin (Stettin), Germans remained in some numbers until the transfer process became more ordered in mid-1946.

Jews

Although the Jewish population was not scheduled for movement out of Poland, unlike other minority groups, the state's nationality policy was not unproblematic towards them, and the thrust to achieve national homogeneity contributed to the intolerance shown towards them by large swathes of the wider population. Furthermore, the tendency to view anti-Semitism as a consequence of Jewish actions was not strongly challenged. So, while the creation of the Office of the Government Commissar for the Productivization of the Jewish Populace played an important role in training Jews for work, it was rationalized, at least in part, by the view that the concentration of Jews in certain professions and lines of work contributed to anti-Semitic sentiment. It was therefore deemed necessary to move them to other activities. No clear policies were formulated to challenge the opinions of wider society, or to explain to the public how Jewish concentration in certain economic activities was connected with the way that Jews were incorporated into the Polish polity during previous generations.

Furthermore, Jews were not, in practice, afforded the full equality promised by the PKWN manifesto, the Prime Minister and others, since this frequently conflicted with the strategic goals of the PPR/PZPR. In the initial period of 1944–47, this is most clearly seen in the ambivalent attitude taken by the state apparatus in response to various outrages including the Kielce and Kraków pogroms (discussed above). Indeed, Szaynok (2004: 193) has pointed out that PPR policy towards the Jews was dependent on its own strategic needs, whether to win Western approval or to discredit the Polish Government in Exile (as occurred after the Kraków pogrom).[45]

In the immediate postwar period, Jewish life was re-established in Poland, with a concentration in Lower Silesia. The Jewish population was 240,489 in June 1946, with the arrival of Jews from the USSR, before falling to 88,257 in 1948 as Jews left/fled to the West or to Palestine.[46] The arrival of Jews from the USSR reinvigorated communities. Schools were opened under the auspices of the CKŻP and, by 1 August 1946, 36 schools with a total of 3,300 children existed (Datner 1994: 105). Hebrew and Yiddish were on the syllabus, though from the end of 1946 Polish was the language of instruction in several schools. By 1947 the Jewish Religious Congregation supported 38 synagogues, organized religious schools, and helped the aged (Cała 1998: 249). However, the mass flight undermined the efforts of the previous years. The shift in late 1947 and early 1948 to a *soft* ethno-nationalist policy by the Government exposed Jews in Poland to greater assimilatory pressures. Their position became more tenuous with the Soviet-sponsored antipathy to the newly established State of Israel expressed in 1948 and the subordination of Jewish organizations to the Polish State in 1949 and 1950.

Belarusians

The Belarusian minority was earmarked for population transfer to Soviet Belarus as a result of the September 1944 agreement. However, there was a widespread view that the Belarusians had a weakly developed sense of national identity and could be easily assimilated into Polish majoritarian norms. This was the view elaborated in 1935 in an internal paper of the Ministry of Internal Affairs, which argued that:

> there is no desire amongst the Belarusian national minority at grass-roots level to set themselves apart ethnically, on the contrary, they want to merge with the Polish majority. We can see this phenomenon in the area of elementary education, where the Belarusian peasant not only does not demand Belarusian schools to be opened, but, faced with a choice of two schools, Polish or Belarusian, opts to send his children to the Polish one.[47]

This was the position discussed in Knoll's 'secret' document of 1943. And it was the view adopted in the late 1940s by the PPR and, later, the PZPR. It was to have a significant impact on the Belarusians themselves, and the way that structural violence affected them.

Following the September 1944 agreement between the PKWN and the Belarusian Soviet Socialist Republic, 36,388 people left the Białystok voivodship and the northern part of the Lublin voivodship for Belarus between 1944 and 1946. A total of 27,409 were Belarusian (Sienkiewicz and Hryciuk 2008: 233)[48]. Mironowicz (1993: 133) argues that the population transfer agreement and its tight timeframe (initially from 15 October 1944–15 February 1945) created an atmosphere of impermanence in the lives of Belarusians in Poland, especially in the Białystok voivodship.[49]

Small acts of resistance occurred. In December 1945, a representative from the PUR reported that, 'in spite of a large number of free farms, the settling of repatriants is simply undoable during the winter since most farms, houses and farm buildings are partly or totally devastated by the evacuating

Belarusians and the local populace'.[50] For those transferred, such acts were frequently the only possible way to demonstrate opposition to moving.

The sense of impermanence was exacerbated by the decisions made during the PPR's Voivodship and Powiat-Secretaries Conference of 10–11 October 1944 in Lublin, which confirmed the intention to create a state without minorities and reiterated the policy of population transfer agreed earlier, on 9 September. The commitments made at this conference were soon felt within the Białystok voivodship with the commencement of population transfers and the closure of Belarusian cultural and social institutions. Between October 1944 and December 1947 virtually all Belarusian schools were shut down. Many of these schools had only just reopened following liberation from Nazi occupation (Mironowicz 1993: 192).

Furthermore, although Polish partisan activities were muted in late 1944, due to the large Soviet presence in the Białystok voivodship, by the beginning of 1945 several formal and informal armed groups had emerged. In the main, these groups limited their contact with the Belarusian minority, confining their activities to requisitioning supplies (food, etc.) from the Belarusian peasants, and punishing them (more on this below) if they handed over to the Government the demanded quotas. Since the communist authorities had difficulty in extracting taxes from ethnic Polish villages in the voivodship, a disproportionate tax burden fell on the Belarusians.

By the end of 1946, the removal of Belarusians from Poland had run its course. Relatively few people had been expelled (in the context of postwar expulsions/transfers). Instead, the assertion of Polish culture and Polish values was emphasized and the presence of Belarusians was simply denied. For example, in the Białystok powiat, the starosta (mayor), Alfons Kaczmarek, asserted, in early 1948, that:

> In the area covered by the powiat there are no national minorities left. There is a certain number of people who possibly were previously considered Belarusian but at the present moment in all official events underline their Polishness. These elements inhabit in the most part the borderland gminas in the eastern part of the powiat.

The starosta of the Sokólski powiat was more direct: 'In the area of this powiat there are no national minorities'.[51]

However, despite these denials, the presence of the Belarusian minority was unofficially recognized in the form of widespread negative stereotypes. Belarusians were, as Mironowicz (1993: 154) points out, stigmatized as 'ruskies', 'simple', 'orthodox' and 'from here'/'locals' (tutejszy). Tellingly, as early as June 1946, the president of the Białystok MO (Milicja Obywatelska – Citizens' Militia) demanded that all those who spoke Polish poorly be removed from office – a clear signal of the intent to 'Polonize' the security apparatus.[52] Research conducted by Mironowicz (2000: 40) clearly shows that Poles maintained control of key positions and decision-making within the emerging communist state apparatus. He notes, for example, that, although the membership of the PPR in 1945 in the Białystok powiat was mostly composed of Belarusians, the key positions of the governing body were held by Poles.[53] For, while some Belarusians were functionaries within the emerging communist apparatus, they did not determine policy and remained vulnerable to changes in the Government's nationality policy as well as to insurgent violence.[54] The early affiliation of some Belarusians to the PPR can be explained by their need for protection from the increasingly hostile Polish underground. However, Belarusian over-representation in the lower echelons of the security apparatus confirmed for many Poles the stereotype of Belarusian-communist. But even though Belarusians were over-represented in the membership of the PPR, it is not possible to conclude that most Belarusians were or actively supported the communists, even though they had good reasons to affiliate themselves to the PPR and, later, the PZPR.

By 1949, the 'single road to socialism' policy which framed Polish–Soviet relations at this time, combined with the shift from 'hard' ethno-nationalism (characterized by population transfers/expulsions) to a 'soft' ethno-nationalism (focusing on integration and assimilation), produced a slight change in how the state treated the Belarusian minority.[55] In the summer of that year the Central Committee of the PZPR ordered that Belarusian schools be re-established. But rather than being a mere matter for the educational authorities, the entire administration, party committee, militia and the office of public security became involved. There would be Belarusian schools in the Białystok voivodship, but they would be closely policed by the organs of the state to ensure that they did not form the foundations for a Belarusian renaissance. Indeed, of the schools that had been created by 1950, most were primary schools (39) and three were middle schools. The 'Belarusianness' promoted was a denationalized, folkish culture, which blended easily with the local peasant culture, and the schools largely functioned to aid assimilation and to allow the state to monitor the population. Furthermore, the number of schools created remained substantially below the number existing in October 1944. No other Belarusian institutions were created at this point.

Ukrainians

The redrawing of the eastern border of Poland left around 700,000 Ukrainians in the country (compared to 5.5 million prior to the Second World War), and they were scheduled for resettlement in the Ukraine itself.[56] Though the initial period of the transfer of Ukrainians to the Ukrainian SSR proceeded fairly harmoniously, poor conditions in the places of settlement there persuaded many to return, and this had a negative impact on those who were supposed to depart. Increasing resistance to the transfer programme, together with the emergence of Ukrainian nationalist forces (such as the OUN-UPA) on the Polish side of the border, engendered an increasingly violent response from the Polish authorities. Willingly or not, the Ukrainians were to be removed from Poland. Łemkos were frequently treated as Ukrainians by the Polish state authorities and were also transferred to the Ukraine.[57] This was despite reports from officials that Łemkos were loyal to the Polish State and an order from Władysław Gomułka to end the forced resettlement of the Łemko population (Snyder 2003: 190).[58] By 13 February 1945, Vice-Minister Władysław Wolski reported to the Council of Ministers of the Provisional Government that 70,000 Ukrainians had been transferred, 150,000 registered and some 400,000 scheduled for departure.[59] Physical violence and the fear of such violence, together with various economic pressures, including unrealistic mandatory agricultural targets, played an important role in encouraging Ukrainians to leave (Jasiak 2001: 177).

By July 1945 the Voivod of the Rzeszów voivodship, E. Kluk, in an announcement to Ukrainians in the province, called for an end to the violence, blaming the murders and spilling of blood on both Polish and Ukrainian fascists, and explaining that 'democratic' Poland wished to foster good Polish–Ukrainian relations and would crush the fascist groups.[60] Those who refused to leave were identified as enemies of 'democratic' Poland and the Ukrainian SSR, and described as kulaks, bourgeois, clerics, and reactionaries.[61] However, the killings and beatings which took place in 1945 and 1946 were not just carried out by 'fascists', as Kluk suggested. During that period, NKVD forces were operating in Ukrainian-inhabited areas of eastern Poland and were responsible for several massacres, which claimed hundreds of lives, including the killing of 400 Ukrainians on 6 April 1945 in the village of Gorajec. In addition, groupings that were formerly part of the Polish Home Army (wound up in January 1945) were responsible for attacks on Ukrainian villages. Some of these attacks were supported by Poles from nearby villages such as the massacre that occurred at Pawłokom on 3 March 1945 (Jasiak 2001: 178). The third significant force in the conflagration of 1944–46 was the UPA, which targeted PUR officials, other state officials, the railway infrastructure and telephone lines and burned villages from which Ukrainians had been deported. A substantial number of Ukrainians aspired to a fully independent Ukraine, and rejected both Poland and the Ukrainian SSR. Indeed, during the spring and summer of 1945 the UPA temporarily halted the population transfers in Rzeszów, leading to the dispatch of three Polish infantry divisions with instructions to destroy the OUN-UPA, resettle the Ukrainian population, and clear a 50 kilometre wide area along the border with the Ukraine. In total, some 4,670 Ukrainian civilians are estimated to have been killed in the transfer operation (Szcześniak and Szota 1973: 421–432).[62]

In addition, attempts were made to resolve the problems in a nonmilitarized fashion. On 24 July 1945 a conference took place at the Ministry of Public Administration in Warsaw, in which Ukrainian minority delegates participated, though none from the UPA.[63] The fundamental problem from the Ukrainian perspective was the population transfers, which they argued had to be voluntary. Thus, in a document entitled *Memoriał ludności ukraińskiej* (Petition of the Ukrainian Populace), Ukrainian representatives outlined the problems which the minority faced in Poland and articulated hopes for education, social associations and agricultural reform. The underlying assumption was that they had a future in Poland. Such a view was at odds with the Polish administration's objectives, though at the July conference the Poles suggested that Ukrainian requests would be met following the completion of the population transfers. The illusion that the transfers were 'voluntary' was sustained. Indeed, the possibility of some Ukrainians settling in the 'Recovered Territories' was broached, but not taken up.

By 1 August 1946, 482,500 people had been transferred from Poland to the Ukraine. The final period of the transfers, from 5 April 1946, took place under a specially created military unit, 'Operation Group Rzeszów', which devoted two-thirds of its personnel to the resettlement effort and had the remit to root out all armed resistance. The year 1946 also saw the final assault on the Ukrainian Greek Catholic Church by the Soviets. Bishop Ya Kotsylovsky and his staff were arrested and sent to Kiev. Ya Kotsylovsky was later sent to Siberia where he died soon after (Subtelny 2001: 162).

The transfers out of Poland ended on 15 June 1946 as the Ukrainian SSR advised that it was not prepared to extend the deadline or to provide transport. Of those transported, Jasiak (2001) argues that only 90,000 left of their own free will, as per the transfer agreement. The rest were coerced to varying degrees. Over 150,000 Ukrainians were still in Poland, and they were viewed by the Polish authorities with considerable suspicion. Despite the efforts of Polish officials, the Ukrainian SSR would not extend the June 1946 deadline. During the summer of 1946 the notion of shifting Ukrainians to the Recovered Territories gained some ground, with plans being devised by the state administration (Jasiak 2001: 183). By February 1947 more specific plans were being created within military circles and, on 27 March 1947, General Stefan Mossor presented to the State Security Commission (Państwowa Komisja Bezpieczeństwa) his ideas to shift the Ukrainian population to the north and west of Poland. On 28 March General Karol Świerczewski, Assistant Minister of Defence, was assassinated in the Bieszczady mountains by the UPA. The following day the Politburo decided to 'promptly resettle the Ukrainians and mixed families to the recovered territories (mainly northern Prussia) in a dispersed manner and no closer than 100 kilometers from the border'.[64] This was the beginning of Action Vistula (Akcja Wisła).[65]

Action Vistula had the twin goals of destroying the Ukrainian armed resistance and resettling the Ukrainian population to facilitate their assimilation. Interestingly, a sliver of legal justification for the project was claimed by reference to a pre-war statute, 'Executive Order of the President of Poland on the State Borders' of 23 December 1927 (amended 9 July 1936), which empowered voivods and village mayors to forbid people to enter a border zone. The definition of the border zone could be extended for reasons of national security. This dovetailed with other laws that prevented defined persons from entering border districts (Misiło 1993: 56).

Action Vistula aimed to solve the Ukrainian question by liquidating Ukrainian culture in Poland. Those to be removed to the 'Recovered Territories' had been identified following orders given to military leaders in south-eastern Poland in January 1947 to draw up lists of Ukrainian families and Ukrainian mixed marriages. Religion, background and, according to Snyder (2003: 198), a 'U' in Nazi identity documents, helped to identify Ukrainians. In practice, the operation had at least 19,000 men at its disposal, drawn from infantry divisions and internal security personnel. The operations against the UPA saw the utilization of Soviet anti-partisan techniques, in which soldiers pursued UPA units until they were destroyed. Trapped UPA insurgents often preferred suicide to capture.

In terms of the resettlement process itself, soldiers encircled a village, and a list would be read out, naming those to be transferred. It was frequently a very brutal affair, with significant numbers of casualties and several villages burned to the ground. In addition, given that members of the UPA were excluded from the February 1947 amnesty, and that the director of the operation, General Mossor, had been given wide-ranging powers to achieve the operation's objectives, UPA partisans could be, and were, summarily tried and executed. Military courts sentenced at least 175 Ukrainians to death for assisting the UPA. Others were sent to the Jaworzno camp, which had been an affiliate camp of Auschwitz-Birkenau during the war years, and in 1947 functioned as a transit camp, as well as a concentration camp. A total of 3,873 Ukrainians, including 916 women and 107 children, arrived in Jaworzno, where 158 died as a result of food and clothing shortages and diseases such as typhus.[66] Torture at the camp of those suspected of collaborating with the UPA was routine. During the course of Action Vistula, from 28 April to 31 July 1947, 140,660 people were relocated (Snyder 2003: 200), 630 members of the UPA were killed and 820 arrested (Jasiak 2001: 187), and a further 27 people, mainly old people and infants, died on trains during the resettlement process. The resettlement programme was comprehensive; all Ukrainians were subjected to it, including PPR members, police and members of the various public security institutions, some of whom had fought against the UPA-OUN. The final part of the state project to remove Ukrainian culture took place between July and September 1949, when the state treasury seized all property left by Ukrainians in south-east Poland, including community institutions and property belonging to the Greek Catholic Church.

Thus, the structural violence against the Ukrainians brought together two policy objectives. First, the drive to national homogeneity necessitated the physical removal of Ukrainians from Poland. When this was no longer possible due to the Ukrainian SSR's refusal to extend the transfer deadline, internal relocation was suggested as a solution, which allowed the state to isolate Ukrainian families in Polish environs, strangle Ukrainian culture, and offer assimilation as the only existential path. Second, the drive to hegemony over the entire Polish territory necessitated the destruction of the opposition, especially armed groups. This bitter and costly task was ultimately won by force of arms and through the destruction of the Ukrainian environment of south-east Poland by forced population resettlement, which deprived the UPA of sympathizers.

Autochthonic populations

Although the Council of Experts on the Question of the 'Recovered Territories' advocated granting full citizenship to those of Polish origin who had been German citizens, the process of rolling this out was delayed by several months as the Government aimed to expel the German population. During the period before verification of Polishness was introduced, autochthonic populations were caught, to varying degrees, in the anti-German actions. The harshest example was that of some 15,000 Silesian miners deported to the Donetsk region in the USSR as slave labour in the spring of 1945 (Dudek and Paczkowski 2005: 222).

Between 1945 and 1947 the arrival of Poles from the east (former Polish lands now incorporated into Belarus and the Ukraine, as well as from the depths of Russia) placed additional stress on the rural autochthonic population, as the new arrivals were frequently allocated farms occupied by autochthones. Thus, for a period of time in 1945–47, one farm was frequently occupied by two farmers, both claiming rights over it. In total, 24,000 farms were affected. The problem emerged as a result of the September 1944 land reform, which confiscated the property of Germans, and the initial identification as German of over 10,000 people later 're-Polonized'. It was not until the decree of 6 September 1946 that the Polish Government decided that those farms which had not been abandoned should remain with the autochthones as long as they passed the nationality verification test.

The autochthones were also affected by the law prohibiting the use of German in public, and by the Polonization of place names and personal names. Some 280,000 Polonized their names (Kulczycki 2001: 215). The process of 're-Polonization' continued in earnest in late 1948 and early 1949, as programmes were launched in schools and workplaces to promote fidelity to majoritarian norms and culture. Nevertheless, autochthonic assimilation remained problematic and was frequently viewed by the new population from the east as simulation.

Within the postwar Polish state there was no place for the nationality ambivalences which the sociologist Stanisław Ossowski detected in August 1945 (Ossowski 1967: 275). The notion that nationality was conditional was anathema to both the PPR and oppositionists, who essentialized and fixed

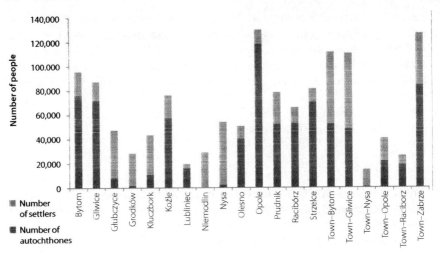

Figure 4.1 Population in Opole Silesia according to origin (31 May 1949).

Source: AAN, PZPR 237/VII/2619, p. 77.

nationality. Autochthones' strength in their regional identity was seen as problematic as, for many, it exhibited disturbing elements of Germanness, which had to be purged to reclaim these people as true Poles.

Figure 4.1 shows the population profile of Opole Silesia in 1949, separated into those who arrived in the region mainly from lands east of the contemporary Polish borders and the autochthonic population. In some places, such as the Opole powiat, the autochthonic population, due to the limited number of settlers, was able to maintain greater social cohesion and a sense of community. Elsewhere, where the proportion of settlers to autochthones was greater, the autochthones were exposed to greater assimilatory pressure and demands to suppress cultural or identity markers that could be viewed as Germanic.[67]

Subjective violence

The subjective violence that afflicted members of minority communities was linked to the general ethno-nationalist sentiment which existed in the immediate aftermath of war. By uncovering groups which were victims of subjective violence it is possible to comment on the socio-cultural tensions in operation in Poland during the period 1944–50.[68] For example, violence against Jews can tell us something about anti-Semitic sentiment *and* the connection between subjective and structural violence. So, while Kenney (1997: 108) is correct in his contention that 'Poles relieved their frustrations related to the war and the rise of communism with ethnic antagonism', further factors shaped how frustration transmuted into violence, including the nationalist narratives promulgated by the PPR.

Germans

The subjective violence inflicted on the German population, in the first instance intimately tied to the war, continued after the fall of Nazi Germany. The Germans in Poland from May to August 1945 were exposed to widespread subjective violence as the Soviet Army and, to a lesser degree, Poles, coerced them to leave through assault, murder and widespread rape.[69] The violence was allowed to continue by the Soviet authorities and tacitly supported – it was not directed, but proceeded from within the ranks. In addition, from June 1945, the Polish Army attempted to clear the border zone of Germans through summary expulsions.[70] In this period the random violence of military units was aligned with, and complemented, the sanctioned violence. With the convening of the Potsdam Conference and subsequent technical agreements, the role of terror in encouraging Germans to leave was reduced. People were still beaten, coerced, poorly treated, raped and killed, but, at least in theory, their expulsion was now regulated by some minimum standards of treatment, and the scale of outrages declined.[71] Nevertheless, many Germans who arrived in the British zone of occupation advised the British authorities of the poor treatment they had received. As late as August 1946, five months after the start of Operation Swallow and twelve months after the agreement at Potsdam, Germans expelled from the Liegnitz district complained of being robbed and suffering poor treatment.[72] Indeed, J. Buchanan, a British official who interviewed expellees in January 1947, was of the view that 'the refugees who did not lose much in the transit camps or internment camps were those whose property had been taken previously to their going into the camp'.[73] The British also received other testimony which detailed beatings, confiscation of property and forced labour on farms at the Potolice camp.[74]

The journey from the interior of Poland to the departure points at Kaławsk and Szczecin was particularly difficult for the Germans during the first half of 1946. Although there were Polish guards on these trains, incidents of varying degrees of seriousness occurred. A British official stationed in Poland for Operation Swallow concluded that 'the Polish guards winked at these incidents'.[75] Arriving at Kaławsk, the Germans were faced with a customs procedure that confiscated much of their property – illegitimately, in the view of a British official stationed there.[76]

The network of camps set up to hold Germans was an ideal environment for subjective violence to flourish. Many camps had been created by the Nazi authorities during the Second World War. While the architecture of the camp system was inherently brutal, camp guards and directors accentuated its harshness to varying degrees through beatings and, in some instances, murder. Indeed, the Director of the Łambinowice camp in Lower Silesia, Czesław Geborski, was eventually indicted for his criminality in 1959. On 4 October 1945 he ordered guards to shoot anyone who tried to escape from a burning barracks. At least 48 people were killed (Naimark 2001: 130).

Jews

The course of violence against the Jewish population is especially instructive. Jews returning from the USSR were prone to random attacks and many were killed. The railway network was particularly dangerous. In 1945 alone, according to the Bulletin of the Central Committee of Jews, 353 Jews were murdered in Poland. [77] Engel (2005: 425) argues that 'it does not seem possible to determine with any reasonable degree of certainty the total number of Jews killed by Poles in the years following the liberation' (1944–46), and suggests that the total number of casualties falls in the range of 500–600, 'with the probability of a greater or lesser figure declining sharply with distance from that range'. [78] These attacks have to be placed in the context of widespread lawlessness. Jan Gross (2000: 196) argues:

> given the general level of disorder at the time, and that many of the victims were killed not as Jews but as targets of political violence or armed robbery, only a fraction of [the killings] can be attributed to anti-Semitism.

Nevertheless, Gross qualifies this remark, 'one must be aware of the circumstances of each episode: robbers often chose their targets on the basis of ethnicity'. [79]

This seems to have been the case in Bolesławiec, where, in December 1945, a Jewish family was robbed by a group of 'bandits' and then murdered. [80] Jews were seen as easy targets and, while anti-Semitism may not always have been the primary rationale for attacks on Jews, the pervasive anti-Semitic atmosphere in the immediate postwar period, stoked by property restitution, myths of ritual murder and established stereotypes which were not seriously challenged, provided a legitimating backdrop to anti-Jewish actions.

David Engel's (1998) examination of patterns of anti-Jewish violence reveals that Jews were victims of partisans as well as unorganized groups and individuals. Engel (1998: 77) argues that the 'peak periods of violence – March–August 1945 and February–July 1946 – both appear to have coincided with periods during which the number of Jews in Poland was increasing'. The response of the CKŻP was to encourage Jews to abandon small towns and rural land holdings and move to the cities, which were more secure. This removed Jews from the reach of those Poles who felt threatened by the possible restitution of property belonging to Jews. Following the pogrom in Kielce in July 1946 the CKŻP organized a Special Commission which aimed to provide 'adequate protection and defence of Jewish institutions and thereby assist the authorities in their defence of the lives of the Jewish population in the country' (Gross 2000: 195). [81] The Kielce pogrom, in which 42 Jews were murdered, was the event which prompted many Jews to leave for Palestine. Subjective violence affected the Jewish population and, in prompting Jews to leave, brought ethnic homogeneity closer to realization. However, the flight of Jews also highlighted the limited commitment and capacity of the new state to protect (some) citizens from criminal actions. Indeed, through the Special Commission, some Jews were armed by the state – recognition of the fact that it had yet to establish its monopoly on violence. Arming Jews also helped the PPR to avoid the 'accusation' that it was pro-Jewish, as Jews were now able to defend themselves and institutions such as synagogues, training centres and community centres from attack.[82] Jewish institutions were guarded by Jews and a *de facto* Jewish militia existed in Lower Silesia, where a sizeable proportion of surviving Jews and those returning from the USSR either settled or spent a period of time (Egit 1991: 65).

By August 1946, subjective violence against Jews was on a downward trajectory and the actions of the CKŻP in defending Jews must take some credit for this. However, as Engel (1998: 79) indicates, in August 1946 anti-Government underground organizations recognized that, following the Kielce pogrom, worldwide attention was focused on Poland. A number of partisan pamphlets argued that anti-Jewish actions were not, at least for the time being, aligned with the strategic goals of the underground. A WiN pamphlet declared, 'at the present moment it is not in our interest to fan the flames of anti-Semitism' and contended that 'Jew Communists' were attempting to exploit anti-Semitism to show to the 'outside world that the presence of Russian security forces in an intolerant Poland is necessary in order to educate the Poles in the spirit of "democracy"' (Engel 1998: 79).

The sharp reduction in anti-Jewish violence in the late summer of 1946 seems to have been connected with the reduction in the number of Jews in Poland presenting fewer targets, the efforts of the CKŻP and the tactical shift of the anti-Government underground – a shift which reflected the underground's understanding of world opinion rather than any fundamental shift in their ethno-nationalist vision. By late 1947, however, the ascendancy of communist power exposed the community to different stresses, most notably assimilation to the Polish identity promoted by the state. This enforced conformity affected all minority communities remaining in 'homogenized' Poland.

Belarusians

The subjective violence inflicted on members of the Belarusian minority ranged from theft and beatings to murder. The perpetrators included Soviet soldiers, Polish soldiers and members of the oppositional underground as well as Polish civilians. In the autumn of 1944, NKVD soldiers intimidated Belarusians into leaving for the Belarusian SSR, often with excessive zeal. By January 1945 the Polish underground in the Białystok voivodship recommenced actions against the Belarusians, largely as a result of a decline in the number of Soviet and Polish troops in the region. Polish partisans stole foodstuffs and inflicted punishment beatings on those deemed to have assisted the Soviets or the Soviet-backed Polish Army.

The activity of the partisan group, Special Action Group – National Army Association (PAS-NSW), encouraged many Belarusians to view the communist authorities as significantly less hostile towards them than the Polish underground. The PAS-NSW, under the command of Romuald Rajs (pseudonym 'Bury'), forced Belarusians to leave Poland, and, during January and February 1946, murdered 87 Belarusians, maimed several dozen others, 'pacified' 6 Belarusian villages and, in the village of Zaleszany, locked people in a building before burning it down.[83] In total, 422 Belarusians are thought to have been killed in the mid- to late 1940s in the Białystok voivodship. Of these, 296 were civilians, 66 were members of the security forces (citizens' militia and Office of Public Security) and 60 were members of the PPR/PZPR (Iwaniuk 2005: 101).

In such a dangerous environment Government closures of Belarusian schools and institutions were, understandably, uncontested and a general policy of quietism was practised by the majority of the peasant Belarusians, both to avoid expulsion to the BSSR, and to avoid contact with hostile Polish underground cells.

Ukrainians

Like the Belarusians, Ukrainians faced four possible sources of violence against them: Soviet troops (including the NKVD), Polish troops, Polish civilians and the Polish underground. All four were guilty of outrages. Soviet, NKVD and Polish soldiers' violence against the Ukrainians took place in the context of population expulsion and the pacification of the Ukrainian armed resistance. There were, as indicated above, actions which went far beyond the legitimate use of force. These included the massacre of entire villages, summary executions, beatings and robberies. During the population transfer to the Ukraine, Szcześniak and Szota (1973: 421–432) maintain that 2,268 families were victims of robbery, over 3,000 farm animals were confiscated, 47 people were either hanged or drowned and over 4,500 civilians killed. Those who remained in Poland during Action Vistula were exposed to further violence in holding camps such as Jaworzno.

Autochthonic populations

Subjective violence against autochthonic populations was often the result of their being identified as German, sympathetic to Germans, or insufficiently Polish due to their coherent and strong regional cultures, dialects and social practices. Consequently, many were exposed to the same forms of violence that afflicted the German population, including rape, murder and beatings – first by Soviet soldiers and, later, by Polish soldiers and civilians.

Aligning subjective and structural violence

Subjective violence tended to reinforce the structural violence inherent in the project of creating a nationally homogeneous state. During the period 1944–47 subjective violence was loosely 'managed' by the PPR through its publicization of the benefits of national homogeneity and 'controlled' through selective interventions according to PPR and state strategic needs. These interventions were responses to both domestic and international pressures and varied depending on the population groups considered. For example, subjective violence against Germans was reduced in 1946 after British complaints that the commitments undertaken at Potsdam were not being fulfilled. The attacks on Germans had their own geography: the greater the degree of British supervision, the less unregulated violence there was. But, by the time British liaison teams arrived in Poland, the period of 'wild' expulsions and camps had passed. Excesses at Kaławsk and Szczecin did decrease, though they were not eliminated. Subjective violence revealed to the German populace, in the harshest manner, that they had no future in Poland and complemented the structural necessity to expel them. Similarly, the Belarusians and Ukrainians in the period up to 1947 were schooled to accept that they had no future as Belarusians or Ukrainians in Poland – by both state policy and the widespread unregulated violence which affected them.

In short, the prevalence of subjective violence directed against minority communities, both those scheduled for transfer out of Poland and those free to remain, was aligned with the structural violence which affected them. However, beatings, murder and robbery of members of minority communities could not be tolerated when the objective of national homogeneity was more or less achieved. From 1948, with the PZPR hegemonic, the PZPR's explanatory models to account for outrages became redundant. Attacks on Jews could no longer convincingly be attributed to 'fascist bands' loyal to the Polish Government in Exile, when those bands had been defeated, amnestied or no longer existed. Direct attacks on Germans, Ukrainians and Belarusians became intolerable, as those who remained were reclassified as autochthones, or as people being 're-Polonized'.[84] Thus, with the expulsion window closed, subjective violence had no strong benefits for the PZPR and considerable costs. In other words, the emphasis had shifted from drawing hard boundaries between Poles and other nationalities to highlighting commonality and a shared Polishness, though the PZPR reserved the right to define individuals and/or groups as insufficiently Polish.

A further factor contributing to the reduction in the tolerance of subjective violence was the less pressing need to channel social anger towards minorities, as the PPR had achieved its objective of holding power in 1947 and expelling minorities. Subjective violence also threatened to challenge its platform, which promised a better future, as well as undermining its claim to offer stability and security. The *effective* tolerance of widespread subjective violence until 1947 can be understood as a temporary tactic, exploiting the unique circumstances of the postwar period, in which the PPR and its Soviet allies allowed society (and their own personnel) to give vent to their frustrations and vices on people who were not to be incorporated into the body politic, or whose incorporation was marked by significant ambivalence. After this point, subjective violence would be tightly policed.

Thus, the shift from a regime of violence characterized by high brutality and high mortality in the period 1944–47 to one which was less overtly violent, owed more to the achievement of the structural (and, indeed, societal) goal of national homogeneity than a simple supersession of violence with power. Violence continued apace, but it was the structural violence of the social system that dominated. The state authorities maintained constant vigilance over society and the Ministry of Public Security made frequent interventions to sustain 'communist' social relations. Indeed, as indicated above, 1949 saw a substantial increase in the prison population as the 'class war' intensified.

The legacy of ethno-nationalism was that negative stereotypes of minority communities remained widespread and this reservoir of antipathy was a resource which the PZPR (and factions within it) could mobilize for their own objectives. The repeated use of representational violence was the natural corollary of power transparency of the communist system. It played the key role of diverting the social anger, which was naturally directed at the PZPR during the course of the PRL. Even within the highest echelons of the PZPR, non-ethnic Poles were described as 'badly born',[85] and it was clearly understood that a non-ethnic Pole could not lead the Party. 'Badly born' referred, in the main, to those who had a Jewish background, but also included those who were descended from any of the other national minorities found in Poland.

However, to understand fully how violence, social anger and PPR/PZPR policy related to each other in postwar Poland, it is necessary to consider the important role of the Roman Catholic Church in shaping the discursive landscape and the PPR's relationship with it. It is to this that we now turn.

5   Securing the Church

Contemporary Polish scholarship, analysing the relationship between the Roman Catholic Church and the state, highlights the growing state repression of ecclesiastical institutions throughout the period 1944–50. Dudek and Gryz (2006: 13) describe the communists as pursuing a 'salami strategy' in their relationship with the Church. By this they mean that the communists adopted a policy which steadily and continuously reduced the Church's scope for manoeuvre through a series of legal and administrative regulations.

However, there are considerable problems with the use of the 'salami' metaphor. First, it underplays the degree to which the PPR attempted to establish a good working relationship with the Catholic Church, especially in the period up to autumn 1947. Second, it obscures the degree to which the Polish episcopate found some agreement with the PPR over the new territorial configuration, and benefited from the reconfiguration at the expense of the 'German' Roman Catholic Church as well as Protestant churches. Third, it promotes a problematic narrative of continuous and increasing state oppression of the Catholic Church and downplays tensions and ambiguities within the PPR and, later, the PZPR. Furthermore, the 'salami' metaphor cannot adequately accommodate the real differences between PPR policy towards the Church in Poland and the Vatican, especially in the period up to autumn 1947, and therefore obfuscates the way in which the Church was able to pursue its own policy objectives by being relatively free from Vatican supervision.

In short, conceptualizing the relationship between the Church and the state purely as one of repression overlooks Church–state co-operation, the degree to which the PPR not only elicited support from the Church, but also required this support and, more controversially, the degree to which the Polish Church was able to exploit its relationship with the PPR in its expansion to the west and north in the immediate aftermath of the Second World War. Indeed, Diskin (2001: 2) argues that Dudek's (1995) reliance on a totalitarian model to understand Church–state relations underestimates 'the power of the Church and overemphasiz[es] its defensive activity'.

The following analysis will show that the Catholic Church had considerable scope for manoeuvre in the fairly fluid political situation of 1944–47, and somewhat less in the subsequent period of 1948–50. It will also demonstrate that the PPR and the PZPR, though ideologically hostile to the Catholic Church (and other denominations and religions), recognized that, since around 96 per cent of the population was Catholic, it had to come to an understanding with the Church, while not jettisoning its social and political programme. As *Trybuna Wolności* (a publication of the PPR Central Committee) put it, on 1 March 1946, 'the Catholic Church is an inseparable part of authentic Polish reality'.[1] Catholicism was understood by many within the PPR as being part of Polishness. Indeed, even the traditional anti-clerical ethos of the PSL was muted, as PSL leader Stanisław Mikołajczyk also recognized the crucial role that the symbolic and cultural power of Catholicism could have. The PPS alone maintained its traditional suspicion of the Church in the immediate aftermath of war, but it was only following the 'merger' with the PPR to form the PZPR in 1948, together with the changed international situation, that its hostility towards the Church was more closely aligned with the perceived political interests of the state.

Mutual benefits, mutual suspicions 1944–47

In principle, the PPR upheld the 1921 Polish constitution, which in articles 111 and 112 guaranteed freedom of conscience and religion respectively and in article 114 proclaimed the leading position of the Roman Catholic Church. The 1921 constitution also contained a contradiction. Article 120 instituted compulsory religious education, while articles 111 and 112 forbade such compulsion. In 1945, this contradiction was resolved in favour of articles 111 and 112, and the Ministry of Education issued a circular to exempt from religious education those pupils whose parents did not want them to receive it (Monticone 1986: 12). In September 1945 the state also legislated that only civil marriages were legal, bringing Poland into line with many western European countries and earlier, in December 1944, the PKWN abolished the religious oath of office given by civil servants and replaced it with a secular oath.[2] For many in the Church these changes were seen as hostile moves but, when placed in the wider European context, they can be seen as neither radical nor particularly aggressive. Rather, they indicated the continuation of the secular pan-European project of separating Church from state, which had stalled in Poland. For the Church, however, these were clearly not welcome developments.

The one action that would, on the surface, indicate a significant breach with the Catholic Church was the unilateral rejection of the 1925 Concordat with the Holy See on 12 September 1945. The rationale for this was that the Vatican had not fulfilled its obligations. Article IX of the Concordat declared that 'no part of the Republic of Poland should be controlled by a bishop residing outside Poland's national frontiers.' Pius XII's appointment of the German Hilarius Breitinger as Apostolic Administrator for the Archdiocese of Gniezno and Poznań for the German population there in

1942, together with the wartime consignment of the Chełmno diocese to the German Bishop of Danzig (Gdańsk), Karl Maria Splett, constituted breaches of the Concordat according to the Polish Government.[3] Indeed, the Polish Government in Exile on 12 November 1942 had declared, in relation to Breitinger's appointment, that 'Pius XII's decision is tantamount to the acceptance of illegal German demands and comprises an unfriendly act towards the Polish people'.[4] Further reasons for the annulment of the Concordat included the Vatican's refusal to recognize the Warsaw Government, the continued presence at the Vatican of the Ambassador of the Polish Government in Exile and the Vatican's failure to realign ecclesiastical boundaries with the frontiers of New Poland. Indeed, until 1954 the 'Recovered Territories' appeared in Vatican publications (such as Annuario Pontificio) as part of Germany (Diskin 2001: 30).

The PPR sought to exploit the international tension within the Catholic Church. So, while it maintained cordial relations with the Church and Church officials in Poland, it was uncompromisingly hostile in its relationship with the Vatican, and sought to promulgate the view that the Vatican favoured the Germans over the Poles and Poland. Such a view also found a following within the Polish Church. The hierarchy in Poland attempted to exploit the animosity between the Polish Government and the Vatican for its own ends. If the PPR viewed the Catholic Church instrumentally, the Church in Poland was not adverse to adopting a similar approach towards the PPR and the state.

The best example of the Church's instrumental opportunism is the Polish Primate August Hlond's use of the special plenipotentiary powers granted to him by Pope Pius XII on 8 July 1945, which allowed him to conduct Church affairs in an undefined 'Poland' in any way that he saw fit. From the Vatican's perspective, granting the resident Episcopal Head such powers would give the Church flexibility and allow it to survive in conditions which it assumed to be hostile. The Primate returned to Poland and was informed by Piotr Jaroszewicz, Deputy Head of the Political-Education Section of the Ministry of Defence (and PPR member), that the Government's main goals were the reconstruction of the country and the incorporation of the 'Recovered Territories', and assured that the Church had nothing to fear (Siebel-Achenbach 1994: 201). In late July and early August, Hlond advised clerical colleagues of his plans to assume ecclesiastical control of the 'Recovered Territories' from the 'German' Roman Catholic Church, arguing that it was the 'will of God'. The 'will of God' in this case was neatly aligned with Polish Church, state and national interests but apparently had not been revealed to the Pope.

On 12 August 1945, Hlond arrived in Wrocław and met with Catholic German bishops, advising them that the Pope had approved the plan to replace the Breslau Metropolitan with apostolic administrators. No Germans were going to be tolerated. He referenced this decision to the fact that Polish Government officials would not allow German clerics to remain and that the best interests of the Church were at stake. The German bishop, Ferdinand Piontek, who had only assumed his post in Breslau (Wrocław) in July, following the death of Cardinal Bertram, pointedly asked Hlond whether the transfer of the diocese was the wish of the Holy Father, to which Hlond replied in the affirmative (Siebel-Achenbach 1994: 203).

At the request of Bishop Piontek, Father Johannes Kaps journeyed to Rome and informed the Pope of Hlond's actions on 10 October 1945. Pius XII was surprised by Hlond's actions, since he had not specifically instructed him to take such steps. The Polish Primate recognized that the special plenipotentiary powers granted to him, and the serious communication difficulties between Rome and Poland, together with the appeal that the 'reclaiming' of former 'Piast' lands had for the Polish Church, provided the opportunity for a radical shake-up of ecclesiastical boundaries.

By late 1946, most German clergymen had departed with their congregations for the reduced Germany. Piontek himself left under duress in July 1946. The Polish Church was encouraged to claim former German churches, and was provided with state funds to repair Church property. In 1946 this amounted to US $40,000 (Diskin 2001: 53). By 1948 the Polish Government had given 2,895 churches in the 'Recovered Territories', most of which formerly belonged to the German Protestant churches, to the Roman Catholic Church in Poland. The Polish Church also received German Churches' properties within the pre-war boundaries of Poland itself, mainly in Wielkopolska.[5] The allocation of property to the Catholic Church did not include the handing over of farmland formerly belonging to German Churches. This land was regulated by the laws of March and September 1946 relating to the 'Recovered Territories' and was parcelled out by the state.[6] The Church and monasteries were exempted from the 1944 agricultural land reform bill and priests were invited to come to the 'Recovered Territories'. Indeed, as early as September 1945 the Government representative in the Wrocław region, Stanisław Piaskowski, met with the Apostolic Administrator and expressed the desire that the Church and the state should work together to redevelop the region.

The state's 'liberal' policy towards the Catholic Church found expression through its approval of the re-emergence of the Catholic press and educational institutions. The Catholic University of Lublin began to function again in autumn 1944. On 25 March 1945, at the instigation of Archbishop Sapieha, *Tygodnik Powszechny* was published under the editorship of Jerzy Turowicz, religious education was adopted in state schools as an optional subject and, by September 1946, some 54 Catholic schools had been authorized by the state (Patrick 1991: 252). Church-sponsored hospitals were permitted to operate, and the Church-backed social help organization 'Caritas', while not legally registered, was allowed to function without harassment (Diskin 2001: 54). Żaryn (2003: 75) points out that 'the local authorities on many occasions financially supported local divisions of Caritas, and even bought liturgical equipment such as chasubles, copes or surplices'. By 1947 Caritas ran around 1,000 kindergartens and 400 kitchens, organized summer camps for tens of thousands of children and played a very important role in satisfying the basic needs of people in virtually all parishes in the difficult years following the war (Kloczowski 2000: 314). In July 1946 the journal *Znak* appeared and, by 1947, there were some 70 Catholic titles in circulation (Żaryn 2003: 83).

The Church lost approximately 20 per cent of its personnel during the war, and in the immediate postwar period experienced a manpower shortage. In 1946 there were 10,344 priests, rising to 10,528 in 1947 and, by the end of 1948, there were 23 seminaries training 1,754 students (Diskin 2001: 11). This included seminaries in the 'Recovered Territories' at Gorzów and Wrocław. Catholic priests from former Polish lands in the east accompanied their congregations west, and other priests were sent west to look after several parishes. The contribution that the Catholic Church made to the incorporation of the 'Recovered Territories' into Poland cannot be underestimated. As Diskin (2001: 13) argues, 'Church activity in the western territories was highly successful and made a genuine contribution to the settlement project in these territories and to the re-establishment [*sic*] of their Polish character.'

The practical basis of Church–state co-operation in the period up to late 1947 was the shared objective of 'Polonizing' the 'Recovered Territories', and in some respects the state and the Church needed each other to achieve their goals. For example, the arrest of the German Catholic bishop Karl Maria Splett on 3 August 1945, for 'activity directed against the Polish nation', was aligned with the Polish Catholic hierarchy's aim of removing German clergymen (Patrick 1991: 252). The expulsion of the German population ultimately made the German Catholic bishops' position untenable and allowed the Polish Church to assume control. This, in turn, allowed the state to illustrate the Polishness of the 'Recovered Territories' by pointing to the presence of the Polish Catholic Church in those areas. Furthermore, by supporting the Church, the PPR hoped to substantiate its claims to Polishness, and to neutralize a possible powerful source of resistance to its agenda.

Initial co-operation was fairly good. In February 1945 Katowice bishop Stanisław Adamski issued a pastoral letter welcoming the Soviet Army and expressed gratitude to the Provisional Government for making possible 'the free practice and nurturing of the Catholic faith'. Jakub Berman, the communist leader responsible for cultural affairs, was pleased by this letter, commenting, 'they [the clergy] are looking realistically and searching for a way to create a symbiosis between the Church and the Polish State'.[7]

Archbishop Sapieha went further. He attended a banquet with Soviet officers to mark the re-opening of the Jagiellonian University, met with Minister of Defence Michał Rola-Żymierski, attempted to stop armed resistance against the new authorities and, in July 1945, issued a pastoral letter in which he appealed for moderation and criticized 'noble outbursts' which 'could lead to heavy losses in the country' (Dudek and Gryz 2006: 12). However, Sapieha also assisted those who did not listen to his appeal and intervened with the authorities on behalf of those arrested for so-called political crimes. The church–state policy of co-operation occasionally found expression in unexpected places. For example, Government representatives participated in the Corpus Christi procession in Warsaw in 1946 and priests attended to the funerals of state officials in the immediate postwar period.[8] At the regional level, in 1946, the PPR instructed all town and rural commit-tees to participate in organizing Christmas celebrations for young people and children, with the aim of enhancing the image of the PPR.[9]

Even more surprising, given the chaos, dislocation, food shortages and insecurity in the immediate postwar period, is the fact that during 1946 an estimated 4 million people participated in pilgrimages within Poland, 2.1 million of whom journeyed to Jasna Góra (Diskin 2001: 23).[10] In July of that year the Catholic Church dedicated the Polish Nation to the Immaculate Heart of the Virgin Mary. The act was performed in parishes on 7 July, in the dioceses on 15 July and by Primate Hlond with the bishops and a crowd of the faithful at Jasna Góra on 15 September 1946. Symbolically, it helped to link the idea of Polish patriotism with Roman Catholicism, and is a good illustration of the Church's ability to act fairly freely in the immediate postwar period. There can be no doubt that 1945 and 1946 witnessed an astounding religious revival that was supported in various ways by the state and, at the very least, was not checked.

For the Polish episcopate, the early postwar years were a period during which the Church's area of manoeuvre was demarcated; for the PPR it was a period in which it attempted to promulgate its Polishness and distance itself from its atheist image (while not discarding its secular vision of the state) in order to attract adherents. Primate Hlond, for instance, pursued a strikingly independent course when he returned to Poland. Arriving in Poznań on 21 July 1945, he did not attempt to meet local officials and announced that a mass to mark the end of the war would take place the following day. This clashed with a previously publicized parade to commem-orate the first anniversary of the establishment of the PKWN. The mass attracted 15,000 people, the parade around 3000, clearly showing the PPR leaders that the Church remained a powerful social force.

Yet, despite co-operation in some areas, with PPR officials participating in religious events, and Church officials taking part in state events, both sides recognized that disagreement and conflict were inevitable. The first significant rift was the change in the marriage law, which the Church rightly viewed as challenging its view of, and power over, family life. Indeed, as Dudek and Gryz (2006: 18) argue, senior Church leaders were more upset by the marriage law than by the termination of the 1925 Concordat. The reason was that the rejection of the Concordat reframed the relationship between the Polish state and the universal Roman Catholic Church, and the state's hostility to the Vatican had the short-term benefit of allowing senior

Polish Catholic clerics, most notably the Primate, to act in an independent manner and expand the ecclesiastical boundaries of the Polish Church to the west. The marriage law, on the other hand, directly challenged the authority and influence of the Church in Poland itself.

In December 1945, at the episcopate meeting in Jasna Góra, clerical antipathy to the new marriage law was freely expressed, with the bishops contending that the law was passed without the participation or support of the nation. And, in practice, the implementation of the law was not immediately successful, as the 1947 amendment made clear. The amendment attempted to break the clergy's boycott of the state law by allowing clerics to perform a marriage ceremony only if a civil marriage had already been contracted and a certificate issued. This was supported by a system of heavy fines for recalcitrant priests. Through late 1945 and 1946, the Church issued a series of pastoral letters which were critical of the Government. In February 1946 it called for a Poland based on Catholic principles and, in May 1946, it crossed over from speaking about matters mainly relating to human dignity to a clearly political position when it spoke out against arrests, executions and the curtailment of democratic freedoms.[11] Nevertheless, until 1947 it was mutually beneficial to delay head-on confrontation. Aware of the privileged status it enjoyed, the Church largely distinguished between ideological questions and practical matters, and the PPR was keen to neutralize the Church, but not through a frontal offensive (Diskin 2001: 14/43).[12]

The tension between the Church and the state was expressed in numerous ways. For the PPR, the Church, as well as being a crucial ally in cementing the Polishness of the 'Recovered Territories' and in assisting it to develop its own Polish credentials, was also seen as a reservoir of reaction, a zone of safety for reactionaries, and an obstacle to the creation of a secular, modern communist Poland. This view was not without basis, as a minority of priests actively supported and sheltered the armed opposition in the period 1944–47. Hlond himself received monthly reports from WiN, and Sapieha met with people engaged in underground activity (Dudek and Gryz 2006: 12). The Church tried to use its influence against the Democratic Bloc in the 1947 election. On 20 October 1946, for example, priests read out an announcement calling on the faithful not to vote for parties opposed to Christianity. But while the Church's sympathy and support for the armed underground was arguably only reactionary from the perspective of the PPR, its stance on anti-Semitism was more problematic.

The Catholic Church failed to extinguish the myth of ritual murder that adversely affected the Jewish population, and did not speak out clearly against anti-Semitism, anti-Semitic violence and the pogroms in Kraków in 1945 and Kielce in 1946. Indeed, following the Kielce pogrom, *The New York Times* reported that Hlond blamed the Jews in the Government for anti-Semitism. The Primate contended that anti-Jewish violence was due to Jews in Government imposing a regime on the country which the majority of people did not want.[13] This assertion does not bear up to scholarly scrutiny, as Engel (1998) demonstrates.[14] The only exception among senior Church figures was Bishop Kubina of Częstochowa, who took an unambiguous position and clearly stated that claims about ritual murder were 'lies', and condemned unequivocally anti-Semitism and the murder of Jews in a proclamation issued on 7 July 1946, which was jointly signed by Częstochowa city and county officials. At the plenary conference of the Polish episcopate in September 1946, Kubina's proclamation was declared to be unacceptable 'on grounds of fundamental intellectual and canonic principles of the Catholic Church'.[15]

For those who continue to view the Catholic Church as an unambiguous supporter of democracy in the immediate aftermath of war, its policy towards Jews – and other minorities, for that matter – provides evidence to the contrary.[16] To be clear, the Church did not extend an equality of respect to all Polish citizens, and thereby worked to marginalize some groups from what it deemed to be the legitimate *Polish* polity.[17] Indeed, the failure to speak clearly against the myth of ritual murder, the support which the Catholic Church offered to the myth of the Jewish-communist and its own ethno-centrism not only provided the discursive legitimization of crimes against members of minority communities, but it also made the PPR's drive for national homogeneity somewhat easier. 'Excesses' could easily be ascribed to 'reactionaries' influenced by the Church, while the PPR could claim to be doing all it could to protect minorities which were not to be expelled. The Church was in many respects a useful ally in the bid for national homogeneity, an ally that was prepared to tolerate medieval superstition in its attempt to weld the Polish population to itself. It attempted to outflank the PPR on the Right, but the result was merely to align itself with PPR nationality policy and to foster an illiberality in the political culture of which the PPR was the chief beneficiary.

Increased tensions 1948–50

The relationship between the Church and the state in the period 1944–47 was marked by co-operation, policy alignment and a great deal of simulation and pretence. Neither side trusted the other, though for that brief period they did need each other. The state nevertheless attempted to limit its need for the Church. In November 1945 it formed the PAX movement under the leadership of pre-war Polish fascist Bolesław Piasecki. Piasecki had been arrested by the NKVD and was interrogated by General Ivan Serov, who authorized the creation of the lay movement of Progressive Catholics as a way to limit the influence of the Polish Church, as well as to illustrate that Catholics in Poland supported the Government. In this endeavour the state was successful and, through PAX, won the support of several thousand clergy, who participated in events under the banner of progressive Catholicism.[18]

The creation of PAX has been seen as a hostile act against the Catholic Church in Poland, but more accurately it should be seen as an expression of the limit of action to be taken to ensure Church co-operation. Indeed, as Prażmowska (2004: 163) points out, Hlond tacitly supported the radical nationalists led by Piasecki until 1947, when the Church informed Piasecki's group that it no longer appreciated their efforts. The emergence of PAX has to be placed alongside the financial, material and political support given to the Church by the state. And, given that PAX had tacit support from the Church until 1947, while both the state's and the Church's nationalistic objectives were aligned, it only constituted a brake on the Church's expansive goals when the interests of the Church and state began to diverge substantially, starting in autumn 1947. Nevertheless, PAX was always a danger for the Church and the fact that Hlond was prepared to deal with Piasecki illustrates the degree to which Church policy utilized ethnonationalism as a means to connect with society and to embed itself in the new Polish lands.

If PAX constituted a boundary demarcating the Polish Church's scope for manoeuvre (a boundary hardening after autumn 1947), so, too, did policy emanating from the Vatican. So, while Pius XII had to accept Hlond's northward and westward expansion of the Polish episcopate, he certainly did not make the Polish Church's position in Poland easier. The Pope's Christmas message of 1945, which constituted a criticism of those who harmed Germans following the Nazi defeat, his 2 June 1946 demand that camps holding Germans be closed down and his appointment of Bishop Maximillian Kaller as spiritual head of expellees in Germany, were all seen as evidence of the Holy See's pro-German bias. This provided a further rationale for the Catholic Church in Poland to emphasize its Polish credentials both to remain connected with the Polish populace and to sustain working relations with the PPR and the state.

However, with the hegemony of the PPR following the fraudulent election of January 1947, and the formation of the PZPR in December 1948, the degree of mutual dependency between the Church and state was much reduced. By 1948, co-operation with the Church as a method to gain legitimacy was no longer necessary. Indeed, by mid-1948 the Central Committee had instructed voivodship committees of the party to highlight 'the anti-Polish position of the Pope' in order to undermine society's trust in the episcopate, and to attempt to increase divisions within the Catholic camp.[19] In this new context, the Church in Poland found it increasingly difficult to accommodate the Vatican's pronouncements and to maintain cordial relations with an increasingly hostile state.

On 21 February 1948 the Pope released *Jura Antistitum circa sacerdotes ex Germania orientali expulsos*, which specifically referred to 'expelled' Germans, a phrase which angered the Polish authorities, and called for the German Church to find positions for clerics removed from parishes to the east. This was followed on 1 March 1948 by a letter to the German bishops, in which the Pope sympathized with the plight of the expellees, describing their fate as 'unprecedented'. The Polish Government, keen to highlight the pro-German bias of the Roman Catholic Church, widely promulgated the papal pronouncements which were most likely to offend Polish sensibilities. Like the attack on the PSL a year earlier, the PZPR attempted to show that only it could be trusted to defend Polish national interests. Indeed, at the 7 May 1948 meeting of the secretariat of the Central Committee, it was argued that the Pope's message could be politically exploited in the same way as James Byrnes' Stuttgart speech was used against Mikołajczyk in 1946.

Hlond, however, was not to be outflanked on this issue. On 24 May 1948 Hlond issued an open letter to settlers in the 'Recovered Territories', declaring that 'on no grounds whatsoever will the Church desire to diminish the territory of the Polish Republic. . . . It is the intention of the Church not to permit Poland to be diminished by Peace Treaties'.[20] Even though the Pope had not expressed support for the Oder-Neisse line, Hlond implied that he had, in order to refute the allegation of the Roman Catholic Church's pro-German orientation. The Vatican continued in its policy of not appointing permanent bishops in the 'Recovered Territories'. The Vatican would not at this point endorse the western frontier that the Primate defended but it did not censure Hlond for his open letter. Hlond's letter was published on 27 May 1948 in the *The New York Times*, thereby gaining a readership in the English-speaking world. The letter attempted to minimize the distance between the position of the Polish Church and the Vatican, but there can be no doubt that the gap remained substantial. As Siebel-Achenbach (1994: 209) points out, '[t]he Vatican had put itself in an unenviable position of having conferred powers to a Cardinal who had consistently acted against the spirit, if not the letter, of the wishes of the Pontiff'. The state's manipulation of the Pontiff's enunciations encouraged the Catholic Church in Poland to highlight its fidelity to the national project unfolding in the 'Recovered Territories', which further assisted the state in its Polonization programme in the west and north. Indeed, the *The New York Times* reported that, on 12 June 1948, Hlond had declared that the 'Church stands by Polish people wherever they settle'.[21] It would be wrong to suggest that the Polish Church was bullied into this position, since it coincided with the ethno-nationalist vision that the Church held for the new lands, and for Poland more generally.

Nevertheless, the Catholic Church in Poland was faced by increasing Government hostility to the Vatican, and remained vulnerable to the claim that it did not prioritize Poland's interests, being a mere tool of a pro-German ecclesiastical institution. For example, the placing of 'interim' bishops in the 'Recovered Territories' rather than permanent bishops was interpreted by the state authorities as a lack of commitment to those areas. Although such a claim was nonsense – given Hlond's rapid replacement of German bishops in 1945, and the 1 million złoty allocated from the Primate's curia to rebuild Breslau/Wrocław cathedral – it did have significant propaganda value. However, the danger to the Polish Church should have been clear. The state was marshalling ethno-nationalist arguments, the same ones that the Polish Church had itself championed in the early postwar years, to ensure that the Church acted in the 'right' way. This policy served the state, as it both aided its nationalist project and encouraged the widening of divisions between the Polish episcopate and the Vatican.

A further factor changing the nature of Church–state relations was the diminution of Soviet support for a policy of co-operation. In Poland, PPR plans to pursue a harder line towards the Catholic Church were set out in late 1947. In both Czechoslovakia and Hungary in 1948 there was a hardening of the state's position *vis-à-vis* the Catholic Church.

In the spring of 1947 a general review of Polish state policy towards the Church and the articulation of future policy had been undertaken. The document, entitled *Comments on the issue of the Roman Catholic Church in Poland* (Uwagi w sprawie Kościoła rzymskokatolickiego w Polsce), set out how the PPR understood the Church.[22] It argued that the Church constituted a serious obstacle to the PPR programme as a source of ideological opposition, that it transmitted reactionary ideas to the masses and how, in some sense, it constituted a dangerous state within the state. It also conceded that the Church constituted a bastion of Polish tradition and culture and that traditional ideas of patriotism were understood to be linked to Roman Catholicism. From this analysis the author of the document concluded that it was necessary to take action against the Church and recommended four key policies. The first was to separate the perceived connection between patriotism and the Roman Catholic Church among the intelligentsia; the second was to promote secularism among the masses; the third was to reduce the cultural influence of the Church; and the fourth was to remove the class basis of the Church – essentially to liquidate the petite bourgeoisie.[23]

During the summer of 1947 no serious action was taken against the Catholic Church. The most notable event was the secularization of the military oath on 3 July 1947, which brought the military into line with civil practice. This situation was to change fairly quickly in the autumn. Following the episcopate conference that took place in Jasna Góra between 5 and 7 September 1947, and in an attempt to evaluate the state's policy towards the Church, the episcopate released a 'Letter to the Faithful' calling on them to boycott the non-religious press and oppose the atheistic indoctrination of youth. It also condemned the 'violation of the religious character of Sundays and holy days' (Dudek and Gryz 2006: 27). The episcopate argued that the state was hostile towards the Church, pointing to the incitement of the PPR and affiliated organizations to act against it, and to the role played by press censorship and paper allocations in undermining its ability to confront and argue with the state in the public arena. It further contended that the state infringed civil liberties and freedom of conscience by making it compulsory to join Government parties. This last point was not strictly true, and it should be noted that the Church's notion of freedom of conscience included the universal provision of religious instruction in schools.

Just as the Church felt itself to be under attack from the state, the PPR felt under attack from the Church. The 'Letter to the Faithful' was seen as part of a Church offensive on the PPR programme. On 1 October 1947 the Central Committee of the PPR met to discuss what action could be taken to neutralize what was seen to be a hostile Church. The era of soft power had definitively ended. It was decided that parish priests throughout the country would be interviewed by representatives of the security organs, with the co-operation of local mayors, to ascertain their views on the points raised by the bishops. The censorship of the Catholic press would increase and its access to illegal sources of paper would be cut, thereby handing the PPR control of the volume of publications. Legal paper sources would also be tightened, with Jakub Berman discussing the issue with paper suppliers. It was also decided to *limit* (rather than ban) the number of masses trans-mitted by radio. A further decision made by the Central Committee held that local government and ministries must become aware of what resources were being channelled to the Church, with the obvious intent to reduce this transfer. This is indeed what happened. Money which had been allocated to rebuild historic church buildings was withdrawn.[24] Over 400 priests were interviewed by officials of the Office of Public Security (UBP). The UBP attempted to persuade the priests to sign declarations distancing themselves from the views of the bishops (Dudek and Gryz 2006: 28). In addition, it was decided that the *ad hoc* and liberal treatment of religious associations would be formalized. Organizations such as Caritas would now have to be regis-tered with the state authorities.

Two weeks later, between 13 and 15 October 1947, the Ministry of Public Security (MBP) further discussed how to limit the influence of the Church. The tone of the meeting was set by the Minister of Public Security, Stanisław Radkiewicz, who argued that the Church was 'the most organized reac-tionary force acting against the democratic camp. This is the strongest force in Poland against which we have not yet pitted ourselves. We must beat down such an enemy as the clergy.'[25]

Julia Brystygierowa, director of Department V of the MBP, whose remit included dealing with Churches and faith associations, presented an exten-ded paper entitled '*The offensive of the clergy and our tasks*' (Ofensywa kleru a nasze zadania) to the voivodship heads of the UB in mid-October 1947.[26] She argued that it was necessary to deal with priests in the under-ground, and to initiate a systematic programme to sieve through Church institutions and personnel, and called for a much harder approach, demanding that it was necessary to jettison the view that 'a monastery cannot be worked over'. She also called for pressure to be applied to Church suppliers and supporters, investigations into the resources of the clergy, strong actions to prevent the clergy from interfering with workers and youth organizations, and the creation of information networks and the limiting of the Catholic press.

By January 1948 Minister Radkiewicz's decision that Department V should be empowered to carry out tasks against the Church had been approved by the politburo of the PPR. This facilitated the moving of MBP staff from other departments to Department V, and the intensification of efforts against the Church. As Gryz (1999: 21) points out, '[a]bout 2,000 operatives of the MBP, supported by over 4,000 informers, took part in the infiltration of, and the struggle against, the Church at the end of the 1940s'.

Yet, even in 1948, scope for dialogue still existed. So, while the pastoral letter of 15 April 1948 to the youth of Katowice warned young people not to let their souls be ensnared by the materialists (i.e. PPR), it also called on them to respect those who aimed to create better conditions for the workers. On 23 April the bishops wrote to President Bierut, appealing for the continuation of dialogue between state and Church. On 28 September, a pastoral letter called the populace to work hard to rebuild the country. This should be viewed as a counterbalance to a letter issued the previous week (22 September) that expressed disappointment that religious education was becoming increasingly marginalized.[27]

August Hlond died on 22 October 1948 and was replaced by Stefan Wyszyński. On 28 October the public health service law was passed, effectively nationalizing health provision in the country, and thus removing Catholic hospitals from Church control. This law also transferred hospitals run by other organizations to state control. Despite the generality of the law, the Church felt increasingly isolated and repressed by state authorities. By November 1948 no less than 81 priests were imprisoned (Dudek and Gryz 2006: 31).

However, the growing tension between the Church and the state was not just the result of the PZPR's latent hostility to organized religion. The Vatican, concerned about growing secularization and the disdain shown to it by governments across east-central Europe, issued a decree on 30 June 1949 forbidding Catholics to join communist parties or conduct activities which promoted atheistic communism. This increased pressure on the Polish Church, which up until then had allowed communists to participate in Church activities. Seeing an opportunity to exploit divisions between the Church in Poland and the Vatican, the PZPR passed a law in 1949 criminalizing priests (with the possibility of up to five years' imprisonment), who refused the sacraments to people because of their political or scientific opinions.

The state's consolidation of control continued in earnest in 1950. In January of that year, schools run by the Church were brought under state control. The legal status of Church buildings in the 'Recovered Territories' was modified. Rather than being the property of the Church on which the state levied taxes, the property was classified as state property, rented to the Church, giving the state and the PZPR greater leverage over the episcopate.

On 20 March 1950 all church estates over 50 hectares were seized by the state. Exceptions were made for the Poznań area, Pomerania and Silesia, where the threshold was twice as high at 100 hectares. One of the rationales behind this move was to restrict the Church's sources of income, as well as to punish the Church for the Vatican's failure to recognize Polish sovereignty over the 'Recovered Territories' (Monticone 1986: 17). In addition, tax rules relating to the clergy were changed, and all income not used for ritual purposes became liable to income tax. Thus, although the Concordat (which contained clauses absolving the clergy from income tax) had been discarded several years earlier, it was only in 1950 that the state actually broke with the 1925 agreement on this issue.

Throughout 1949 and 1950 the Church and the state remained in dialogue and, by April 1950, a *modus vivendi* had been reached which, despite the pressure exercised by the state in 1948 and 1949, was not particularly punitive to the Church. Indeed, the 'Lublin miracle' reminded the state of the Church's power, when, in July 1949, an icon of the Virgin Mary was 'seen' to shed tears. Though not officially recognized by the Church, hundreds of thousands of Poles journeyed to Lublin to witness the 'miracle'. The pilgrimage was only stemmed when the state authorities banned the selling of bus and train tickets to the city. The event is generally understood as a symbol of opposition to the state's programme.[28] It is in this context that the *modus vivendi* was formulated. It demarcated the area which the state was prepared to grant the Church, and highlighted the contribution that the Church was expected to make to the achievement of state goals. Some of these goals were aligned with the Polish episcopate's policy objectives. It was agreed that the Church would:

1   oppose German revisionism and work to bring about Vatican recognition of the Oder-Neisse line;
2   request the Vatican to appoint permanent Polish bishops to the 'Recovered Territories';
3   ensure that the clergy did not oppose the development of co-operatives;
4   not guide religious feeling against the state; and
5   teach people to respect state authority and law.

It was also agreed that the Pope would remain the supreme authority on matters of faith and ecclesiastical jurisdiction, Catholic associations would have access to the press, the public would enjoy freedom of worship and that the state would not restrict religious instruction in schools. The state also approved the continuation of the Catholic University in Lublin. However, by September 1950, Primate Wyszyński accused the state of violating the April agreement, pointing to the situation in schools and the effective liquidation of Church control of Caritas and, together with Cardinal Sapieha, he wrote to President Bierut outlining their concerns.[29]

The situation of the Roman Catholic Church in Poland deteriorated sharply after the autumn of 1947. Its relationship with the state was not to improve substantially until the thaw of 1956, though, during the course of the PRL the Church remained under constant surveillance and pressure from various state organs. During that time, the Polish Primate himself was placed under house arrest (from 1953 to 1956). Yet, despite the decline in Church–state relations, the Church in the period of 1948–50 still maintained considerable scope for manoeuvre, until the major offensive against it in 1950. Its utility as an ally in the expansion of the Polish state to the west and north was much reduced when the German Democratic Republic recognized the Oder-Neisse line on 6 July 1950, and the hardening of the East–West Cold War confrontation made any boundary changes increasingly unlikely in the short to medium term. The Church did not surrender to the legal, administrative and fiscal pressure applied to it, or retreat to a purely defensive position. Its ability to withstand state pressure was due to three key factors. First, its strong association with what was understood to be Polishness – an association that only increased, despite the desire of the PPR and PZPR to weaken it – in the period of national homogenization and population transfers. It therefore enjoyed continuous and widespread social support. Second, both Polish Primates, first Hlond and then Wyszyński, were able to remain fairly flexible in their dealings with the state. In the first instance, Hlond was able to align his desire to expand the Polish Church to the west and north with the state's desire to quickly Polonize those regions. In the second instance, both Hlond and Wyszyński were able to avoid direct conflict with the state, and, although the Church was identified as enemy number one by the Ministry of Public Security from the second half of 1947, and programme after programme was launched to neutralise it, good leadership allowed the Church to operate fairly freely up to, and sometimes beyond, the area demarcated for it by the state. The Church in this period was never a passive target of state policy. The third reason why the Church was able to withstand state pressure was that, unlike the Orthodox Church in the pre-war Soviet Union, or the Uniate or Orthodox Church in postwar Poland, the pressure applied against it, even after 1947, was relatively weak. In other words, even in the harsher times of 1948–50, the Catholic Church remained 'special'. To illustrate how special, we now turn to the ways in which the state dealt with other religious bodies and communities in the period 1944–50.

Not 'special', not 'Polish': non-Roman Catholic denominations

Although the shift of Poland westwards and the loss of its eastern areas reduced the number of non-Catholics in the country, there remained sizeable minority communities who were members of the Uniate, Orthodox or Protestant Churches. Indeed, religion was used as a marker to identify people's national identity. In the Białystok region, NKVD functionaries drew up lists of people who belonged to Orthodox congregations as a

prelude to transferring them to Belarus as Belarusians. Uniate congregations were generally seen as Ukrainian, and likewise identified by military
units prior to moving them to the Ukraine. Protestantism was also seen as
unPolish and was understood as being part of Germanness. Judaism was
also viewed with some suspicion, though this was tempered by the fact that
Jews were not scheduled for expulsion/transfer out of the country.

Thus, on a general level, the PPR and, later, the PZPR tended to view
religion through the prism of nationality. While this worked to the benefit
of the Catholic Church, it was nothing short of disastrous for minority faiths
whose congregations were scheduled for expulsion and whose specific
cultural traditions were seen as incongruent with the homogenizing project
unleashed in the aftermath of the Second World War. As indicated above,
even Catholicism deriving from a foreign national culture (German) had
no place in the new Poland – a view shared by the Polish episcopate and
the PPR.

Protestant Churches

Protestant Churches in postwar Poland included the Evangelical Augsburgian Church, the Evangelical Christian Baptist Church and the Evangelical
Reform Church among others. In general, these Churches were seen to
have a tenuous connection with the Polish nation and were associated in the
popular imagination with Germanness. As Kazimierz Urban (1994: 66) has
observed in connection with pre-Second World War Poland, different
nationalities were frequently linked to different faiths and denominations,
which led to a politicization of religion. The Polish state itself sought to
establish which of the Protestant Churches had an 'anti-Polish' character,
and attempted to limit radical expressions of sentiment in those Churches
most strongly associated with German communities.

The relationship between the Evangelical Augsburgian Church and the
Polish State was fairly tense throughout the course of the Polish Second
Republic, despite the efforts of the Evangelical Bishop Juliusz Bursche to
demonstrate loyalty. His endeavours often met with hostility from German
Evangelical communities within Poland. In 1936, two legal acts attempted
to regulate the status of the Church, but the strong antagonistic reaction of
German communities meant that, in practice, the relationship between the
state and the Evangelical-Augsburgian Church was not satisfactorily
resolved prior to the outbreak of the Second World War.[30]

At the beginning of hostilities, 120 out of 210 Evangelical-Augsburgian
ministers in Poland claimed to be Polish (Kloczowski 2000: 301). During the
course of the war, Augsburgian clergy were removed from central Poland
(the *General Gouvernement*) by the German occupation authorities that
sought to separate German and Polish parishes. A total of 36 clergymen
were sent to concentration camps, where some lost their lives, including
Bishop Bursche. During the Nazi occupation many parishioners signed the

Volksliste, which, in the immediate postwar period, 'proved' to the Polish authorities their disloyalty to the Polish nation. Indeed, the decree of 28 February 1945 sought to remove from Polish society so-called bad elements, largely those described as Volksdeutsche.[31]

On 21 January 1945 Augsburgian clergy met in Częstochowa to discuss the rebuilding of religious life in Poland. At the meeting it was agreed that a council should be established to guide and organize the rebuilding process, a body which was approved by the Ministry of Public Administration on 9 March 1945. On 29 June 1945 the clergy met once more and charged a deputy bishop, Jan Szeruda, to lead the project. Despite these organizational developments, the Church remained in crisis as a result of population expulsions and the taking over of Augsburgian churches and other property by the Catholic Church and state institutions. The Polish Government policy later developed to affirm that property that had been 'abandoned' became state property, and that only property which was being used by the Augsburgian Church at the time of the property decree of 19 September 1946 should remain with the Church. An amending decree of 4 July 1947 confirmed that the Church could be active wherever its parishioners existed. In the 'Recovered Territories', on the other hand, all Augsburgian property was seized by the state and was largely transferred to the Roman Catholic Church.

As early as October 1945, deputy bishop Jan Szeruda clearly perceived collaboration between the Polish Government and the Roman Catholic Church in marginalizing the Evangelical Augsburgian Church. In a note to Edward Osóbka-Morawski on 12 October 1945, Szeruda contended that state institutions (state government, local government, militia and public security organs) in collaboration with Catholic clergy were seizing Augsburgian property, identifying the Ausburgians as German and attempting to convert the faithful to Roman Catholicism. Szeruda's complaint referred not only to what was happening in central and eastern Poland, but also in the 'Recovered Territories'.[32]

Catholic hostility towards the Evangelical Augsburgian Church had been succinctly expressed by the bishop of the Katowice diocese earlier in 1945. Bishop Adamski, in a letter to the Vice-Voivod of the Silesia-Dabrowskie voivodship, argued that there were relatively few Poles within the Augsburgian Church and that this, together with its anti-Polish orientation, justified the liquidation of the Church.[33] The Catholic clergyman was largely successful, at least in the short term, as the Vice-Voivod forbade the religious activities of the Evangelical Augsburgian Church in the voivodship. Following a strong protest from the Augsburgian Church to the Ministry of Public Administration, the Vice-Voivod was requested by Warsaw to moderate his policy in May 1945 (Urban 1994: 74).

However, the association of Protestantism with Germanness remained extremely problematic during the early postwar years. One response of the Protestant Churches was to form a special council with representatives from the Evangelical Augsburgian Church, Evangelical Christian Baptist Church, Evangelical Reform Church and the Methodist Church in October 1945, to provide a point of contact for overseas Protestant Churches to direct assistance to the Churches in Poland. A further council was also formed in October 1945 – the Christian Ecumenical Council – which included representatives from the non-Roman Catholic Christian Churches and engaged in dialogue with representatives of the state on matters of denomination reforms and social reforms and made pronouncements on the socio-political changes during the period 1945–50.[34] Despite these institutional developments, Protestants faced continuing problems as a result of being seen as insufficiently Polish. For instance, Father Feliks Gloch of the Evangelical Augsburgian Church was moved to write to the Ministry of Public Administration in August 1945 on the problems faced by Mazurians as members of the Evangelical Augsburgian Church. He argued that the 'militia not only interferes but assists in terrorising the Mazurian population. In the view of the militia and the Department of Public Security every Mazurian is a German, and Mazurians are just Protestants'.[35]

Other Protestant Churches were similarly treated, with property confiscation and social marginalization being the main policies. Indeed, within the Ministry of Public Administration, a special Office of Consultants considered the personnel and position of the various Churches and made policy recommendations. In January 1946 the Office of Consultants declared that it considered that the leader of the Evangelical Christian Baptists did not have a 'good war' in that he and other leaders had worked with the Germans, glorified Hitler and delivered speeches in honour of the Nazis. Consequently, it argued that the Baptists did not deserve equal rights with other denominations (Tomaszewski 1991: 48), and requested that the Ministry of Public Administration restrict the activities of this Church.

In 1945 many Baptist churches and other properties were seized by organs of the local administration, without direct approval from the Ministry of Public Administration, and either transferred to the Catholic Church or put to other uses. These seizures were resisted by strong protests being sent by the Baptist Church to the Ministry of Public Administration, though without much success. So, while the lack of a legal basis of some property transfers was admitted in correspondence between the Ministry of Justice and the Ministry of Public Administration, the property was not returned.[36]

The Baptists were repeatedly described as being anti-Polish. In March 1946, for example, a militia commander in Łódź wrote to a mayor of a ward in the centre of that city, maintaining that Baptists did not fire their weapons for the Polish Army during the war and, with the arrival of the Germans, became members of the SS and persecuted Poles.[37]

The narrative that Protestants were anti-Polish provided a strong pretext for the suppression of the various Churches, seizure of Church property and marginalization of the Protestant faithful. Only after 1947, with attempts to

'Polonize' the autochthonic population, did the full frontal assault on the Churches ease, and this, in part, was due to the efforts of some of the Protestant clergy in actively assisting with 'Polonization' and limiting contact with Protestant Churches outside Poland. In short, as Urban (1994: 79) points out with regard to the Evangelical Augsburgian Church, the clergy increasingly adopted a pro-Polish position. Yet, despite this, the association of Protestantism with Germanness remained pervasive in the popular imagination and continued to function as a mechanism of marginalization.

Greek-Catholic Church

The Greek-Catholic (Uniate) Church's main centres were in western Ukraine and south-east Poland. The annexation of a large chunk of former Poland to the Ukrainian SSR brought most Greek-Catholics under Ukrainian administration, though prior to the population transfers of autumn 1944 a sizable minority remained in Poland. In the Ukraine, traditional Russian and Orthodox hostility to the Uniate Church was expressed almost immediately with the arrest of all Uniate bishops in April 1945 and the deportation of around 500 priests. In March 1946 the remaining Uniate clergy requested to join the Russian Orthodox Church. As Miner (2003: 189) argues, 'refusal to take part in the forced union with Orthodoxy would spell arrest and deportation for recalcitrant priests'. That same month, in the Ukraine, three seminaries were shut down, most instructors arrested, and 9,900 primary schools and 380 secondary schools which had been run by the Uniate Church were closed.

For the Soviets, the assault on the Uniate Church was part of a wider agenda to destroy the Ukrainian nationalist movement, which had strong links with the Uniate clergy. The Soviets skilfully used the Orthodox Church, placing Orthodox clergy in former Uniate parishes. But the Russian Orthodox Church required little encouragement on this issue, given its longstanding view of the Uniate Church as a schismatic instrument, turning the faithful away from Moscow towards Rome.

Soviet hostility to the Uniate Church was faithfully reproduced in Poland, often by Soviet personnel. As detailed in Chapter 5, in 1946 Bishop Ya Kotsylovsky and his staff were arrested and sent to Kiev, and Ya Kotsylovsky was later deported to Siberia where he died. Subtelny (2001: 162) reports that, according to Ukrainian nationalist sources, 36 Uniate priests were killed in the Przemyśl region alone, in the period up to 1946. Uniate clergymen were identified as sources of resistance to the population transfer programme, which was highly understandable, given the Soviet assault on the Uniate Church in the Ukraine itself.

Greek-Catholicism had been effectively neutralized as an opposition force by 1946 due to Soviet action against the Uniate Church in the Ukraine, population transfer, the killing of priests and concomitant intimidation in

Poland. Indeed, given that the canonical structures of the Greek-Catholic Church had largely been destroyed in the Ukraine through ruthless repression, and in Poland through the population transfer programme and the dispersal of Ukrainians in Action Vistula, the Polish Government did not pass any official decrees or laws against the Church, as it was convinced there was no possibility of a revival (Hałagida 2003: 53). The 1949 decree transferring Uniate Church property to the state indicated that the authorities saw the issue of the Greek-Catholic Church as closed (Syrnyk 2007: 229).

Of the approximately 140,000 people relocated in Action Vistula, some two-thirds were Greek-Catholic (Hałagida 2003: 53). In the main, for many Ukrainian Greek-Catholics the 'Catholic religion was more important than Eastern ritual, [and] they baptized their children, buried their dead and were wed in Roman Catholic churches' (Syrnyk 2007: 244). Roman Catholicism was a path towards Polonization and the 'battle for souls' had a strong nationalistic element.

Nevertheless, the Uniate Church in Poland did not completely disappear. Its clergy were under continuous surveillance by Department V of the Ministry of Public Security. Several clergymen were interned at the camp at Jaworzno. After Action Vistula, which transferred Ukrainians and Łemkos to the north and west, and deliberately broke community and friendship ties in its resettlement programme, the activity of the Uniate faithful was closely monitored. State policy towards both the Greek-Catholic Church and the Orthodox Church, as Syrnyk (2007: 228) has observed, was determined not so much by ideological concerns, but by national imperatives. The state also supported actions which increased antagonism between the two Churches, including the creation of networks of informers.

The Roman Catholic Church also had a substantial impact on the Greek-Catholic Church. Pius XII's conferment of plenipotentiary powers on Primate Hlond invested him with authority over the Greek-Catholic Church in Poland. Many Greek-Catholic clergy were accepted into Roman Catholic clerical circles and were permitted to perform the lower functions of a reverend. Married priests were also permitted to perform religious functions, though the proviso was that their wives had to remain in their old place of residence (Hałagida 2003: 54). In Pomerania, though not in Silesia, the Roman Catholic Church allowed the Uniates to share churches for special religious festivities (Syrnyk 2007: 230). The question of whether the actions of the Roman Catholic Church constituted an act of charity in saving the Uniate clergy from penury and possible repression, or the exploitation of circumstances to complete the domination of a Church virtually destroyed by oppression, remains moot and requires further investigation. However, many Greek-Catholic clergy gave up the priesthood and commenced different careers, as accountants and teachers amongst others. In addition, many within the Roman Catholic clergy, especially those from the east, exhibited unfriendly attitudes towards the Uniates. As Syrnyk

(2007: 245) suggests, the sentiment guiding many within the Roman Catholic Church was both related to the issue of nationality (Pole versus Ukrainian) and to a sense of superiority as expressed in the Latin phrase: *greca fides nulla fides* (Greek faith is no faith).

Orthodox Church

The situation of the Orthodox Church was somewhat more complex, as it was the most ethnically diverse Church in postwar Poland. It was also of considerable significance with regard to Polish–Soviet relations, just as it had been in the pre-Second World War period.

The Orthodox Church was constituted by self-headed (autocephalous) Churches in each country and lacked the form of international hierarchy that characterizes the Roman Catholic Church. Following independence, the Polish State anticipated the establishment of a new Polish Auto-cephalous Orthodox Church. However, the Patriarch of Moscow did not wish to lose his western reaches, and most of the Orthodox bishops in Poland sided with Moscow, given their cultural and national links to Russia. In response, the Polish state named a Metropolitan compliant to its wishes in 1922 who declared autocephaly in July of that year. He was subsequently assassinated by an Orthodox clergyman in 1923. The Orthodox bishops then elected Dionysius Valedenskii as the new Metropolitan. Dionysius sided with Moscow, and this time the Polish state took the issue to the Patriarch in Constantinople, the senior Orthodox hierarch, who, in an effort to demon-strate his influence, sided with the Polish state. The Patriarchs of Antioch, Jerusalem and Alexandria also recognized Polish autocephaly, in part because they felt that 'the Russian Church had lost its freedom under the Communist regime' (Miner 2003: 115).

The Orthodox hierarchy in Poland reluctantly accepted its new status, aware that the political situation in Russia restricted the action of the Moscow patriarchy. Discussions on the legal status of the Church lasted throughout the 1930s, and were only finally settled by Presidential decree in November 1938. The Church, during this period, was viewed as an instru-ment which could advance state objectives. The policy of the Voivod of Volhynia, Henryk Józewski, in particular, as Snyder (2005: 148) shows, sought to 'domesticate this foreign organization, while convincing the Orthodox that Poland was their home'. Part of this policy was to remove Russian influence on the Church, hence the bid to create the Polish Autocephalous Orthodox Church and then to get the blessing of the Constantinople Patriarchate.[38] In addition, Polish State policy sought to Ukrainianize the Church as a way to defend against the Russian threat, outpace Ukrainian nationalists and create a beacon for Orthodox believers in the Soviet Union.[39]

Following the Second World War, Polish state policy relating to the Orthodox Church partly inverted the pre-war position. Metropolitan

Dionysius was now pressured to abandon the 1924 autocephalous status and submit to the authority of the Moscow patriarchy. He refused and was ultimately removed from his position.

However, in 1948 the Moscow Patriarchate recognized the autocephalic status of the Polish Orthodox Church.[40] Most of the Orthodox faithful resided in the Białystok voivodship and had, during 1944 and 1945, largely been identified as Belarusian, with their Orthodox faith being used as an objective marker by NKVD 'repatriation' units. In the context of the state's national homogenizing agenda and population transfers, these people emphasized their Polishness, though in reality national consciousness was not highly developed and most of the population had a more localized sense of identity.[41] Similarly, the Orthodox Metropolitan Dionysius, throughout the period prior to his removal from office, sought to demonstrate his loyalty to Poland. A broadcast from Moscow on 26 June 1946 reported that the Metropolitan had donated 100,000 złoty to the President of the KRN to assist wounded Polish soldiers.[42]

Due to the transfer of Ukrainians out of Poland, the redrawing of the eastern border and, after 1947, Action Vistula, the Orthodox Church in Poland could not carry out its pre-war function of being a magnet for, and symbol of, Ukrainian national aspirations. The Polish Government went to some lengths to ensure that the Orthodox Church took on an increasingly Polish aspect and worked to prevent Orthodox institutions becoming a focus for a possible Ukrainian revitalization in the 'Recovered Territories'.

Following Action Vistula, the nationality of Orthodox people in the 'Recovered Territories' was closely monitored, and decisions as to whether an Orthodox parish would be created in a particular place were, to a large extent, predicated on whether its parishioners were seen to be Polish or Ukrainian. Indeed, if the populace was deemed to be Ukrainian, consultation with the UB (Office of Security) was routine. For example, a letter sent from the Voivod of the Wrocław voivodship to the Ministry of 'Recovered Territories' on 19 January 1948 declared that, 'there is no point or necessity to form Orthodox parishes in [a number of towns in Lower Silesia] as all believers of Orthodox religion are of Ukrainian origin and are settlers of Action "W" [Action Vistula]', while six months later the Voivod wrote to the Ministry arguing that, 'because of the Polish nationality of the Orthodox believers I do not object to the forming of an Orthodox parish in Jawor'.[43]

The emergence of the Orthodox Church in the 'Recovered Territories' began in 1945 and, by 5 June, an Orthodox administration was established which a month later became a diocese headed by Aleksander Kalinowicz. By 1947, with the arrival of people from the east, a network of Orthodox communities had been established. Representatives of the socio-political section of the Wrocław voivodship participated in a ceremony consecrating a church in Wrocław. In the April 1952 resolution of the political bureau of the Central Committee of the PZPR it was concluded that 'the [Orthodox] clergy are generally loyal to the state and influence the wider population in the same spirit', and that the loyal Orthodox should have the support of authorities in carrying out religious ceremonies.[44]

However, the pastoral role of the clergy was highly circumscribed, as the state tightly restricted their function to the performance of their religious duties. Every decision made in relation to the wider parish involved consultation with the state authorities. The control over the Orthodox clergy was further tightened in the early 1950s: in 1951 orthodox clergy had to confirm their citizenship, and in 1953 all priests had to declare 'faithfulness' to the PRL and be registered with the state.

The Catholic Church and social anger

The privileged position of the Catholic Church and the freedom that it enjoyed, especially prior to being identified as enemy number one by the Ministry of Public Security in autumn 1947, allowed it to pursue with some success its own particular policies. Indeed, its drive to incorporate the 'Recovered Territories' would have been somewhat more difficult had relations between the state and the Vatican been more cordial. Yet, as the encouragement that Primate Hlond gave to radical nationalist Catholics led by the pre-war fascist Bolesław Piasecki indicates, the Catholic Church's nationality policy closely mirrored that of the PPR. The Catholic Church in Poland conceived its mission as demanding that it replace the German Catholic Church in the west and north, pressuring the Orthodox Church in the east and maintaining an imperious disdain for Judaism. Since faith broadly dovetailed with nationality, the Church's objectives and practice supported, rather than contested, the state's guidance of social anger. For the Catholic Church in Poland, non-believers were second-class people and, in the case of German Catholics or Protestants, barriers to the consolidation of its influence in the 'Recovered Territories'.

Although reference to differences of denomination and faith can account for the Catholic Church's orientation in the aftermath of war, in practice, the ethno-nationalism of the Polish clergy played a key role. Hlond himself was at the forefront of this movement, recognizing, as soon as he returned from Rome with special plenipotentiary powers, the opportunity to re-draw the religious map of Poland. So, while Hlond and the rest of the hierarchy exhibited continuous antipathy to the PPR and the communist-dominated state apparatus, their actions and many of their nationalistic proclamations linked them to the PPR's nationality policy. Indeed, the Catholic Church in Poland has to be seen as a key sponsor of the social anger regime which the PPR attempted to guide. In short, without the Church's ethno-nationalism (which it justified by reference to the formula of Pole = Catholic), the ability of the PPR to move against minority communities would have been diminished.

The greatest irony of this is that, although the Catholic Church saw itself as being repressed by the state, as constituting a key part of the anti-PPR opposition and embodying the true Poland, it unwittingly contributed to legitimating and securing the PPR in power by its ethno-nationalist policy and actions. For it was through the manipulation of social anger and the 'guiding' of subjective violence towards 'safe' targets such as minority communities that the PPR assuaged hostility which could have been directed towards itself. The Catholic Church may have been enemy number one after 1947, but it was the PPR's most useful Polish ally, especially in the period 1945–47.

6   Rupturing homogeneity?

Class and national identities

The drive to achieve national homogeneity took place within a changing international context. The goodwill between members of the Grand Alliance had all but evaporated by 1947 with the announcement of the Marshall Plan in June and the launch of Cominform at Szklarska Poręba in October.[1] Increased tensions between West and East introduced new considerations about how nationality policy in Poland (and, for that matter, elsewhere in east-central Europe) was to be developed, and how relationships with the West were to be conducted. The language of nationality remained a useful medium of communication, as the ideal of nation-state homogeneity still commanded international support, but it could not disguise the different ways in which nationality was conceived and only thinly veiled the deeper disagreements regarding key issues such as the pan-European need for skilled labour. In addition, whereas until 1947 the ideal of national homogeneity functioned both as a state objective and a method to secure social acquiescence within Poland, it later gained a more contingent and instrumental aspect, directed to audiences outside Poland, largely in the West.

Two issues highlight the flexibility of nationality policy and how it was manipulated to achieve state objectives after 1947. First, during the course of 1947, German citizens claiming Polish background appealed to the Polish Government in Warsaw to be allowed to 'return' to Poland. They sought Polish intervention with the British occupation authorities in Germany and the British Foreign Office, to enable a transfer programme to be initiated. Through the Minister of Foreign Affairs, the Polish Government first broached the notion of transferring German citizens of Polish background to Poland in a meeting with British Foreign Secretary Ernest Bevin in April 1947, and the subject was to remain a point of contention between the Polish and British governments through 1947 and 1948.

The second issue was closely linked to the Soviet-bloc policy of providing sanctuary to political refugees from Greece in the period 1948–50. During those years, the Polish Government made substantial investments in accommodation, food, training and rehabilitation facilities for several thousand political refugees from Greece. Both of these policies illustrate a retreat from the *hard* ethno-nationalism of the immediate postwar years. *Hard* ethno-nationalism is distinguished by its greater reliance on coercion (often physical) and exclusion, whereas *soft* ethno-nationalism includes policies aimed at integration, assimilation and inclusion within the mainstream of society. Both forms imagine a polity defined by its national constituency, the main difference is that *hard* ethno-nationalism seeks to separate various national groups, whereas *soft* ethno-nationalism privileges a specific national identity and demands that all within the polity assimilate with it. Neither form allows space for minority cultures to develop freely.[2] The post-1947 shift to *soft* ethno-nationalism witnessed extensive 're-Polonization' campaigns among autochthonic population groups. The softer line found clear expression in the Polish Government response to the issues of 'Poles' in Westphalia and Greek refugees. Government policy also emphasized economic reconstruction and a single path to build socialism.[3]

Capturing Polonia in Westphalia?

The cessation in early 1947 of 'Operation Swallow' – the transfer pro-gramme moving Germans from within the boundaries of the new Poland to the British zone of occupation in Germany – and the settling of people from the east in the 'Recovered Territories' largely completed the mass popula-tion transfer/expulsion programmes of the immediate postwar period.[4] After August 1946, the provisions of the Potsdam Agreement regulated the removal of the Germans. However, for the Polish Government, the wider project of creating an ethnically homogeneous state remained to be completed. There was still the task of 'returning' to Poland the tens of thou-sands of Poles who had left the country prior to the war or earlier, and now resided in various countries in Europe and beyond. Though this issue had attracted attention earlier, the end of the expulsion/transfer process forced it to the top of political agenda.

In April 1947 Polish Foreign Minister Zygmunt Modzelewski met with British Foreign Secretary, Ernest Bevin, in Warsaw. Modzelewski informed Bevin that the Polish Government was willing to accept into Poland Poles who were classified as 'Reichsdeutsche' living in Westphalia. Bevin's main reason for agreeing to the meeting with Modzelewski was to express the British Government's concern about the way in which the election of the previous January had been conducted, and it seems that Modzelewski's transfer idea was not, at this point, recognized as particularly significant.[5] Subsequent Foreign Office documentation suggests that Bevin did not give any form of assurance that the Polish scheme would be possible.[6] Never-theless, the Polish Government believed that the British had agreed to facilitate the population movement. Thus, what *The New York Times* correspondent Sydney Gruson identified as 'a minor crisis in Anglo–Polish relations', originated in at least a partial misunderstanding, though it must be noted that Modzelewski had a reputation among Foreign Office officials for being 'brazen in his efforts to blackmail and in his lies'.[7] This 'misunder-standing' remained a continuous problem in Polish–British relations throughout 1947 and provoked a flurry of activity in the Foreign Office and the British Element of the Control Commission in Germany. Briefs reached Cabinet level in London.

The Polish administration maintained continuous pressure on the British to ensure that 'Westphalian' Poles could move to Poland. The Polish press was extensively used to explain to the Polish public the issues and principles at stake. In the Polish daily *Rzeczpospolita* on 6 August 1947 Vice-Minister Władysław Wolski (the official responsible for repatriation affairs and a long-time communist) stated that the transfer programme had been agreed at the Bevin–Modzelewski meeting of the previous April. The clear implica-tion was that the British were failing to substantiate a promise, and that the Polish Government was doing all it could to get Poles back to Poland.

The tone became more aggressive the following month. On 7 September, Władysław Gomułka, the Polish Deputy Prime Minister, gave a speech in Szczecin strongly criticizing the British point of view.[8] The next day, the PPR organ *Głos Ludu* published an article which argued that:

> It seems peculiar, this anxiety on the part of the British not to let any 'Germans' into Poland. They do not want to accept from us real, thor-oughbred Germans even up to the amount they undertook to accept formally ... they would like to retain such 'Germans' whom we consider to be Poles and who even sent their delegation to Warsaw in order to ask the Polish government to enable their return to their country.[9]

The Polish Government remained unhappy that 'Operation Swallow' had been ended, in its view prematurely, given that the 1.5 million Germans that the British counted included thousands who had infiltrated the British zone of occupied Germany by unofficial channels. In conflating the two issues – the expulsion of Germans and refusal to allow 'Poles' to leave Germany – the Polish Government promoted a narrative that depicted the British as pro-German and, more importantly, anti-Polish. At the same time, the PPR was engaged in its fierce attack on the PSL and Mikołajczyk, using similar rhetoric; in this case Mikołajczyk was being depicted as a Western stooge. The propaganda that the Polish Government issued relating to the Westphalians made a significant contribution to shaping a narrative which positioned Poland as facing hostile Western forces and a rhetorical environ-ment that made the PPR's accusations against the PSL and Mikołajczyk seem significant, at least for some of the population.

In October 1947 a party of British parliamentarians visiting Poland were informed of the ongoing Westphalian issue, obviously with the hope that these Left-leaning representatives would pressure the British Government on their return to the United Kingdom.[10] The Polish Government was convinced that people it claimed for its own in Westphalia were 'Poles' and, through its Military Mission in Berlin, took the issue to the Control Commission, contending that:

> [The Westphalian Poles] or their fathers have left Poland at a time when every year thousands of Poles had to migrate driven by economic difficulties. Regarding it as a temporary emergency these emigrants continued to regard themselves as Poles and indeed within the 'Union of Poles' in Germany deployed a clearly national activity [*sic*].[11]

This view does have some support. Kulczycki (1997) charts the development of the Polish coal miners' union in the Ruhr from 1902–34 and notes that many did not take advantage of the opportunity to gain Polish citizenship after the First World War, despite provisions in the Treaty of Versailles which allowed them to do so. The Polish authorities in the 1920s were of the opinion that 'the distinction between Poles who opted for Polish citizenship and those who did not had no meaning. The consulate regarded German citizenship as a temporary expedient for Poles until conditions favouring migration ripened' (Kulczycki 1997: 220). Polish citizenship would be granted so long as appropriate documentation and recommendation from the Polish Trade Union (Zjednoczenie Zawodowe Polskie, ZZP) or other Polish organizations was received. However, it has to be noted that in the prewar period, given the surplus of labour in Poland, the 'return' of Poles to Poland was not encouraged. Nevertheless, the PPR echoed the view of previous Polish governments in recognizing these people as Poles, but unlike previous administrations, sought to facilitate their return.[12] Indeed, by politicizing the issue of 'Poles' in Westphalia and elsewhere in Western Europe, and demanding that these people were allowed to 'return' to Poland, the PPR was also highlighting to the Polish public the inadequacies of the Second Republic, which 'created' over-population in Poland through its capitalistic social relations. The PPR implied that the regime of 'forced' economic migration would be consigned to the dustbin of history along with its socio-economic plan. Thus, the demand for Westphalians and other 'Poles' elsewhere in Europe fused the PPR's ethno-nationalist contention that Poles should be in Poland with the longstanding Marxist argument that 'over-population' was a bourgeois mystification concealing the tendency of capitalist social relations to create 'a reserve army of labour'.[13]

However, the British did not agree that the Westphalians were Poles. A British report into the matter (6 May 1947) argued that the Westphalian Poles 'have enjoyed German nationality for 150 years. In the circumstances, reference to a Polish minority in Westphalia seems altogether devoid of reality. These persons are as much German as any other German in Germany.' The report added that the expressed desire of 20,000 of these people to leave Germany 'can no doubt be attributed solely to present conditions in Germany', which were very difficult.[14] Subsequent British enquiries were less definitive, but did not seriously contest the assertion that the Westphalians were German. Foreign Office official Francis Bourdillion conducted extensive research into the issue and came as close as the British ever came to supporting one of the Polish assertions. He argued that the Westphalian Poles originated in the main from the Prussian Partition and 'migrated to Westphalia mostly between 1890 and 1910'.[15]

The British understanding of the issue highlighted the important economic role that the Westphalians played in Germany. In a telegram sent from the Commonwealth Relations Office to the governments of Canada, New Zealand, Australia and South Africa on 30 August 1947, the British acknowledged the

> serious effect on the supply of labour to essential industry in the British Zone, including Ruhr mines, and the problem that, should the West-phalians be allowed to leave, it would set a precedent for people of minority origin to exit to other countries, and be detrimental to efforts to rebuild the economy.[16]

Discussion of the Westphalian issue continued in the Foreign Office throughout the late summer and early autumn of 1947. In September, Robin Hankey, head of the Northern Department at the Foreign Office (he had been attached to the British embassy to Poland during the war years and immediately afterwards as a counsellor), contended that:

> We should resist firmly Polish attempts to remove miners who have been happily established for very many years in our zone, that we should prevent them from building up an artificial agitation in our zone in favour of our miners leaving.[17]

The British were beginning to take the view that the issue of nationality was a cipher for the Polish desire to obtain quality labour. Indeed, in October 1947 Hankey concluded that 'this is largely an artificial Polish agitation created by getting Warsaw stooges into certain key trade union positions in Westphalia and supported by such community organizations as can help'.[18]

The value of Westphalian labour was certainly something that concerned the Poles. In August 1947 Dr Jakub Prawin, head of the Polish Military Mission in Berlin, had suggested swapping German Silesian miners for Westphalian Poles on a head for head basis. This proposal was, however, immediately withdrawn by the Polish Government (it seems it was Prawin's own suggestion) on the grounds that 'those individuals who wished to return to Poland should be accorded the right to do so irrespective of whether acceptable Germans were sent to Germany in return or not'. The British had looked favourably on the proposal, provided that they could 'send inspectors to Poland to satisfy that the Germans offered in exchange are fit and genuine miners'.[19]

On 27 September 1947 the Polish Ambassador maintained the pressure on the British Government in a letter to Foreign Secretary Ernest Bevin, in which he highlighted the importance for Poland of obtaining the Westphalian Polish labour:

> At a time when the manpower of every single Pole has so great a signifi-cance for the country's reconstruction, when there is work for everyone and, lastly, the desire to reunite on Polish soil all Poles wishing to work for the benefit of their country, the Polish Government considers it their duty to assist in every way to facilitate the return of the Poles of Westphalia to their native land.[20]

The obvious implication for the British was that a refusal to come to some sort of agreement on the Westphalian issue would be understood as under-mining the reconstruction of Poland and seen as a hostile act. The British were well aware of the Polish interest in securing quality labour. Jakub Prawin had previously emphasized to potential transferees that the terms of employment in Poland for skilled workers in heavy industry – i.e. miners – were very good.[21]

Given the shortage of skilled labour, the Polish Government needed to attract workers from abroad in order to reinvigorate the economy. This need was compounded by its desire ultimately to release those Germans in skilled work who had been retained in Poland because of their importance to the wider economy. Polonia (Poles settled outside Poland) provided a potential reservoir. However, exploiting this source demanded an emphasis on the Polishness of the Westphalians, and, for that matter, 'Poles' in France, Belgium and elsewhere, as it was only through the language of nationality that to demand quality labour became a legitimate enterprise. And in this the Polish ethnic understanding of nationality was closely aligned with its labour recruitment policy. The slogan 'Man in the right place' now underpinned Polish arguments for the Westphalians to be allowed to come to Poland in the same way as it framed and 'justified the expulsion of Germans from the "Recovered Territories"'.[22] Just as the autochthones maintained a Polish heart, according to PPR and PZPR propaganda, so too did migrants from Poland to Germany, whether this migration occurred 50 or 150 years previously.

Like Polish state policy in the pre-war period, in the postwar period, Poles in Westphalia were assessed to see how they could best serve Polish *raison d'état*.[23] In the aftermath of the Second World War, Polish officials sought to facilitate their 'return' for both economic and political reasons. Communications between the Polish representatives in Berlin and Warsaw described the Westphalians as 'our miners', clearly illustrating the impor-tance of the labour issue to the Polish Government.[24]

In contrast, the British adopted a liberal vision of nationality in relation to the Westphalians, contending that they had assimilated and become

German. This perspective supported the British policy of holding onto quality labour and allowed the British to perceive clearly the logic of the Polish position. Prawin's offer of a head-for-head exchange, for example, was seen as admission that the Poles had been 'keeping back able bodied Germans for bartering purposes, instead of transferring them with others under the Control Council Agreement of November 1945'.[25] The fact that the whole episode had been launched by Zygmunt Modzelewski, whom the British considered to be untrustworthy, helps to account for the rather undiplomatic pronouncements of Robin Hankey among others within the Foreign Office.

A letter dated 10 December 1947 from the Political Division HQ of the British Element of the Control Commission in Berlin to Pat Dean at the German Department of the Foreign Office succinctly summarized how the British understood the entire issue:

> Nor can there be any doubt that the Polish government are interested in the manpower aspect. They want coal miners, and so do we, but they are trying to have their cake and eat it, since they have retained a considerable number of German miners who ought to have been expelled under 'Operation Swallow' and are simultaneously trying to deplete our manpower reserves in the Ruhr.[26]

The Polish petition to the Control Commission in Germany was rejected by the Legal Directorate of the CCG on 17 October 1947 as it considered the Westphalians to be German citizens. It did not exclude an *ad hoc* solution and asked the Control Commission's Political Directorate to come up with a suggestion. The Manpower Division of the CCG (BE) meanwhile had researched how many people wished to move to Poland and recorded that only 1,000 people had reported to the Polish Registration Office in Bochum and the Polish Repatriation Mission at Iserlohn. The Poles, however, claimed that 12,000 people were ready to leave, and that same month (October 1947) the Manpower Division established that 4,160 were men, 4,279 were women, 3,650 were juveniles. A total of 672 were coal miners, with the rest involved in inessential employment. A Manpower Division official contended that 'a fair number of these may have registered in the hope of obtaining some special advantage and I do not think they would be willing to go forward for repatriation when the time came'.[27]

With this information, the British decided to accede to individual requests, conditional on manpower requirements in the British zone of occupation, and hold out against a mass population transfer programme. Nevertheless, the Polish Government maintained pressure, highlighting for domestic consumption the fact that it was attempting to safeguard Polish national interests against an imperial power. On 17 December 1947 at 17.30 on Radio Warsaw, Deputy Premier and Minister for the 'Recovered Territories', Władysław Gomułka, declared that Westphalian Poles were being prevented from returning to Poland by the British and concluded that, 'Poland is not a colonial country and therefore she cannot allow the British to decide the fate of Poles living in Germany'.[28]

Yet, in essence, the British interest won out. Mass migration was ruled out, direct Polish agitation in Westphalia was prohibited and individuals were given the option to leave for Poland and become Polish citizens. A description of the arrangements for transfer and the bureaucratic formalities that the 'Westphalians' would have to complete before leaving for Poland was sent to the Polish Military Mission in Berlin on 28 January 1948.[29] These arrangements were later finalized through a series of talks between Brigadier Staveley, head of the Entries and Exits Branch in the British Zone, and Colonel Marecki of the Polish Mission.[30]

Though the full extent of Polish demands had not been met, the several months of pressure had played a useful role in showing to a domestic audience that Poles abroad were of concern to the Government, had heightened the sense that the West favoured Germans over Poles, reiterated the contention that only the PPR was prepared to look after Polish national interests and provided a concrete example of how the Second Republic had failed. At the international level, the 'Westphalian' issue looked somewhat different. Claims regarding the existence of a Polish minority in Westphalia were seen as a covert method of securing valuable labour, and the anti-British rhetoric which accompanied the Polish campaign sharpened the division between East and West, identified by Churchill, in his 'Iron Curtain' speech at Fulton, Missouri, and by others in 1946. Indeed, the loss of quality labour was seen as potentially disastrous for the British zone of occupation in Germany. Yet the conflict only came about due to the prior consensus on the desirability of national homogeneity in east-central Europe. Discourses of nationality channelled discussion of Westphalian Poles, even if they were merely a cipher for the critical issue of labour.

British consent to move people to Poland was given in January 1948 and the Poles responded with some speed. On 10 February Władysław Wolski hosted a conference at the Ministry of Public Administration in Warsaw, attended by key personnel to be involved in the transfer, including Vice-Director Kirszenstein of the Central Coal Industry Board, Leon Szybek of the Ministry of Foreign Affairs, Mścisław Olechnowicz from the State Repatriation Office, Colonel Marecki from the Polish Military Mission in Berlin, Jan Pietkiewicz from the Ministry for the 'Recovered Territories', Kazimierz Lewandowski from the Ministry of Trade and Industry and Roman Szymanko of the Ministry of Labour and Social Security. Wolski highlighted the importance of achieving the transfer of Westphalian Poles to Poland without problems.

> This is a serious issue because the running of the entire re-emigration operation from Westphalia will depend upon how we handle the first

Westphalian arrivals, to what degree we take care of them, how we arrange homes and ensure work for them.[31]

Colonel Marecki then summarized the events of the preceding months, acknowledging that 'the re-migration of Westphalians apart from its social character has a strong political aspect'. Marecki admitted to colleagues at the conference that Polish hopes of securing quality skilled labour had been largely thwarted by the Control Commission and the British:

Our plan aimed in the first instance to transfer miners and only in later stages to transfer other workers and possibly their families. The decision of the British authorities went in the totally opposite direction.[32]

Marecki described the Westphalians and outlined potential problems which their arrival in Poland may cause. He argued that the Westphalians maintained their Polish national consciousness and had a strong sense of working-class solidarity. However, he expressed apprehension that, since the Westphalians had lived for so many years in Germany, they had become 'soaked through with a German mentality, which might annoy us'. Marecki was also concerned that the Westphalians may be 'sworn at as Hitlerites or Germans because they have a slightly German accent'.[33]

So, while the Polish Government used every opportunity to claim the Westphalians as Poles, those closely connected with the project expressed concern that they would not be viewed as such in Poland itself. Despite this apprehension, Polish officials saw them as being of the right class and came to the conclusion that 're-migrants' from various European countries would become both economic and political assets. Marecki then highlighted the Westphalians' class credentials:

The majority of Westphalians, casting aside those not able to work, even if there [in Germany] they pass for unqualified people, in light of practice and observation these people turn out to be fully capable of working in the most important industries. The reason for this is that all of the Westphalians are of the traditions of industry.[34]

Westphalian farmers were also praised for their 'strong sense of class' and 'high standing in terms of the culture of farming'.[35]

It was coal miners that attracted the most interest, however. By the time of the meeting at the Ministry of Public Administration, some 500 miners from the estimated 10,000–12,000 among the Westphalians had elected to move to Poland. The good treatment of the 're-migrants' would, it was thought, attract those people (skilled labour) that Polish officials wanted. Marecki optimistically opined that 'the mining and metal industry will fully benefit in 1948 from the Westphalians'.[36]

However, the projections of Polish officials were not fulfilled and, as early as 4 March 1948, Colonel Marecki complained to Major Williamson at the Manpower Division. He disagreed with 'the principle that the return of Westphalian Poles to their homeland should depend on the difficulties of German industry', and argued that, 'owing to such proceedings mostly unproductive Westphalian Poles, being decisively a burden to the economy of the British Occupation Zone, are being allowed to leave the Zone'.[37] No doubt the British recognized the irony of Marecki's complaint, given that throughout 'Operation Swallow' the dearth of 'productive' Germans being sent to the British Zone by the Poles was a constant issue. Marecki's intervention failed to change the profile of those electing to move to Poland. The first train of Westphalians included 'a considerable proportion of the so called weak element (elderly, invalids)'.[38] Indeed, in the period of the Westphalian operation (6 April 1948 to 16 October 1948), a total of just 4,223 Westphalian Poles arrived in Poland, considerably below the estimates of Polish officials, who put the figure at around 12,000.[39]

Nevertheless, the Westphalian incident should not be considered a failure of Polish policy. Through the efforts to bring in people from Westphalia, the Polish Government was able productively to channel ethno-nationalist arguments in the international arena. By maintaining that Westphalians remained Polish, despite having German citizenship (some had even fought in the Wehrmacht), the Polish Government was able to access the pools of quality labour that were required both to rebuild the country and to replace non-ethnic Poles (mainly Germans) in skilled work, though not to the extent that Polish officialdom had hoped. By politicizing the issue at all levels – ministerial through to press reports – the Polish Government was able to demonstrate to the Polish population its commitment to build a new Poland, one freed from the regime of economic migration which characterized the interwar period. A further factor underpinning Government policy was the fact that the so-called 'return migrants', given their dependency on the PPR/PZPR for housing and work, were likely to become loyal supporters of the state. This calculation bore fruit with the 'remigrants' from France in particular, during the 1950s and 1960s.

The policy towards re-migrants, including those arriving from Westphalia, France and Belgium, constituted a *soft* ethno-nationalism. It celebrated the Polishness of Poles abroad, promoted a narrative of an exile consequent on the shortcomings of the Second Republic and promised an attractive future for the Polish worker. The return of these 'migrants' was highly politicized and served to depict the West, and Britain in particular, as pro-German and anti-Polish. This propaganda sought to demonstrate to a domestic audience the fact that the PPR-dominated Government would defend Poland's national interest in the face of what it identified as the West's pro-German policies. It also aimed to discredit those parties (and individuals) that maintained links with and hopes in the Western powers. Through the arrival of potentially loyal citizens, the Government also sought to strengthen the link between the socio-economic revolution and the national revolution.

Refugees from Greece

While the 'Westphalian' issue marked the shift to a soft ethno-nationalism, Polish acceptance of the political refugees from Greece, as part of the wider Soviet-sponsored project of offering asylum, highlighted the flexibility of Polish nationality policy in the context of bloc geopolitics. This is not to suggest that the arrival of refugees from Greece signalled an end to the ethno-nationalist project, rather that the refugees' status as non-Polish was parenthesized by their status as working class and peasant heroes, and the fact that they were not native.[40] As such, their categorization as political refugees shielded them from the strong assimilationist pressure placed on Poland's remaining indigenous minority communities during the late 1940s and throughout the duration of the PRL.[41] However, the primary rationale for accepting these refugees was geopolitical.

Postwar Greece attracted considerable interest from both East and West. The British were determined that the country would remain within the Western sphere of influence and Churchill was prepared to make deals with Stalin to ensure that this took place. At the meeting between Stalin and Churchill on 9 October 1944 in Moscow, Churchill produced his 'naughty document'.[42] This meeting should not be too hastily dismissed, as it constituted a serious attempt by Churchill to secure 'a free hand in Greece, so that British troops could land . . . and pre-empt a Communist coup without fear of Soviet recrimination' (Reynolds 2004: 460). The British Prime Minister listed the states of central Europe and the Balkans, and allocated to the USSR and the UK/USA a percentage of influence in each state. Nevertheless, Sebag-Montefiore (2004: 486) is correct in his contention that, from Stalin's perspective, Churchill's note was 'surely a bemusing attempt to negotiate what was already a *fait accompli*' in relation to Eastern Europe. Despite this, Churchill's formulations provided the framework for two days of discussions on the proportion of influence in Bulgaria between Soviet Foreign Minister Vyacheslav Molotov and British Foreign Secretary Anthony Eden.

As early as 9 August 1944, the War Cabinet and the Foreign Secretary discussed the issue of Greece. Eden had outlined Britain's strategic interest in Greece and had contended that a takeover by Greek Communists could result in a massacre, which would damage British prestige and lead to Greece becoming part of the Balkan Slav bloc under Russian influence (Gerolymatos 2004: 58). The British were prepared to prevent such an eventuality, and, in December 1944 airlifted an army division from Italy to Athens to secure victory in the Battle of Athens (Gerolymatos 2004: 154). If only for his own political reasons, Stalin was faithful to the arrangement he had made with Churchill in October 1944 in relation to Greece. Table 6.1

Table 6.1 Allocation of influence according to the 'naughty document'

State	Proportion of influence
Romania	90% Russian – 10% UK/US
Greece	10% Russian – 90% UK/US
Yugoslavia	50% Russian – 50% UK/US
Hungary	50% Russian – 50% UK/US
Bulgaria	75% Russian – 25% UK/US (subsequently adjusted to 80% – 20%)

Source: Churchill 1985: 198.

illustrates how influence was allocated by Churchill, and approved by Stalin.

The British, and later the USA, aided the anti-communist faction during the course of the Greek Civil War, to ensure that Greece remained in the Western sphere of influence.[43] The USSR did have the option of backing the National People's Liberation Army (ELAS) and later the Greek Democratic Army, in which the leading role was played by the Communist Party of Greece.[44] Stalin gave his reasons for not aiding the Greek Democratic Army to the General Secretary of the Communist Party of Greece, Nikos Zachariadis, in the early 1950s. He pointed out, in 1949, that he did 'not advance the Red Army into Greece in 1944 because he did not want to clash with the British, [noting that] the Soviet Union did not have a navy for such an undertaking' (Gerolymatos, 2004: 127). The Yugoslavian communists under Tito were not constrained by such concerns and did support the Democratic Army. Nevertheless, the Greek communist leadership looked to the USSR.[45] Following the Yugoslav–USSR split in 1948, military aid to the Greek communists from Yugoslavia was withdrawn.

In 1948 the Democratic Army was in serious military difficulties and, in autumn of that year, the decision was taken to evacuate civilians to the safety of countries of the socialist bloc. British and, later, US support played an important role in the success of the anti-communists.[46] By the autumn of 1949 the Democratic Army had lost the military initiative and had to face the harsh reality of military defeat and exile. A further factor in the defeat of the Democratic Army was the disastrous change in military tactics in the summer of 1949. Guerrilla warfare, which had served the Democratic Army fairly well, and which was very flexible, was replaced by positional warfare. Within two months the war was over, as Greek Government forces overwhelmed the Democratic Army with superior firepower, a greater number of men and the use of American-sourced napalm. On 16 October 1949 the radio station of the communist-controlled temporary government gave the order to retreat. Both soldiers and civilians were evacuated from Greece to communist countries of east-central Europe and to the USSR.

The Greek Civil War and its aftermath were brutal. It is estimated that over 150,000 people lost their lives during the conflict between 1946 and 1949. Those who survived and remained in Greece and were suspected of having been, or were found to have been, on the Democratic Army side faced a very bleak future. Approximately 3,000 were shot and a further 60,000 were placed in prisons or labour camps (Pudło 1995: 134). Thus, for many, exile offered the only real possibility of escaping persecution. In the period 1948–49, between 55,000 and 100,000 left Greece for life abroad.[47]

For the governments of the communist camp, including the Polish Government, providing sanctuary for Greek political refugees enabled them to highlight what they believed to be the illegitimacy of the 'fascist' Greek Government. As early as 1947, the PPR's propaganda department published a text for distribution at PPR schools, analysing the international situation, in which the Greek Government was described as a monarchist-fascist regime that only came to power thanks to English bayonets.[48]

The communist camp continuously drew attention to the Greek Government's harsh treatment of the opposition. Later, the communists of east-central Europe, together with the USSR, contested the illegal withdrawal of citizenship by the Greek Government from those who fled or were evacuated. By maintaining that those who had left Greece were *political* refugees, communists sought to occupy the moral high ground and criticize the West for failing to uphold those very values that it allegedly cherished and wished to promote. The exile of the Greek refugees was also used to deflect Western criticisms from the communists' own questionable practices. However, it should be noted that the offer of sanctuary to the Greeks also served to show the solidarity and fraternity celebrated in communist propaganda to an oppressed group. The hand of friendship extended to the Greeks cannot be reduced to simple geopolitical manoeuvring; for those involved it was (also) a realization of closely held ideals.

In Poland, the theme of Western hypocrisy was continuously developed and promulgated during the late 1940s and early 1950s. The Polish Society of Friends of Democratic Greece was formed in 1948 to improve the Polish population's knowledge of what was happening in Greece. It included amongst its membership a number of high-profile personalities, including the famous Polish poets Władysław Broniewski and Julian Tuwim, Zofia Nałkowska and KCPZPR member Ostap Dłuski. Polish academics were also involved in promoting knowledge of the conflict in Greece, and, in 1949, issued a protest against the 'massacres by the Athens fascists'. The academics saw a clear link between what was happening in Greece and the Nazi occupation: 'We state that the Athenian regime by murdering former partisans because they had fought against the Germans and collaborators is continuing the work of the Hitlerites'.[49] By framing the issue in this way, the protest was sure to be registered by the Polish public, who clearly understood what the work of the Hitlerites looked like.

The evacuation of people from Greece was co-ordinated by representatives of the 'free' Greek Government, in collaboration with representatives from communist states, including Poland. Refugees were sent to the various countries of the communist bloc. The movement to Poland went through three distinct stages.

The first phase of evacuation to Poland started in late 1948 and finished in early 1949. It was exclusively composed of children, who were removed from areas close to the front.[50] The second phase took place in 1949 and 1950, as a consequence of the defeat of the Democratic Army. It was composed of fighters and auxiliary staff, as well as civilians. The final phase reunited families which had become separated during the evacuation to eastern Europe and the USSR. Table 6.2 summarizes the movement of people to Poland.

Most of the refugees left Greece via Albania (76.6 per cent), where they boarded ships taking them to Poland. On the ships a sign written in Greek declared: 'The Polish nation welcomes heroes of the Greek nation' (Wojecki 1989: 22). The notion that the Greeks were heroes was also promulgated at the December 1948 Congress amalgamating the PPR and PPS to form the PZPR. The propaganda department of the PPR's Voivodship Committee in Łódź prepared a number of slogans celebrating socialist internationalism, one of which declared: 'Hail to the heroes of the Greek Democratic Army'.[51]

In Poland, the Central Committee of the PZPR was clear that the refugees had to be well cared for. It therefore devoted considerable resources to ensure that the needs of the refugees were swiftly met. It was immediately acknowledged that the refugees were in a very poor condition and needed a great deal of help. Not only was the treatment of the refugees politicized by the ongoing propaganda battle with the West, but the refugees themselves were idealized as heroes fighting for communism. They were therefore entitled to the best treatment that could be provided for them. And to ensure

Table 6.2 Refugees to Poland 1948–50 according to role played in the Civil War

Date of arrival	Number of people	Partisans	Civilians
10 and 27/10/48	1,013	–	1,013 children
04/49	2,200	–	2,200 children
13/7/49	752	752	–
25/8/49	2,100	1,200	900
13/12/49	2,750	1,900	850
11/1/50	1,500	1,400	100
14/7/50	1,400	900	500
6/8/50	780	500	280
Total	12,495	6,652	5,843

Source: Wojecki 1989: 22 from data provided by Perkilis Huliars, the first leader of the Association of Greek refugees in Poland.

that they were well cared for, senior communists took control and oversight of the entire Greek settlement and rehabilitation effort. Vice-Director Antoni Alster of the Organisational Department of the Central Committee of the PZPR wrote, in early 1950, to the secretaries of Wrocław, Szczecin, Rzeszów, Katowice, Gdańsk and Poznań voivodships to highlight the entire issue. He pointed out that:

> On the terrain of [your] voivodship there are groups of Greek partisans and their families. They are taking advantage of the right of asylum which is an expression of international solidarity of the Polish working class with the Greek working class and nation, which is carrying on an heroic struggle against Anglo-American imperialists and their agents.

Alster then advised the voivodship secretaries that the Greek refugees were mainly of peasant origin and did not know the Polish language. He called on the relevant party institutions and state organs to assist the refugees.[52]

The effort to settle the refugees in Poland and to provide for their needs was co-ordinated by the Communist Party of Greece and the voivodship secretaries, with oversight being maintained by KCPZPR member Ostap Dłuski. It is worth noting, however, that in the late 1940s the arrival of refugees from Greece was a state secret. Polish workers at reception points in Lower Silesia were forbidden to reveal the nationality of the incoming children – or how many there were – and had to pledge an oath of secrecy. In order to maintain secrecy, the refugees frequently arrived in Lower Silesia at night. In addition, those refugees arriving on the initial transports were described as Romanians, Spaniards or even Americans en route home to their own countries. The policy of secrecy was the result of concern about the response of the wider international community to the evacuation (especially of children) and due to the potential impact that news of evacuation could have on the military situation – at least until October 1949. It is also likely that the Poles were initially apprehensive about the response of Polish society, given that it had been subject to ethno-nationalist propaganda for several years. Secrecy was also maintained over the arrival of later transports of refugees.

The refugees were not expected to stay in Poland long, and certainly not for decades. Rather, it was thought that the refugees would return to Greece in the not-too-distant future, fully prepared to renew the fight for democracy (as defined by the Poles and their Soviet allies). As Pudło (1995) has observed, the refugees were initially seen as essential human capital that would stimulate the emergence of a democratic polity in Greece. And with this view in mind, the fit and able among the refugees were at first accommodated in barracks and given military training under the guidance of the Communist Party of Greece. Part of this training included essential ideological orientation.

The Polish authorities initially settled the refugees from Greece in the under-populated 'Recovered Territories', and particularly in towns near the new Polish–German border such as Zgorzelec and Police. The situation of these towns, away from established Polish communities, both aided secrecy and helped to sustain the fiction that the refugees were displaced people on their way to their home countries. From 1950, the Polish state recognized that greater efforts were required to enable the Greeks to live in as normal a manner as possible, and so initiated training in the Polish language and in trades, crucial to allow the Greeks to participate in the Polish economy and make a living. Many Greeks were given employment at State Agricultural Farms, where they formed an important part of the workforce, and thereby made a contribution to implementing the PZPR agricultural policy in the western part of the 'Recovered Territories'. In addition, a significant number of Greeks found work in factories. Of the 4,000 refugees in Zgorzelec in 1950, 1,600 worked in the 'Delta' co-operative and the suitcase factory. Most of the others were either invalids, sick people, children or mothers with infants.[53] In Zgorzelec alone, over half of the refugees were reliant on some form of support from the Polish state.

One of the main ways the refugees from Greece were helped was through a special programme channelled through the Workers' Holiday Fund Special Action under the direction of Czesław Todys. The Central Council of Trade Unions launched the programme by decree on 7 September 1949, and it should be seen as an attempt by the PZPR to give concrete expression to the declared international working-class solidarity. The programme was fairly generously funded and had four main aims:

1   To employ in industry all those able to work and to search out and prepare an appropriate number of flats/homes.
2   To teach a trade and employ all invalids.
3   To organize care homes for the elderly.
4   To provide care for all repatriants and make it possible for families to be united.[54]

In early 1950 the Greek refugees themselves expressed thanks and loyalty to the PZPR, and continued to enjoy the support of the Party. The PZPR was not slow to exploit the Greeks' sense of grievance in order to accumulate moral capital in relation to the West. By 1949 declarations were being made by well-known Polish academics, supporting the refugees and condemning the Athens regime; the early 1950s witnessed campaigns against executions; and from the mid-1950s onwards, attention focused on amnesties, easing of prisoners' ordeals in Greek prisons and camps, and the emergence of the 'repatriation-with-honour' campaign. The anti-execution campaign to save left-wing combatants in Greece, for example, had the complete support of the Polish ruling elite and cemented a good relationship between the refugees and the authorities. Emblematic was the campaign to save the life of Nikos Beloyannis, who was ultimately executed in

Greece on 30 March 1952.[55] His name subsequently prefixed the refugee association.

Since their legal position, survival, education and life chances were dependent on the PZPR, and given that they had no malignant historical legacy to deal with in Poland, the Greeks were generally loyal to the ruling Polish authorities. Reports from the nationality section of the PZPR note the lack of anti-Greek sentiment within Polish society. Importantly, they were of the right classes (peasants/workers) and, as Pudło (1995: 140) suggests, elite philo-Hellenism also helped to sustain good relations between the refugees and the Party. As a result of these factors, the PZPR treated them well, both in the period up to 1950 and afterwards.

The acceptance of the Greek refugees was a co-ordinated programme across east-central Europe and the Soviet Union, and indicates that Polish nationality policy could accommodate geopolitical demands. And while, between 1948 and 1950, there was little sense that the Greeks would have to remain in Poland for several decades, as early as 1949 it was clear that some form of integration would have to take place. The fact that most of the refugees could be classified as 'working class' gave substance to declared international working-class solidarity. And, given the relatively few refugees that arrived, the positive perception of them held by wider Polish society, the loyalty the refugees showed towards the PZPR and the fact that they were expected one day to return to Greece, the Government treated them as a privileged national group. They were not expected, or pressured, to discard their cultural identity, as were Poland's indigenous minorities. Indeed, Greek cultural activity was supported. Greek political life was encouraged as it was focused on the situation in Greece, rather than challenging the ethno-nationalist basis of the PRL. Indeed, it was only in 1965 that their legal position was clarified, when the law of 29 March 1963 that stated that the refugees were not stateless, but were Greek citizens, was reiterated.[56]

Cold War considerations

The changing and increasingly troubled international environment post-1945 influenced the practice of nationality policy in Poland and altered the way in which it was articulated. In the immediate postwar period, international consensus on the issue of nation-state convergence was supported by practical co-operation across what was to become the Iron Curtain. Nationality policy in Poland at that time was important to the PPR, predominantly as an instrument of domestic policy, highlighting to Poles its commitment to perceived national interests, and as a method of channelling social anger. By late 1947, the situation had changed radically. Domestically, the challenge from the PSL had been met, the PPR was secure in power, and the activities of the Catholic Church were being increasingly restricted. Internationally, the launching of the Marshall plan, followed in October by the creation of Cominform, signified a parting of ways and growing tension between West and East.

The Westphalian issue straddled the period of multiple roads to socialism and the shift to a single-road policy. It charts the increasing dissonance between East and West, but also demonstrates that co-operation, albeit strained, continued well into 1948. The new political direction that began in earnest in the summer of 1948 placed significantly less emphasis on responding to, or aligning policy with, the perceived concerns of society, and relied more heavily on force to drive through industrialization and agricultural reform.[57] In this context, in which society was increasingly seen as an entity to be acted on rather than worked with, the need to align nationality policy with social sentiment was considerably less pressing, though not jettisoned. Thus, the pan-bloc deal to accept Greek refugees prioritized geopolitical state requirements, as identified through the policy of a single road to socialism.

Nationality policy in the period 1944–50 was not monolithic. Though ethno-nationalist and inflected by perennialist understandings of identity, it both remained responsive to the strategic needs of the PPR/PZPR, and was sufficiently flexible to accommodate the demands of the changing and increasingly tense international environment. The emergence of the Cold War and the harder 'internationalist' line sponsored by the Soviet Union shifted the focus of nationality policy from domestic audiences to the international arena.[58] Nationality policy was a key polemical tool in the late 1940s in the same way that it was a fundamental tool of constructing consent in the immediate aftermath of the Second World War.

7   Conclusion

Jan Gross (2006: 246) argues that 'we must seek the reasons for the novel, virulent quality of anti-Semitism in Poland not in collective hallucinations nor in pre-war attitudes, but in actual experiences acquired during the war years'. According to Gross, these experiences were 'opportunistic', as Poles had benefited from the plundering of Jews during the war and taken on their property and social roles after the war. They therefore defended their gains and saw Jews as threatening their material existence. As I explained in Chapter 3, this argument is problematic. It marginalizes the assistance given to Jews by Poles during the war, and overlooks recent research on Jewish survival, such as Gunnar Paulsson's work on Warsaw. Nor does it account for the degree of violence and hatred directed towards other minority groups in the postwar period. So, while Gross's project was focused on anti-Semitism, by dealing exclusively with that issue we are left with no idea where anti-Semitism merges with a more generalized anti-minority sentiment. The result is that the anti-Semitism of the postwar period is detached from its historical context. What was, in reality, a guided nationwide upsurge in ethno-nationalism is reduced to just one dimension of its complexity – a tragic chapter in Polish–Jewish relations.

I have argued here that a better sense of the postwar violence can be obtained through a comparative framework. One difficulty with Gross's conceptualization is clearly illustrated by reference to the experience of the Belarusian minority. The violence directed against them cannot be 'explained' by the 'revenge' thesis which has had so much traction in relation to the German and Ukrainian populations. Thus, one might ask, was the animosity directed at Belarusians also the consequence of how Poles acted towards them during the war? If it was, then the posited defence of real material interests was less important than Gross suggests, given that the appropriation of Belarusian property and social roles was insignificant. If it was not, then we are left with a series of 'national' histories and no means of comparison or way of developing a broader understanding of the postwar violence directed against minority communities.

This 'exceptionalist' position has, to date, largely dominated the debate about postwar violence, with experts on each minority affirming the uniqueness of the experience of the particular population group that interests them. The result, admittedly, has been some excellent empirical work, but at the cost of overlooking commonalities, linkages and the underpinning ethno-nationalist logic that defined the immediate postwar period. It is probably only due to the dominance of this 'exceptionalism' that Gross's argument has been so seductive. The key conceit of his position is the subtle conflation of temporal progression (time A necessarily leads on to a later time, time B) with the progression of cause A to effect B. Thus, it becomes a common-sense proposition that Polish acquisition of Jewish property and social roles in an earlier period resulted in violence when the higher status achieved through previously Jewish property and social roles is seemingly threatened in a later period. No doubt, the fear of restitution contributed to the level of antipathy expressed towards Jews in the immediate postwar period. However, I have contended here that Gross's argument underestimates the importance of the specificity of the postwar environment, and overemphasizes causal chains originating in the wartime experience. I have also contended that the manipulation of national sentiment by the PPR (and the Catholic Church) played a fundamental role in managing social anger, giving subjective violence which affected Jews and other minorities the imprimatur of sanction. In other words, the scale and intensity of postwar subjective violence was by no means an inevitable consequence of that wartime experience.

Postwar anti-minority violence was rooted in its own time, and drew upon the past as a reservoir of anti-minority sentiment. This reservoir was full, due to both wartime and pre-war exploitation of national differences and stereotypes, and the experience of strained and frequently violent inter-group relations during the war. Representational violence played an important role in creating an environment conducive to outrages taking place. As Leszek Kołakowski argued in 1956:

> A necessary condition for bloody Jewish pogroms, slaughters and atrocities has always been a social atmosphere of emotional tolerance of anti-Semitism, even in its mildest watered-down form. Wherever atrocities occurred, the system of discrimination and suspicion, even if apparently harmless, always gathered reserves of destructive social energy beforehand which nourished and bred criminals.[1]

Medieval superstitions, which the Catholic Church failed to discourage, contributed to anti-Jewish discourse. So, while the population may not have truly believed these myths, the Church's failure to condemn unequivocally anti-Jewish violence and sentiment 'legitimated' action against Jews. This then took the form of a widespread social imperative, since the Church was seen as a bastion of Polishness. Any action taken with an implied sanction from the Church affirmed the national credentials of the actor, in a context when 'Polishness' was highly politicized and overvalued. A further factor encouraging violence was the fact that Jews were often seen as communists, the perceived antithesis of true Polish independence, and clear enemy of the Church. These factors help to account for the intensity and scope of anti-Semitic sentiment in the mid- to late 1940s. But it is important to recognize that the anti-Semitism in the immediate aftermath of war was part of a broader pattern of anti-minority violence.

Recognizing the broader context within which anti-Semitic actions took place helps to show precisely how anti-Semitic violence differed from violence against other minorities, rather than either just asserting or implying it to be so. It is through considering the wider set of social relations unfolding in the immediate aftermath of war that we can come to a convincing account of the period.

The key to understanding the violence in the period 1944–47 is not to overdetermine the experience of the Second World War, but to locate the primary origin of that violence in the actual framing of the social conjuncture through the lexicon of nationality from 1944 onwards. So, while the reasons to which specific individuals may allude in justifying their violent and criminal actions are not uniform, those acts can be understood as the expression of social anger whose meaning only makes sense if the contours of the social anger regime being shaped by the PPR are deciphered. This is to recognize the double aspect of an act – its immediate individual meaning determined by the actor, whether a thief, murderer or rapist, and its social aspect which gives it social meaning and rationality.

As I argued in Chapter 3, the orchestrating of the social anger regime to secure some acquiescence to the PPR project necessarily constructed minority communities as objects of disdain and 'legitimate' targets of subjective violence, notwithstanding PPR declarations of equality for all citizens. The Catholic Church's ethno-religious policy assisted in undermining the position of members of non-Catholic religions and faiths, but so too did the regime of population expulsions/transfers.

This leads to the conclusion that the sponsors of the population expulsions were not only responsible for the expulsions themselves, but also contributed to shaping the social anger regime which proved to be so disastrous for minority members and so successful for the PPR's bid for hegemony. Just as the Catholic Church in Poland bears some responsibility for the scale and scope of anti-Jewish outrages in the immediate aftermath of war, so the British and the Americans bear some responsibility for the anti-German subjective violence during the mid-1940s. Although the British Government and British public opinion condemned the violence, it was sustained by the contention that Germans had no place in Poland – a contention supported by the British. Indeed, despite their wishes, by endorsing the principle of national homogeneity and providing practical assistance to achieving this goal, the British and Americans played an important role in facilitating the PPR's drive to power.

Subjective violence against non-ethnic Poles was allowed to flourish on a mass scale in the period 1944 to late 1947, providing an outlet for social anger in a direction congruent with the PPR's aim of establishing its Polish credentials and gaining greater control. The degree to which the PPR *directly* fuelled animosity against each particular minority varied in intensity, though the general ethno-nationalist narrative adversely affected all indigenous minority populations. Representational violence played a key role in the management of social anger. Once the PPR's primary objective of securing the commanding heights of the state became a reality in 1947, the need to tolerate or respond to society's demands was seen as less pressing by many within the Politburo. The foundation of Cominform and the policy of a single road to socialism underpinned the relative increase in state (intentional) structural violence, and the sharp restriction of subjective violence as expressed by the Polish population. Over the same period, the Catholic Church's utility to the PPR was drastically reduced by the achievement of national homogeneity and the removal of German Catholics from the 'Recovered Territories'. This opened the way for increased repression, as the Catholic Church was identified as 'enemy number one' in late 1947.

The different phases of postwar nationality policy between 1944–47 and 1948–50 do not simply reflect changes in domestic circumstances, they also coincide with the opening of the Cold War and the concomitant increase in East–West dissonance. In the earlier period, despite the complications of two rival Polish 'Governments', consensus on national homogeneity facilitated practical assistance across the 'Iron Curtain', as well as providing resources for propaganda, which was used to cement the PPR's authority, whether as a defender of Polish national interests, or through the flurry of articles arguing that the Western Allies were pro-German.

The earlier period saw the (Warsaw) Polish Government focus its efforts on the domestic arena and audiences. The later period saw nationality policy increasingly responding to the strategic and tactical requirements of Eastern bloc geopolitics. The transition from domestic to international orientation was marked by the 'Westphalian incident', which clearly illustrated the growing tensions between East and West, and how these played out in practice.

The year 1948 marked the beginning of Stalinism in Poland, and the crime of 'national deviation' justified the purge of the PPR and PPS prior to the merger of the two parties. It also saw the commitment to the idea that policy could make reality without consent. The condemnation of Gomułka in 1948, in part due to his insistence that policy should take into account social reality, prefaced the way for harsher action across the policy spectrum. Minority schools were brought under state administration, assimilation was encouraged and national difference reduced to folkish and/or apolitical cultural expressions. The general view maintained was that everyone was now Polish, and any claims to the contrary constituted a political act against the state. In addition, the homogenization of minorities and

Polonization of autochthones continued apace. The only exception to the assimilatory model were the non-native refugees from Greece who started arriving in 1948 and were not expected to remain long in Poland.[2]

Nationality policy in the period 1944–50 was shaped by the objectives of the PPR/PZPR. As these objectives evolved with changing domestic and international circumstances, so too did nationality policy. It shifted from an instrument constructing consent and alliances within Poland (with the Catholic Church) to a tool of foreign policy and moral grandstanding *vis-à-vis* the West.

Yet, despite the shift of emphasis in policy, which started in autumn 1947, the underpinning ethno-nationalist position was not altered, merely implemented in a different way. Assimilation, 're-Polonization' and reintegration rather than transfer/expulsion defined the new reality. Those 're-migrants' who arrived from other places in Europe, such as France, Belgium and Westphalia, were Polish on the basis of their ethnic background and valued for the loyalty they demonstrated. The refugees from Greece were accommodated as working-class heroes, as political refugees and as loyal residents.

The analysis that has been presented here has sought to draw out the connections between social anger, various forms of violence and the consolidation of the PPR's hegemony. The establishment of communist power, it has been argued, did not just 'grow out of the barrel of a gun',[3] but was the result of the effective exploitation of social prejudice, institutional avarice and sanctioned subjective violence. The centrifugal aspects of the PPR's nationality policy played a very significant role in the Party's ascendency.

Consent, in practice, was constructed, even through what oppositionists considered to be dissent.[4] The actions of the Catholic Church illustrate this best, for it was because of its hostility to other faiths and its ethno-religious vision that it aligned itself with the objectives of the PPR. The Church contributed to the construction of an environment in which some people were seen as deserving of disdain and exclusion from the community. These were frequently the very same people that the PPR sought to exclude on the basis of their nationality. By sponsoring programmes of exclusion, the Catholic Church and oppositional nationalists helped to create a polity that was illiberal in content, and which provided increasing opportunities for the PPR to move against its perceived adversaries.

So while the power imbalances between the various actors have to be acknowledged, so too does the fact that many of the actions of the oppositionists ultimately empowered the PPR, despite their intentions. By attempting to exploit ethno-nationalist sentiment, the Catholic Church and others justified intolerance within society, and lent an aura of legitimacy to PPR policy and practice. Ultimately, the orchestration of the social anger regime by the PPR was sufficient to reduce society to an uneasy acquiescence. The less willing could easily be identified and incarcerated by the Ministry of Public Security.

The continued relevance of the immediate postwar period in Poland

The dominant stories of the immediate postwar period in east-central Europe have remained fairly consistent, notwithstanding the fundamental socio-political realignment of 1989. In the main, the We/They boundary has been identified simply as one dividing society from the communist party, while either marginalizing the importance of how communist parties across east-central Europe attempted to reframe divisions within the various states along national lines, or by misreading the precise function of the nationalist turn. Employing phrases such as 'Stalin's Polish puppets' and 'Agents of Moscow' as explanatory categories rather than as mere rhetorical flourishes obscures precisely how communist hegemony was established by managing the social anger regime through nationality policy.

Several authors note the communists' sponsorship of nationalist sentiment in order to strengthen their links with the population. But the common conclusion that they failed in their goal to consolidate these connections misses the deeper importance of communist nationality policy. Certainly, in the case of Poland, the PPR would have been pleased if its ethnonationalism had resulted in the population identifying the PPR as the true repository of the national spirit rather than as a Soviet interloper. The party worked very hard to achieve this objective. However, this was not the only, or indeed the main, goal of PPR nationality policy. As argued here, nationality policy played a fundamental role in shaping the social anger regime. It was not necessary for the population to believe sincerely that the PPR was 'of the nation'. It was sufficient for the PPR to present some groups as definitely not being part of the new polity, and frame these groups as both legitimate and accessible targets for social frustrations. In this the nationality policy of the PPR was largely successful. Indeed, the positioning of members of national minority communities as *homines sacri* empowered the population to act as sovereign against them, while the PPR proceeded to ascend to hegemony. Thus, the story of the communist takeover of Poland has to acknowledge the sanctioned oppression of minorities by members of the wider population, as well as NKVD and communist repression.

Although the maximalist objective of achieving party–nation synthesis was thwarted, the goal of redirecting social anger from the PPR and its Soviet ally was, in practice, achieved. This has a number of implications. First, differentiating between the centrifugal and centripetal aspects of communist nationality policy can help in understanding how the communists achieved dominance. Second, when thinking about the postwar period, one needs to place nationality policy at the centre of investigation, and map the course of subjective violence. Rather than focus on a We/They divide splitting the polity between the communist party and society, it is necessary to explore how the We/They divide was orchestrated across east-central

Europe by both the communist parties and other institutional actors such as the Roman Catholic Church.

A third implication is that a full reckoning with the foundation of communist rule is yet to take place. Many actors who, in the post-communist period, have viewed themselves exclusively as victims of communist repression need to reassess their roles, especially in relation to those groups which were the main targets of the social anger regime manipulated by the PPR. In addition, reflection on the function of the West's policy during the post-war period expands the responsibility for population transfers / expulsions, and suggests not only that restitution claims stemming from that period have a clear international element, but also that processes of memorialization need to explore the full complexity of the historical record. For example, British discomfort over the practice of population transfer existed alongside support for the principle, as Frank (2007) notes. This support had a high cost not only for the Germans, but for all those Poles, Ukrainians and Belarusians who had to be moved – transfers endorsed by Churchill through his insistence on the necessity of the Curzon Line.

A study of the West's role in Poland from the end of the Second World War up to 1947 also provides evidence of the saliency of unintended consequences. Population transfers were justified in part to create a more stable Europe, free from the minority-inspired revanchism of the interwar period, but the supposition that people could be 'in the wrong place', despite centuries of settlement, provided crucial fuel to the anger regime being managed by the PPR. The cost of endorsing national homogeneity was high for the Poles and the West. The Poles almost unanimously supported the principle, but the process of achieving national homogeneity assisted the PPR's drive to hegemony. The West's support for homogeneity diminished its influence in Poland by facilitating the substitution of antipathy to the PPR with the unleashing of animosity against minorities. Illiberal means, in this case, resulted in a very illiberal end.

Notes

1 Introduction

1 Rothwell (1990: 161) argues that Stanisław Mikołajczyk, 'who would almost certainly have been the country's leader under a democratic system, ruefully noted [that the communists] took account of "the moods and undercurrents" of the Polish nation'. In actuality, Mikołajczyk observed that the Nazis did not take into account 'the moods and undercurrents of the nations they swallowed' and, by comparing Nazi and communist systems, implies that the communists did so. The inference made by Mikołajczyk is shown to be correct in the forthcoming chapters. See Mikołajczyk (1948: 279–81).

2 Mevius's text examines the nationality policy of the Hungarian Communist Party. In the introduction Mevius (2005: 2) argues that, '[W]hat is true for Hungary is true for all People's Republics in Eastern Europe. All espoused a form of Socialist Patriotism in which national symbols figured prominently.' Mevius contends that the Hungarian communists were seen as 'agents of Moscow', despite their nationalist rhetoric. He suggests that the Hungarian communists failed to persuade the population that they represented the nation in line with national traditions. No doubt Mevius would extend this argument to Poland. This contention has a great deal of support in contemporary Poland, reflected in Torańska's (1987) book, which has been reissued recently, and several IPN publications. However, the view that communist nationality policy was a failure is problematic. It will be argued here that nationality policy did not fail, as its primary objective was not the maximalist goal inferred by Mevius and others. The fact that anti-communist movements throughout Eastern Europe re-appropriated and re-imagined national symbols says more about the invention of traditions and the socio-economic and political shortcomings of the communist system than about a 'true' national spirit finding voice. Indeed, given communists' appropriation of nationalist iconography in the post-war period, the employment of such symbols by the wider society for new, non-state-approved purposes was one of the few channels through which genuine protest that would galvanize large sections of the population could be expressed. Just as the communists found it difficult to criticize the Soviet Union, they were in a similar quandary when dissent was couched in the language of nationality, and were forced to label adversaries as chauvinists or reactionary nationalists, with limited effect. The issue of whether communists in Poland were 'agents of Moscow' is also problematic, and the phrase should not be used as a shorthand to characterize the immediate post-war Polish leadership, as it underestimates the scope for manoeuvre that the Polish leadership had and the extent to which broad policy recommendations from senior communist officials such as Georgi Dimitrov were enthusiastically appropriated and strongly inflected by the Poles.

In short, phrases such as 'agents of Moscow' and 'Stalin's Polish puppets' conceal as much as they reveal.

3 For the sake of brevity, the analysis here refers to different population groups insofar as their experience helps to illustrate the core arguments made. Consequently, the histories of several minority populations are omitted, not because they are unimportant, but because to elaborate on them in sufficient detail would largely reiterate the main contentions of the study, and would vastly increase the size of the current volume. The minorities not considered here include Czechs, Slovaks, Tatars and Roma people. The fate of Łemkos and Lithuanians is only briefly mentioned.

4 Zaremba's book has attracted a great deal of attention. A major point of discussion in Poland has been whether the PPR/PZPR policy could be classified as 'nationalist' rather than just 'nationally orientated.' In part, the discussion highlights the tension in translating Western theoretical insights (largely articulated in the English language), which Zaremba mobilizes in his argument, into a different language – Polish. Key terms like 'national', 'nationalism' and 'patriotism' are as fiercely contested in Polish as in English, but with slightly different historical resonances, and hence meaning. Indeed, Jerzy Tomaszewski (2000: 85) contends that the Polish word *nacjonalizm* corresponds more closely with the English word 'chauvinism' rather than 'nationalism'. Despite these difficulties, Zaremba's contention that the PPR's nationality policy was nationalist is correct. I would like to thank Professor Wanda Jarząbek of the Institute of Political Science, Polish Academy of Science (ISPPAN), for discussing Polish responses to Zaremba's book with me in November 2006.

5 Prażmowska focuses on the PPR's difficulties in dealing with Poland's Jewish population, as a result of its desire to be seen as a Polish party. It consequently did not highlight its policy towards Jews. Nevertheless, its advocacy of national homogeneity was both clear and not constrained, as I will try to show in forthcoming chapters. See Prażmowska (2004: 168–90).

6 The PPR merged with the PPS to form the PZPR in December 1948.

7 The notion of social anger is discussed extensively in Chapter 3.

8 For a discussion of anti-Semitism in 1956 see Machcewicz (1996). For an examination of the anti-Zionist/anti-Semitic campaign of 1968 see Stola (2000) and Głuchowski and Polonsky (eds.) (2009).

9 NA.FO 371/47607 (N12148).

10 *The Grand Alliance* was the title of volume three of Churchill's six volume study of the Second World War. It refers to the events of 1941 which led to the Soviet Union, United States and Britain becoming allied to fight Nazi Germany.

Davies's 2003 account of the Warsaw Uprising of 1944 is problematic. In his attempt to shift focus to the divisions within the Grand Alliance, Davies downplays divisions within the Polish Army (loyal to the Polish Government in Exile) and within the Polish Government in Exile. So, while General Anders is 'counted among the Rising's most unrelenting critics' (Davies 2003a: 348), we are given little sense of how passionately Anders expressed his disappointment at the outbreak of the Rising. Anders described it as 'a serious crime', 'doomed to be annihilated'. Furthermore, Davies does not highlight that other senior Polish Army officers had serious doubts about it. In an earlier work, Davies is far more persuasive, contending that 'its timing, and its underlying tactical considerations, were woefully misguided. Its political goals were fundamentally unrealistic' (Davies 1981: 475). Also see Ciechanowski (2002: 262–3). Anders' comments are contained in a despatch from General W. Anders to the Minister of National Defence, 23 August 1944, No 2139, PISM, Kol G.A./46.

11 Following the Soviet invasion of eastern Poland on 17 September 1939, Sir William Seeds sent a telegram to his superiors in London on 30 September 1939.

In this note he suggested that, in order to drive a wedge between the USSR and Germany, the Kremlin could be advised that British war aims were not incompatible with the Soviet Union's 'reasonable settlement on ethnographic and cultural lines' of eastern Poland (NA.FO 371/23103/237–38). Seeds' idea that it would be prudent for the British to be flexible on the future boundaries of Poland was endorsed by Sir Ivone Kirkpatrick. Kirkpatrick, in a document that was circulated amongst officials at the Foreign Office, entitled 'The German Peace Offensive', argued that it was 'possible for [the British] to stand for an ethnographical and cultural Poland without standing on Russian toes', and recommended that such a policy should be implemented 'until the Russians have definitely declared themselves against us'. Kirkpatrick also attached a map of Poland to his note to other Foreign Office officials and pointed out that the new Soviet border more or less followed the 'Curzon line' (NA.FO 371/23097/203–09). The map used by Kirkpatrick seems to have been cut from a newspaper, probably *The Times*, as there is advertising on its reverse side. See Chapter 2 for a discussion of the 'Curzon line'.

12   Documents on Polish–Soviet Relations 1939–45, vol 1: 68.

13   The Nazis pursued a policy of ethnic reconfiguration in which the indigenous population was to be subjugated and Polish elites destroyed. Increasingly harsh measures were taken against the Jewish population (leading ultimately to the 'Final Solution' in which over three million Polish Jews were murdered). In February 1940 the NKVD initiated deportations of Poles out of eastern Poland to the Soviet Union. Around 320,000 Poles were deported during the period 1939–41 according to the new Polish–Russian consensus (Sanford 2005: 29).

14   NA.FO 371/23103/237–8. Seeds' view was substantiated by subsequent Soviet actions.

15   The Germans announced the discovery of bodies at Katyń in April 1943. It is now known from Soviet documents released under the Gorbachev and Yeltsin regimes that the decision to massacre over 22,000 Poles was taken by the politburo of the All-Union Communist Party (Bolsheviks) on 5 March 1940 and by Stalin himself. See Sanford (2005).

16   An important reason behind the marginalization of Polish concerns was the Western Allies' recognition that the war was largely being fought by the Soviet Union, and acute awareness of the need to remain on good terms with Stalin. Later, in 1944, the Allied forces' advance through Italy proved difficult and Polish soldiers made a key contribution by taking Monte Cassino in May 1944.

17   NA.CAB 79/66/151–4, NA.COS 254 (43) 4 quoted in Reynolds (2004: 380).

18   See Kersten (1991: 4).

19   Zhdanov co-wrote the 'two camps' speech with Stalin.

20   Cited in Sebag-Montefiore (2004: 584). Jakub Berman (1908–84) oversaw cultural affairs and the security apparatus. He was one of three key leaders in the immediate post-war period (the other two being Bolesław Bierut and Hilary Minc). Berman had been involved with the Communist Party in Poland since he was a student. See Torańska (1987: 203) for further biographical details.

21   Gomułka tried to justify his refusal to become a candidate for the Politburo of the PZPR in his important letter to Stalin of 14 December 1948. The letter has been understood, in part, as Gomułka's attempt to defend himself against a possible show trial by raising the issues of nationality and PPR membership in a way that would have resonated with Stalin. He contended that it was 'necessary to discontinue any further increase in the percentage of the Jewish element within the state as well as the party apparatus, but also to decrease progressively this percentage, especially in the higher echelons of that apparatus' in order to avoid disunity in the future Politburo. Letter reprinted in Głuchowski 2004: 379.

22 COMECON was established at a conference in Moscow held 5–8 January 1949.

23 The position of the Communist Workers' Party of Poland was made very clear in a propaganda poster which depicted a Bolshevik soldier moving across Poland, heading west, with the line '*Z drogi*' ((Get) out of the way). It is reprinted in Davies (2003b).

24 See Snyder (2005). In the USSR an initial liberal nationality policy aimed to secure Ukrainians and Belarusians within the Bolshevik fold. In Poland, with National Democratic centralist policies aiming to assimilate minorities (except for Jews), communist promises of autonomy and cultural freedom were attractive. Snyder explores both the national and international role played by nationality policy in the sensitive eastern borderland areas.

25 The Communist International attempted to promote revolution at the global level and subsumed the concerns of communist organisations in particular countries to this broad objective. It was directed from Moscow and published a Manifesto on 29 January 1919 outlining its goals.

26 The shift in nationality policy was most significant in relation to Upper Silesia and in northern Poland, as the Party rejected the idea that those areas had the right to secede from Poland. Elsewhere, the geopolitical considerations of an ascendant German fascism were less pressing, and vocal support for minorities continued to be expressed during 1936, especially in regions with a significant minority population. In multiethnic Lwów in May 1936 the Congress of Cultural Workers proclaimed the 'Left's desire that the cultural needs of all Poland's nationalities be met' (Shore 2006: 128).

27 Quoted in Polonsky and Drukier (1980: 128).

28 There emerged differences of opinion on the issue of nationality between PPR cadres based in Moscow and those in Poland. Members of the Moscow-based group were more attuned to the line being adopted by Stalin, which saw national homogeneity and national animation as the way forward, whereas many of those in Poland were initially uncomfortable with what seemed to them to be a 'nationalist' line usurping Marxist dogma. Dziewanowski (1976: 162) contends that the word 'communist' was avoided in Poland as Soviet deportations to Siberia and elsewhere in the Soviet Union, during the period 1939–41 had 'made communism less popular than ever'.

29 Quoted in Torańska, (1987: 279).

30 See AAN PPR 190/1–13, 31 July 1942.

31 See Gontarczyk (2003: 153–66). Gontarczyk's text emphasizes the factional struggles within the PPR, and highlights the severe difficulties the Party had in reaching out to the Polish population in the period up to 1944.

32 See Gontarczyk (2003: 219 and 302) for a discussion of the March 1943 statement and the November 1943 declaration by the PPR.

33 AAN PPR 190/11, March 1943.

34 The PPR's scope for action was restricted by the difficult situation in Poland, while the ZPP could respond to the policy signals coming from Stalin, for example, the new 'liberal' Soviet policy towards the Orthodox Church in the USSR. See Miner (2003).

35 APŁ KWPPR 1022/164/1. Polish Army Political Education Main Board publication number 4, 28/9/1944.

36 'War Communism' also had domestic rationales.

37 For an assessment of the current identities of inhabitants of Opole Silesia see Szmeja (2000).

38 It should be noted, however, that the pace of reorientation among communists themselves was very uneven, as the proclamations at the Lwów Congress of Cultural Workers in 1936 indicate.

39   This switch brought communist nationality policy in line with the general historic development of Polish nationalism. Walicki (2001: 22) notes that, following the failed 1830 uprising, the effort to define the nation in republican political terms (a notion promoted by the gentry) eventually gave way to a notion prioritizing a narrow concept of Polish spirit and tradition, which ultimately informed the thinking of the National Democrats in the first part of the twentieth century. The movement towards more essentialized definitions of the nation in Poland during the nineteenth century is charted by Brian Porter (2000).

2   Ethnicity and nation: the international consensus

1   See Siebel-Achenbach (1994: 34) This memorandum can be found at NA.FO 371/31091.
2   The League of Nations came into existence as a result of the post-First World War peace conference, and had a remit to resolve disputes by consent and arbitration, and by collective use of force against aggressors. Its General Assembly met every year from 1920 until 1941 in Geneva. It was dissolved in April 1946 and its remaining operations were transferred to the United Nations in New York.
3   Colonel Beck declared before the League's assembly that 'pending the introduction of a general and uniform system for the protection of minorities my Government is compelled to refuse . . . all cooperation with international organizations in the matter of supervision of the application by Poland of the system of minority protection'; *League of Nations Official Journal* 1934, quoted in Claude (1955: 30). Also see Cobban (1970) and Macartney (1934), who both contend that the sponsorship of minorities by kin-states undermined the League.
4   On 1 October 1939, Orme Sargent of the Foreign Office requested that Fred Savery report on how far the Soviet occupation of eastern Poland corresponded to the ethnographic geography of the region. Savery's January 1940 memorandum can be viewed, in part, as a consequence of British officials' attempts to sustain Anglo–Soviet relations following Soviet aggression against Poland in September 1939.
5   The Curzon line was a proposed Polish–Soviet frontier approved by the British Foreign Secretary, Lord Curzon, during the Soviet–Polish War in 1920.
6   NA.FO 371/24470/358: 15.
7   NA.FO 371/24470/358: 10–11. Savery was generally pessimistic about the level of loyalty that Jews would show to Poland. Even the loyalty of Jews from Galicia and central Poland, who, according to Savery, 'were fairly satisfactory Polish citizens' was queried, as they had, allegedly, come under the influence of 'the communist propaganda of the Jews returned, permanently or temporarily, from Palestine'. For an analysis of Polish–Jewish relations in eastern Poland in the period 1939–46, see Davies and Polonsky (eds) (1991).
8   NA.FO 371/24470/358: 1.
9   NA.FO 371/24470/358: 2.
10   NA.FO 371/24470/358: 4.
11   NA.FO 371/24470/358: 15.
12   NA.FO 371/24470/358: 16.
13   NA.FO 371/24470/357.
14   NA.FO 371/24470/360.
15   NA.FO 371/24470/360(2).
16   NA.FO 371/24472/42 (16 April 1940).
17   NA.FO 371/24470/377.
18   Indeed, the expansion of Poland into Prussia was suggested by Mr Kunicki of

the Polish Ministry of Foreign Affairs in conversation with Fred Savery of the British Foreign Office on 15 January 1940. Kunicki even posited the abandonment of Vilnius. This conversation no doubt informed Savery's memorandum which he submitted to the British Ambassador to Poland at the end of the month (27 January 1940).

19 Lech Karol Neyman wrote under a number of pseudonyms during the Nazi occupation, as part of the Stronnictwo Narodowe (National Movement) and later in the Narodowe Siły Zbrojne (National Armed Forces). After the war he was arrested by the communist government, given a death sentence and executed in Warsaw on 12 May 1948.

20 For a detailed presentation of the Polish debates on the future of Polish borders in the early 1940s see Eberhardt (2004: 176–84).

21 'Uwagi o naszej polityce międzynarodowej, Nr 1' PISM, A.9.Ie/15 dok 55, pp. 3–4.

22 'Uwagi o naszej polityce międzynarodowej, Nr 1' pp. 6. Also, see Snyder (2004) for a consideration of how the USSR exploited nationality policy to undermine the Polish State's authority in its eastern borderlands, especially in the period prior to Piłsudski's *coup d'état* in 1926.

23 The Bund was founded in Vilnius in 1897 and was socialist and internationalist in outlook.

24 'Uwagi o naszej polityce międzynarodowej, Nr 1' pp 9.

25 NA.PREM 3/136/8: 2

26 FRUS Conference at Tehran (1943) p. 594–96. As late as June 1944, during Mikołajczyk's trip to Washington, the Americans continued to mislead the Polish leader as to what had been agreed at Tehran. Roosevelt himself gave no indication that the USA had agreed to the 'Curzon line'. It was not until Molotov's statement of 13 October 1944 that the Poles finally found out that the USA had consented to the 'Curzon line' at the Tehran conference. Also see Kemp-Welch (2008: 1).

27 For a discussion of Polish national myths see Davies (1997).

28 Quoted in Kersten (1991: 44).

29 NA.CAB 66/46/34: 193–5. As Sworakowski (1944) points out, it was British Prime Minister Lloyd George who was chiefly responsible for the 'Curzon Line'. Great Britain, France, Italy and Japan were represented at the Spa conference. The USA participated as an observer.

30 For a full discussion of the discrepancy between the frontier line described by the British in the telegram sent to Moscow and the one agreed to by the Polish Government, see Sworakowski (1944). Sworakowski (1944: 26) concluded that, due to the mistakes and inaccuracies contained in the note to Moscow, it had no value as an 'argument in favour of the present Soviet claims to the territories of Eastern Poland, and particularly their claims to the territory of Eastern Galicia'. The Soviet claim to eastern Poland was also justified by the fact that this area had been incorporated into the USSR in the period 1939–41 as a result of the (rigged) plebiscite of October 1939.

31 PISM, PRM-L, 49/217. Reprinted in *Documents on Polish–Soviet Relations 1939–45*, vol. 2, number 214: 372 (hereafter DPSR).

32 House of Commons Debate, 403/489–90. Reprinted in DPSR 1939–45, vol. 2, number 231: 394.

33 *Proceedings of the Moscow Conference on Polish Affairs*. First meeting held at the Spiridonovka Palace of the Narkomindel, Moscow, 14 October 1944. PISM, PRM-Z, 5. Reprinted in DPSR, vol. 2, number 237: 405.

34 Note on a conversation between M. Mikołajczyk and W. Churchill about Soviet territorial claims and the reconstruction of the Polish Government. PISM, A.11.49/Sow/4-b. Reprinted in DPSR, vol. 2, number 239: 416.

35 The Polish president replaced Mikołajczyk with Tomasz Arciszewski of the PPS as Prime Minister of the Government in Exile.
36 Quoted in Kersten (1991: 113) and (1986: 93). Mikołajczyk's point is clear, although the syntax in the despatch is problematic.
37 Note on a conversation between M. Mikołajczyk and W. Churchill about Soviet territorial claims and the reconstruction of the Polish Government. PISM, A.11.49/Sow/4-b. Reprinted in DPSR, vol. 2, number 239: 419.
38 Hansard, House of Commons, 15 December 1944, pp. 1484.
39 United States Department of State (1955: 214).
40 Churchill (1985: 350). Speech given to the House of Commons on 27 February 1945.
41 Letter from Polish Foreign Minister T. Romer to the British Government, 7 October 1944. PISM A.11.49/Sow/6. Reprinted in DPSR, vol. 2, number 235: 400.
42 Ibid.
43 For a summary of the camp system in Poland after the Second World War see Kopka (2002).
44 Directive of PKWN in Dz. U nr 7 poz 32. See AAN 200 'Introduction to Catalogue'.
45 MSZ 9/6/10 'Umowy repatriacyjne z ZSRR 1944–47' pp. 29.
46 See Mironowicz (2000: 44). The relevant documents are found at the Voivodship Office in Białystok (UWB 231, 13).
47 AAN 522/43/467–78. Also, see pages 480–6.
48 AAN 522/43/460–6.
49 Modrzejewski was not alone in being subjected to pressure after criticizing PUR. In early January 1946 the paper *Radio Świat* published an article by a certain Mr Kański entitled *Hallo, tu mówi Szczecin* (Hello, Szczecin speaking) in which he highlighted problems within PUR's operation. A PUR delegation arrived at *Radio Świat*'s offices and, after heated exchanges, threatened staff with prosecution. The paper subsequently published an article praising PUR. This was forwarded by the Vice-Director of PUR Stanisław Olszewski to Undersecretary Władysław Wolski on 26 February 1946. One of the reasons that PUR was so sensitive to criticism was that such criticism could potentially jeopardize the repatriation movement from the West and stimulate concern in the West regarding the substantiation of the Potsdam Agreement. AAN/522/II/46/135.
50 AAN 522/43/493.
51 AAN 522/43/641–5.
52 AAN 522/43/629–30.
53 AAN 522/43/544–9 and 582–5.
54 AAN 522/43/78.
55 AAN 522/43 224–46 and 199–210.
56 AAN 522/43/245–6.
57 Checinski (1982: 13) contends that sending Jews to the 'Recovered Territories' rendered them invisible to the wider population.
58 AAN 522/43/244.
59 MSZ 9/6/10 'Umowy repatriacyjne z ZSRR 1944–47', p. 25.
60 AAN 522/43/487–9.
61 MSZ 9/6/10 'Umowy repatriacyjne z ZSRR 1944–47', chapter 5.
62 See Paczoska (2002: 272–6).
63 See Paczoska (2002: 209 and 211). These figures derive from statistics compiled by the repatriation authorities. See AAN 522/I/19/160.
64 MSZ 9/6/10: 65–7.
65 Frequently, those soldiers who fought in 'Operation Tempest' (Burza) in 1944 against the Nazis were then incarcerated by the Soviets once the battle had been won.

66 AAN 522/II/467/99.
67 AAN 522/II/467/99.
68 As many were to discover, this resolution failed to be substantiated. See Chapter 3.
69 AAN 522/II/467/98–107. The campaign materials were sent to UNRRA DP headquarters for distribution in the three Western Zones in Germany, as well as in Austria, Italy, Cairo and Paris. For an examination of Polish propaganda in the West see Dudek (2002).
70 AAN 522/II/155/65.
71 AAN 522/II/339/17. The Government in Warsaw had been trying for some time to reduce the influence of liaison officers loyal to the Polish Government in Exile. In August 1945 it even offered to allow officers operating for the Government in Exile to stay at their posts if they declared loyalty to the Government of National Unity. AAN 522/II/425/118.
72 Cited in Kersten (1991: 206).
73 AAN 522/II/467/294. Martin's letter begins by pointing out that some young Polish women made arrangements with German families to take in their illegitimate child, and ends ominously by reporting that, 'if the mother wants to go back to Poland badly enough she finds some way of disposing of the child'. Many of these children were conceived as a result of rape. It is worth noting that the nationality of the child was ascribed via the nationality of the mother. This gave rise to some complications. For example, a German foster mother of an illegitimate non-German child had the child taken away from her and placed in a UNRRA home, despite the child living with the German family for three and a half years. The report does not elaborate on the fate of the birth mother.
74 AAN 522/43/467, 470–1.
75 AAN 522/43/141.
76 Scheider 1953: 33E–41E. Cited in Kraft (2001: 118).
77 AAN MAP 2457. Kraft (2001: 118) argues that since around 200,000 people fled from East Prussia to western Germany up to 1944, the Polish estimates for May are too low by around 120,000.
78 See Nitschke (2004: 134) and Jankowiak (2005: 89).
79 NA.FO 800/490/12 (Private Papers of Ernest Bevin: Poland 1945–49).
80 NA.FO 800/490/50.
81 For an assessment of 'Operation Swallow' see Persson (2001). Also see Frank (2007).
82 NA.FO 1052/324/20A. The planned routes were Szczecin–Lubeck (by sea) at a rate of 1,000 people per day, Szczecin–Bad Segeberg at 1,500 per day, Kaławsk–Marienthal Alversdorf at 3,000 per day and Kaławsk–Friedland at 2,500 per day. This final route was never used.
83 NA.FO 1052/479/236. Note from Combined Repatriation Executive to Swallow Team Kaławsk, 27 March 1946.
84 NA.FO 1052/470: 213. In a report from 7 March 1946 the Commander of the Poppendorf camp, which received expellees, noted a 'strikingly large number of cases of maltreatment', and that the 'majority of women have been raped once or many times' (NA.FO 1052/470: 214).
85 NA.FO 1052/324 38D, 3rd Report on 'Swallow', 9 May 1946.
86 NA.FO 1052/471: 130.
87 NA.FO 1052/324/1.
88 NA.FO 1052/324/18E. The MO (Citizens' Militia) was under the authority of the Ministry of Public Security (MBP). According to Dudek and Paczkowski (2005: 243) 'Security functionaries were not only very young, but also extremely undereducated: in 1945 80% had completed primary education only'.
89 NA.FO 1052/471: 208. 30 July 1946.

90 NA.FO 1052/471: 178. 13 July 1946 Policy HQ CCG(BE).
91 NA.FO 1052/471: 215. 2 August 1946 Major General Erskine to the (British) Control Office for Germany and Austria, London.
92 NA.FO 1032/836 Report on Train No. 165 under 'Operation Swallow'.
93 The *Brichah* was the organized movement of Jews from east-central Europe to Palestine in the immediate aftermath of the Second World War. For an analysis of the *Brichah* see Bauer (1970). The British were aware that the Jewish Committee in Breslau (Wrocław) was playing a key role in facilitating Jewish movement out of Poland. In a report dated 14 June 1946 to the British HQ in Hanover, Major Tobin (referring to Swallow train number 165) opined that, 'to my mind there can be very little doubt that the Jewish committee in Breslau has for its objective the getting out of Poland into the British or American Zones all Jews whatever their nationality'. The issue of Jewish emigration from Poland had been a focus of British attention since late 1945. A report dated 5 October 1945 sent from the British consulate in Katowice to the British Embassy in Warsaw provided details of the movement of Jews out of Poland. NA.FO 688/31/3. A leading figure in the revival of Jewish life in Lower Silesia in the immediate aftermath of the Holocaust noted that Yitzhak Zuckerman spoke with senior PPR figure Marian Spychalski after the Kielce pogrom (Egit 1991: 66).
94 NA.FO 1052/471: 4.
95 NA.FO 1052/323/52. Foreign Office translation of article in *Trybuna Dolnośląska*, 24/25 March, No. 37(58).
96 Nevertheless, as a note dated 1 May 1946 from the Foreign Office to Kenneth Johnstone at the British Council in Warsaw makes clear, the Polish attacks on the British did have an impact, especially after Churchill's Fulton speech. The Ambassador to Poland urged the British Council not to make available in Poland some books which could offend the Polish Government. According to the letter, '[t]he Ambassador thinks that while the best tactics are to pay no attention to the contentiousness of the Poles it is as well to bear in mind that they have an inferiority complex, are highly susceptible, and therefore should be given as few excuses as possible for justifiable complaint' (NA.BW 51/14 LC2069/19/452).
97 In a meeting on 7 September 1945 between representatives of the Polish Provisional Government of National Unity, led by General Karol Świerczewski, and the US POW & DP division led by General Eric Wood, the issue of stoves in box-cars was raised. The placing of stoves in cars was refused by the USA as they were considered unsafe, but Poles being repatriated could have two blankets, which they could keep. AAN 522/II/456/106.
98 NA.FO 1052/353 9A.
99 NA.FO 1052/473 96 and NA.FO 1052/353 9A. See Frank (2007: 262–73) for an overview of the British liaison teams stationed in Poland.
100 Train number 514 was the subject of a parliamentary question on 17 January 1947. The problems were accentuated by the fact that the locomotive broke down, giving rise to further delay, and hence lengthening the time people had to spend in the cold. During the period in question the temperature frequently fell below –20 degrees Celsius. NA.FO 1052/473 96 and 107.
101 The cessation of 'Operation Swallow' did not occur in autumn 1946, despite the problems in the British zone of occupation in Germany, in large part due to the British desire not to adversely influence the Polish elections of January 1947. Following the fraudulent election, the British scope for a firmer policy was somewhat increased as a key policy goal of sustaining working relations with the Polish Government in 1945 and 1946 (free, unfettered elections) had not been achieved. See Persson (2001: 179–206).

102 NA.FO 1052/473 158.
103 NA.FO 1052/473 195, 211, 222.
104 NA.FO 1052/470. Those present included Władysław Wolski of the Ministry of Public Administration, who was responsible for the population transfers, Mr Bader of the Ministry of Foreign Affairs, Robin Hankey from the Foreign Office and Major Ford representing the Prisoner of War and Displaced Persons Division of the CCG.
105 Quoted in Kochanowski (2001: 142).
106 In contrast to the German expellees, the experience of Polish expellees has not, with a few exceptions, commanded the interest of Western scholars. The collection of essays edited by Ther and Siljak (2001) is therefore a very useful contribution. In addition, the mass-marketed atlas of the population expulsions and transfers edited by Sienkiewicz and Hryciuk (2008), and partly funded by the Polish–German Reconciliation Foundation, may help to change perceptions.
107 Approximately 200,000 people who had either emigrated, or were descended from Poles who had emigrated, to Western Europe – chiefly France – also moved to Poland during this period.
108 AAN 200/II/17/13 'Repatriacja z Zachodu i Południa 1945'.
109 NA.FO 688/31/3 (48/6/45) 'Jews in Poland'.
110 NA.FO 371/51127 (WR 3418) Cavendish Bentinck's message to the Foreign Office, 19 November 1945.
111 AAN 201/24/26.
112 AAN 201/24/123. This position was not unproblematic. When the Prime Minister made the same point at a meeting of the KRN on 21 July 1945, a member of the Jewish section of the PPR and member of the Central Committee of Jews in Poland (CKŻP) described it as 'anti-Jewish', indicating that, 'the government, instead of providing assistance and work, wanted to offer the Jews open borders'. Quoted in Gross (2006: 218–19).
113 The notion of 'productivization' of Jews may have been imported from a Soviet idea operative in the 1930s. One of the difficulties in using the concept of 'productivization' in postwar Poland was that there were relatively few people to be made 'productive', given that most of Poland's Jewish population had been murdered in the Holocaust, while pre-war notions of 'Jewish' occupations lived on.
114 Quoted in Bauer (1970: 150), from *Unsere Stimme*, 4 June 1946.
115 AAN 522II/459/34.
116 To summarize, the de facto authorities in Poland were, first, from July 1944, the Polish Committee of National Liberation (PKWN), then the Provisional Government of the Polish Republic (RTRP) and, after June 1945, the Provisional Government of National Unity (TRJN).
117 The Polish Government in Exile continued to function until 1990 when it handed over the symbols of the Polish Republic (presidential and state seals) to President Lech Wałesa in December of that year. In 1992 the post-communist Polish Government recognized the medals and decorations awarded by the Government in Exile.
118 AAN 200 III/36/40 (articles from press: overseas news agency report 1874, 24 July 1946).

3 Manipulating social anger

1 For many, Schmitt's compromise with Nazism rules out any dialogue with his work. Yet, the productive engagement with his *oeuvre* by scholars committed to substantive democracy from the political left and centre indicates the correctness of Chantal Mouffe's (2005: 4) argument that 'it is the intellectual force

of theorists, not their moral qualities, that should be the decisive criteria in deciding whether we need to establish a dialogue with their work'.

2   *Homo sacer* is a figure from archaic Roman law, situated at the 'intersection of a capacity to be killed and yet not sacrificed, outside both human and divine law' (Agamben 1998: 73). Agamben proceeds to elaborate the connection between the sovereign and *homo sacer*, maintaining that they have the same structure: 'the sovereign is the one with respect to whom all men are potentially *homines sacri*, and *homo sacer* is the one with respect to whom all men act as sovereigns'. As will become clear in this chapter and the next, minority communities were positioned as *homines sacri* at least until late 1947.

3   It should be noted that the language of class hardened significantly after 1948 due to the Stalinization of the PZPR and public life in general, the strengthening of the Government, the emergence of the Cold War and the development of bloc geopolitics.

4   NA.HS 4/319.

5   AAN 522/II/531/9.

6   The first draft of the land reform decree was written by the well-known peasant leader Andrzej Witos. The final draft was written by Witos, Minc and two others (Dz.U 1944, No. 4, item 17, amended 17 January 1945, Dz.U 1945, No. 3, item 9). Nevertheless, the reform was not particularly radical as *agricultural* reform, as Korbonski (1965: 69, 76) argues. This was due to the fact that it attempted to marry several different agendas. Namely, it was necessary to take into account the limited pluralism of the PKWN, the need to reassure small and medium-sized landowners and the need to reward patriotic landowners who had struggled against the Germans. The land reform was, on the other hand, part of a set of decrees that carried the ethno-nationalist project forward by appropriating German property, and from this perspective it was most certainly radical.

7   See Góralski (2006). Góralski charts the legal basis of the alienation of German property. In addition to the agricultural reform decrees, the PKWN decree of 12 December 1944 on forest land, together with the amendment of 13 November 1945, shifted German property to the State. Article 2 of the December 1944 decree reads, 'forests and forest land, together with the non-forest land attached to them, and other real estate and moveable goods being the property of persons of German ethnic status enter into the assets of the State Treasury independently of their area'. The decree of 8 March 1946 (Dz.U 1946, No. 13, item 87) on 'Abandoned and Post-German property' nationalized German property in areas formerly in the German Reich and in Danzig (Gdańsk). It also included a clause to expropriate the property of those who defected to the enemy during the Second World War. This decree superseded the earlier law of 6 May 1945 on 'Abandoned and Derelict Property' (Dz.U 1945, No. 17, item 97). The construction of the legal apparatus to legitimate the taking over of German property was completed with the decree of 15 November 1946 on the Seizure of Property of States being at War with the Polish State in the Years 1939–45 and on Property of Legal Persons and Citizens of those States and on the Receivership of such Properties. (Dz.U 1946, No. 62, item 342).

8   Dudek and Zblewski derive their figures from Paczkowski (1993).

9   Prior to the referendum, sentiment among PPS and PPR members was also assessed. In Dobrzelin, in the Łódź voivodship, a report sent to the PPR Secretary in Łódź on 19 May 1946 advised that there was little support in the district for the abolition of the Senate, while land reform and the western border were approved. APŁ KWPPR 1022/73/168.

10   See Curp (2001: 592). The first question of the referendum was 'Do you support the abolition of the Senate?'. The third question was 'Do you wish to keep

Poland's western borders on the Baltic, Oder and western Neisse?'. See Kersten (1991: 255).

11 AAN 522/II/531/6 'Agriculture and Food in Poland: Operational Analysis Paper Number 3, July 1946'.

12 AAN 258/3/49–51.

13 The increase in the number of rapes was not just restricted to the East. As Bourke (2007: 361) notes, in the West there were 500 rape cases involving American soldiers each week in April 1945. Sexual violence in the East was on a much wider scale, however. Bourke (2007: 385) argues that, '[i]t is even more important to recognize that military units operating in nearly identical environs display very different tendencies to act in sexually aggressive ways. In other words, rape is avoidable'.

14 Also, see Checinski (1983: 13).

15 APŁ KWPPR 1022/69/3.

16 Quoted in Polonsky and Drukier (1980: 406). Though some strikes in the aftermath of the Second World War had a political character, most had economic causes. The PPR rhetoric celebrating the working class was insufficient to assuage the material shortages experienced by large sections of the working class, and the working class responded through strikes – as though the Government were a capitalist employer. Between 1945 and 1948 there were, on average, 25 strikes a month, with the peak year for strikes being 1946. They were concentrated in the Łódź, Katowice and Kraków voivodships – places with established labour traditions and long-standing stereotypes of minority populations. See Dudek and Zblewski (2008: 42).

17 APŁ KWPPR 1022/225/4–6. In August 1945, strikers called for Jews to be removed and claimed that conditions were better under the Germans.

18 See Dudek and Paczkowski (2005: 247). They also point out that 'from October 1944 to April 1945 around 4,400,000 letters and 179,000 telegrams were censored'.

19 NA.FO 371/57684 WR15.

20 However, there is general acceptance among historians that Jews were overrepresented in some sections of the Office of Security – *Urząd Bezpieczeństwa* (UB). In 1945, the UB had 25,600 members, including 438 Jews, but Jews held 13 per cent of management positions. The claim made by the Right that the UB was a Jewish institution owes more to preconceived notions than to reality.

21 See Chodakiewicz (2003: 125, 131, 213). He claims that Jewish participation in communist structures led to the abuse of at least 7,000 Poles. For an excellent review of Chodakiewicz's book see Engel (2005: 424–9), who correctly sees it as an attempt 'to rehabilitate the "good name" of a small, extreme political minority by endowing its propaganda with the imprimatur of historical research'.

22 Gross (2006) has been extensively discussed in Poland. See the collection of essays compiled by Gądek (2008).

23 The issue of Polish assistance to Jews has been hotly debated over the last couple of decades. Polish assistance is highlighted here merely to show the problems with Gross's thesis. The asymmetry in the Polish–Jewish relationship during this period is recognized. As Barbara Engelking (2001: 24) has noted, '[t]he Poles did not need the Jews in order to wage their war against the Germans. Meanwhile, the Jews – if they wished to avoid certain death at the hands of the Germans – could not manage without the Poles. They were condemned to suffer the consequences of their neighbours' charity, pity, decency, hatred, indifference or greed'.

24 In order to find Jews in hiding in Warsaw, the Germans publicized a scheme to exchange Jews for Germans interned by the Allies. Jews were invited to the Hotel Polski where they were forced to pay a high price to enter (though this was

often waived), in order to get on the list to be exchanged. Some 3,500 Jews took up the offer. They were ultimately sent to the gas chambers. Paulsson (2002) argues that if the Hotel Polski affair and the Warsaw Uprising of 1944 were excluded (both events being unique to Warsaw), then the notional survival rate for Jews in hiding in Warsaw would be around 61 per cent compared with 40–60 per cent for the Netherlands. Overall, around 41 per cent of those Jews who went into hiding in Warsaw (11,500 Jews) survived the Holocaust.

25 Paulsson estimated that there were approximately 3,000 such 'hooligans' (0.3 per cent of the population) and reckons that around 70–90,000 people helped Jews (20–30,000 did so for money alone). See Paulsson (2002: 111, 131).

26 It should be noted that the image of Jews as being the quintessential communist or capitalist, so familiar in the anti-Semitic literature and propaganda of the period, was reproduced, albeit in a more carefully worded and restrained fashion, in the Foreign Office.

27 'Uwagi o naszej Polityce międzynarodowej' SI. A9.Ie/15 doc. 55.

28 The Polish Government in Exile, through the Polish Telegraph Agency, published an official statement distancing itself from the secret document that was sent to New York on 10 May 1944 and to Jerusalem on 25 May 1944. In this statement, the Polish Government declared that the document was 'contrary to the policy, rulings and plans of the Polish Government', and emphasized that it had not received such a report. NA.FO 371/39524 (Annex A).

29 It may be argued that the Government in Exile was pursuing a policy that was fairly uncontroversial both domestically and in the international context of the period. However, it must be recognized that the Government in Exile had greater discretion in formulating its policy towards minority populations.

30 The section of Karski's report on attitudes towards Poland's Jews was censored by officials of the Polish Government in Exile as it was thought that the severe attitude taken by Poles would not be welcomed by Poland's Allies – Britain and France. See Engel (1991: 259).

31 See Polubiec (1984: 174–9). Doc. No. 24 'Nasz stosunek do Niemców' [*sic*].

32 In July 1944 the PPR had 20,000 members; in December 1944 it had 34,000 members. In early 1945 there was a membership drive and the number increased to 188,900 by the end of July 1945. In December 1945 the figure was 235,000 and by June 1946 it was over 347,000. Many people joined the PPR to advance their careers and secure material benefits. See Kersten (1991: 171), and Coutouvidis and Reynolds (1986: 181, 236).

33 Quoted in Polonsky and Drukier (1980: 407).

34 The RJN formed largely in response to the formation of the KRN in January 1944. The RJN's programme, 'What the Polish nation is fighting for', was released in March 1944, and represented an uneasy compromise position of the PPR opposition parties – the National Democratic, Peasant, Socialist and Labour parties, which constituted the London-based Government in Exile. In particular, as Ciechanowski (2002: 126) points out, the socio-economic policies were seen by the National Democrats as too radical, while the Peasant and Socialist parties felt they did not go far enough. Indeed, these differences were so deep that Tadeusz Bór-Komorowski, commander of the Home Army, reported to London that the members of the RJN lacked 'a common line'. See Ciechanowski (2002) and Kersten (1991: 50).

35 While, in the aftermath of war and later, communist parties in Europe were able to engage with criticisms from the Right and even co-opt Rightists, Leftist deviations were not tolerated. For a brief discussion of the situation in France see Birchall (2004).

36 AAN 295/X/84.

37 NA.HW 12/318.

38 Quoted in Zaremba (2001: 154). The original document can be found at the New Documents Archive in Warsaw (AAN, KC PPR 295/173, k.23). Zaremba notes that this slogan was probably not publicized.
39 Quoted in Polonsky and Drukier (1980: 441).
40 Quoted in Kersten (1991: 301). The PPR warmed to this theme through 1946 and, by 1947, in a text distributed at Party schools, it argued that, 'Bevin together with Churchill is speaking out against our western borders with the aim of raising the spirit of German aggression against Poland'. See APŁ KWPPR 1022/146/26 – 'O sytuacji międzynarodowej'.
41 For a brief account of action taken against the PSL and its sympathizers see Friszke (2003: 126). Members of the PSL leadership such as Stanisław Mierzwa and Kazimierz Bagiński were arrested.
42 NA.FO 800/490/69 Bevin's letter to Cavendish Bentinck.
43 *New York Times*, 22 January 1947, p. 22.
44 APŁ KWPPR 1022/109/150.
45 During Operation Swallow the British frequently complained about the quality of people being brought into their zone of occupation from Poland. For an analysis of the expulsion of the German population, see Nitschke (2004).
46 See Polonsky and Drukier (1980: 425). Gomułka's 'national' vision led him to protest against the repatriation of Polish Jews from the USSR in 1946.
47 Speech given at a press conference in the Belvedere Palace 16/8/45, published in *Rzeczpospolita*, 27 August 1945. Quoted in Zaremba (2001: 154).
48 Dz.U No. 57, item 324, 30 November 1945.
49 Between 1946 and 1951 around 32,000 place names and 3,000 physical objects (lakes, hills, etc.) were Polonized, mainly in the 'Recovered Territories'. In the east, Polonization of place names continued throughout the existence of the PRL, and recent attempts by Belarusian activists to have the older Belarusian names reinstituted have not been particularly successful. For an overview, with documentation, of this issue in the Białystok voivodship see Janowicz (2004).
50 See Tomaszewski (1985a: 35). Data for 1946 derived from census 14/2/1946. Data for Belarusians in 1946 refers to all those declaring themselves not to be Polish in the Białystok voivodship. In this census, 286,500 people did not declare their nationality. The verification category largely refers to potential Poles being assessed by nationality verification panels, mainly in the 'Recovered Territories'. The data for 1950 comes from census 4/12/1950. All these figures should be treated with caution. The adjusted figures for 1931 are more robust, as they take into account the methodological problems of conflating nationality with language spoken. Later censuses are also problematic. The 1946 census was conducted in an environment which was still relatively insecure and, given the population transfer policy, would have produced a deflated number of national minorities. The 1950 figure would also be low, given government policy towards minorities.
51 The Polish president Bolesław Bierut discussed the situation of Jews with the British Ambassador Cavendish Bentinck on 25 August 1945. Bierut confirmed that Jews would enjoy the privileges granted to them under the 1921 constitution. NA.FO 688/34.
52 As early as April 1940 the Polish Government in Exile faced accusations of anti-Semitism amongst its armed forces. On 2 April 1940, Member of Parliament Mr Pritt wrote to the Foreign Office minister R.A. Butler MP regarding anti-Semitism in the Polish Army based in France. An investigation was conducted and Mr Makins of the Foreign Office concluded that, 'it seems quite on the cards that anti-Semitism is in fact quite rife in the Polish Army, but in this particular case [an anti-Semitic speech by a Polish army captain] some allowance must be made for the mess-room exuberance of a Polish officer'. On 27 July 1940 Butler

wrote to Pritt stating that, 'there had undoubtedly been a certain amount of anti-Semitic feeling in the Army. No reports have so far reached us of any active persecution', and referred Pritt to the official Polish Government position. Pritt was not satisfied. By 5 August 1940 General Sikorski tried to end the scandal and declared that any soldier who took up arms for Poland was a Pole regardless of race or religion, and that the military authorities would take active care that these orders would be observed. NA.FO 371/24481 (89/92/104/109/110).

53 In the early twentieth century the notion of 'Piast' Poland was most strongly associated with the National Democracy movement (*Endecja*). The *Endecja* argued that Poland should be nationally and culturally homogeneous. This position contrasted with a multiethnic 'Jagiellonian' solution proposed by Piłsudski and the PPS. See Michlic (2006: 59), and Walicki (2001).

54 MSZ 6/1685/105/9 (Dep Pol Wydz d/s Żydowskich: Organizacja i sytuacja Żydów w Polsce 1945–48). Emil Sommerstein was the chairman of the CKŻP and a member of the PKWN.

55 NA.FO 371/51127 (WR 3452).

56 Adolf Berman was the younger brother of Jakub Berman. Adolf emigrated to Israel in 1950 and became a member of the Israeli Knesset. For an excellent analysis of the complex identities – intellectual, European, Marxist, Jewish – and relationships of the period 1918–68, see Shore (2006).

57 AAN 201/24/2.

58 Rabbi Kahane declared at a meeting on 16 February 1946 with representatives from Britain and the USA that Jews in the Government should not be regarded as part of the Jewish community. NA.FO 688/34. Indeed, the sentiment was mutual. After the Kielce pogrom, Jakub Berman is said to have told Rabbi Kahane, 'If you think I am a Jew you are mistaken. My father and my mother were Jews and it so happens that I am working for my ideal in Warsaw' – quoted in Bauer (1970: 114).

59 On the issue of illegal migration see Aleksiun-Mądrzak (1995, 1996).

60 In January 1950 the AJDC's operations ceased. That same month the CKŻP, which represented the various political orientations of Polish Jews, was replaced by the Social Cultural Organisation of Jews in Poland (TSKŻ), which had the goal of 'transmitting socialism to the Jewish community'. See Sienkiewicz and Hryciuk (2008: 152).

61 MSZ 6/1685/105/91 (Dep Pol Wydz d/s Żydowskich: Organizacja i sytuacja Żydów w Polsce 1945–48).

62 Strauchold (2001) analyses this particular issue in detail.

63 Cited in Kulczycki (2001: 207).

64 See Strauchold (2001: 57–9). Also, see Izdebski (1946: 1–2).

65 AAN PZPR 237/VII/2620/30.

66 The PZPR formed in 1948 as a 'merger' of the PPR and the PPS.

67 AAN PZPR 237/VII/2619/108.

68 AAN PZPR 237/VII/2619/110–11.

69 AAN PZPR 237/VII/2619/111 (point 3) Voivodship Committee of the PZPR in Olsztyn 6/11/1949.

70 AAN PZPR 237/VII/2620/1.

71 Noted in Kulczycki (2001: 208). Also, see Stelmachowska (1946b).

72 AAN PZPR 237/VII/2620/28 Ministry of Culture and Art letter to the Politburo of PZPR, 31 December 1949.

73 See Berlińska (1999).

74 To be clear, by endorsing the expulsion of the Germans and the rationales behind this expulsion, the Polish Government in Exile and its followers in Poland contributed to a political narrative which promoted notions of collective responsibility and the legitimacy of violence against 'enemy' population groups.

In short, the Polish Government in Exile parenthesized its commitment to liberalism. This would not have been problematic had the London-based government been in control of the situation in Poland, as the limiting of *individual* rights of Germans would have been an isolated incident contributing to perceived greater security. However, since the Soviet Army and the PPR were in command, the collectivization of responsibility formed part of an intolerant political culture which drew the Friend/Enemy boundary in accordance with *raison d'état*, as operationalized by the PPR and its Soviet Ally. Whereas the expulsion of Germans was a long-standing policy of the Government in Exile, the underlying premise that some people were non-people to the Polish State would have been dangerous to anyone opposed to the emerging communist-dominated state.

4 Violence

1 Though Kenney (1997: 53) argues that, outside the forests, 'within the cities, it would be more appropriate to speak of a war of nerves and expectations, one that did not necessarily engage the concerns of rank and file Polish workers'.
2 See Harvey, 1999: 32, 159–60, for example.
3 The concept of non-intentional structural violence echoes Žižek's (2008: 10–11) notion of objective violence, as both formulations describe violence 'that is no longer attributable to concrete individuals and their "evil" intentions, but is purely "objective", systemic, anonymous'. Intentional structural violence, on the other hand, would be subsumed within Žižek's (2008: 1) notion of subjective violence, 'violence performed by a clearly identifiable agent'. However, it is important to differentiate those violent acts which aim to sustain the dominant social relations from those violent actions which also have identifiable authors, but have no such objective.
4 The role of *intentional structural violence* in sustaining the dominant social relations is shown by Benjamin's (1997: 239–40) consideration of strikes. He notes the general permissibility of the individual strike, and the impermissibility of the General Strike, which challenges the legal system that permits individual strikes. An individual strike is accommodated as the right to non-action (not work); the General Strike is seen by the state as violence being used to advance class aims (through extortion). The state normally responds to a General Strike by sending out the army or special police units to sustain the dominant social relations (i.e. intentional structural violence). Both types of strike tend to emerge from the structural violence of the dominant social relations (inadequate pay, poor working conditions, blacklisting, sackings, lack of autonomy, etc.), and intentional structural violence may be employed during both individual strikes and a General Strike. But during a General Strike, unless the state is prepared for a reconfiguration of social relations, then intentional structural violence is assured. Benjamin's essay on violence has generally been read as a meditation on the tension between violence which preserves the law and that which posits it.
5 State violence to eliminate the opposition could and did range from 'education' programmes to imprisonment and, at the extreme end, execution of those whose actions and views were inimical to the social order being created.
6 'Subjective violence' has been the focus of numerous research agendas since the 1960s. Horowitz (2001: 34–43) provides a summary of the main explanatory frameworks used to understand such violence at the group level. These include models which highlight grievances due to the relative deprivation of some social groups *vis-à-vis* others, and theories which emphasize frustration and aggression. The line of argument pursued here seeks to explore the relationship between subjective and structural forms of violence.
7 The agents of subjective violence *tend* to be individuals pursuing their *own*

agenda rather than groups acting in the name of the state. Though both intentional structural violence and subjective violence have identifiable authors, only intentional structural violence aims to ensure the continuation of a specific set of social relations.

8   This categorization of the various forms of violence can help to highlight the extent to which a particular set of social relations is dependent on directed coercion and may provide the basis for an ethical/normative critique. Some systems seem to rely more heavily on intentional structural violence of varying intensities, while in others non-intentional structural violence dominates.

9   A possible concern with such a broad definition of violence is that it may be read as idealizing 'self-development and self-expression' in an ahistoric fashion. However, such a definition immediately highlights the pervasiveness of violence in all societies without prematurely excluding some forms which may warrant attention. For example, Engels' (1993: 107) notion of 'social murder' is frequently overlooked, as is non-intentional structural violence in general. This seems to be a mistake. The key problematic is to isolate how violence is actually manifested in society through the dominant social relations. It should also be noted that some forms of 'self-expression' within a particular society are deemed to be illegitimate, for example, murder, rape, robbery. Illegitimate forms of 'self expression' tend not only to challenge the legal basis of society, but transgress the ethical boundaries of what specific societies deem to be acceptable conduct. In addition, illegitimate forms of 'self expression', if manifested at a mass scale, become significant centrifugal activities which have the capacity to tear society asunder and to produce a state of lawlessness. However, the sanction against illegitimate activities varies across time and space. This may be, on the one hand, due to the limited ability of law enforcement agencies to curtail them, and on the other, the result of some actors seeking to benefit from the concomitant widespread social dislocation and apprehension.

10   However, it should be noted that subjective violence is sometimes a form of 'counter-violence'. In other words, it may be a response to structural violence. See Sartre (1982: 133).

11   See Clastres (1994: 139–67). The essay 'Archeology of Violence: war in primitive societies' was first published in 1977 in *Libre*, no. 1, Paris, Payot (pp. 137–73).

12   In an earlier book – *The Origins of Totalitarianism* – Arendt conceives totalitarian states (including communist states) to be intrinsically violent, and maintains that the concentration camp is a key part of the totalitarian order. The concept of structural violence which is implicit in that text is absent from her later 1970 work on violence. This absence is shown most clearly in her misreading of Sartre's position on violence. Without a notion of structural violence, the 'counter-violence' that Sartre 'endorsed' becomes, for Arendt, the initial violence, when in fact the opposite is true. For a critique of Arendt's position on Sartre's views on violence see Gordon (2001). For a detailed analysis of Sartre's ideas on violence see Santoni (2003).

13   While many communist leaders in the mid-1940s acknowledged the weakness of their party, it was, in part, acknowledgement of the distance they had to travel to ensure that their party became a mass party. In short, it was an appeal to party members to increase their efforts to engage with the mass of the population. Often such acknowledgements are read simply as evidence of a *lack* of legitimacy.

14   AAN MBP 1744 17 4, AAN MBP 1744 2 123. Members of the UPA were excluded from the amnesty.

15   AAN MBP 1744 1 21.

16   AAN MBP 1744 1 22, 45. Anti-state sentiment was detected in the questions which prisoners asked guards. 'Hostile' questions were seen as evidence of

enemy agitation within the prison. Those identified as agitators were isolated. 'Hostile' questions which prisoners commonly asked included: Why did Anders lead the Polish Army out of the USSR? What is really the case with Katyń? Why did the Red Army not help the Warsaw Uprisers? Why did the Soviet Union cross the Polish border in 1939? Why is everything so expensive, and why is there no fish or meat in the markets? Is it true that the Soviet Army carried out various violations in Poland?

17 AAN MBP 1744 1 22, 50. The British were aware of the incarceration of people for political reasons. On 21 December 1951 political prisoners at the Jaworzno camp (formerly a sub-camp of Auschwitz) were secretly photographed by a British official. This remarkable photograph shows the prisoners marching and closely guarded by soldiers with sub-machine guns. See NA.FO 371/100718.

18 Quoted in Gross (2006: 155).

19 Quoted in Gross (2006: 156).

20 The Department of Public Security was created by KRN decree on 21 July 1944 with the establishment of the PKWN. On 1 January 1945 it assumed ministerial status. Under its authority were: the Citizens' Militia (MO), prisons, camps and internal troops. It also assumed responsibility for counter-intelligence. The MBP was, during the period considered here, under the supervision of personnel from the Soviet Union, who created a complex system of advisers. The Soviets also undertook independent action in the period 1944–47 in Poland, including the arrest of 16 key leaders of the Polish underground (loyal to the Government in Exile) in March 1945, and the deployment of NKVD troops – especially in the eastern border region. Soviet military counter-intelligence operated its own jails and camps in Poland, holding an estimated 47,000 people in the years 1944–46, of whom 25 per cent were Polish underground soldiers. See Dudek and Paczkowski (2005).

21 As in Poland, in Czechoslovakia Soviet soldiers were guilty of countless outrages. See Glassheim (2001: 197–219).

22 In 1946 Stefan Wyszyński was bishop of Lublin. Following the Kielce pogrom he met with Jewish representatives and argued that 'the matter of blood was not definitively settled' – a reference to the myth of ritual murder. The only interpretation of this statement is that the victims of the pogrom were at least partially responsible for their gruesome fate at the hands of a murderous anti-Semitic mob. It is also worth noting that Wyszyński made these comments almost 700 years after Pope Innocent IV issued a papal bull in 1247 declaring that the accusation of ritual murder against Jews was false. Noted in Gross (2006: 148).

23 See Sienkiewicz and Hryciuk (2008: 83). This volume includes both maps and photographs of the transfer/expulsion process, and is sure to become a basic reference work.

24 APŁ KWPPR 1022/94/3–4. Officials suspected that people were using PUR transports for personal purposes and called for records to be kept of people going backwards and forwards. If those who travelled to and from the 'Recovered Territories' for their own personal reasons were excluded, the recorded number of people who returned to the Łódź voivodship due to the problem of insecurity would be somewhat less.

25 Deportations of Poles to the USSR occurred throughout the areas conquered by the Soviet Army in 1944. For a discussion of the situation in the Białystok region see Zwolski (2005). Also, see Piesakowski (1990).

26 The standard narrative about violence directed against the Polish population contends that the system of camps and prisons constituted a regime of terror that subdued the population into acquiescence. To be clear, coercion was significant. However, it is important not to foreclose prematurely the discussion of how the

PPR attempted to construct consent and responded to, and tried to anticipate, social demands.

27   AAN 258/3/10.

28   Micgiel (1992: 287) quotes a 17 January 1947 memo from the PSL Main Secretariat to the US Ambassador in Warsaw, which recorded a member of a (PPR) propaganda group telling inhabitants of Stara Dąbrowa village that 'anyone can kill a Polish Peasant Party member and not be punished for it at all.'

29   The March 1945 'meeting' was arranged by General Ivan Serov of the NKVD. Serov had earlier been responsible for population transfers in the Crimea. In Poland, Serov assumed the post of senior adviser to the Ministry of Public Security in February 1945, which, as Głuchowski (2009: 107) points out, 'effectively made him the first Polish security chief'. Sixteen men were arrested in March, including Leopold Okulicki, leader of the Home Army, and Stanisław Jankowski, delegate of the Government in Exile in Poland. Both perished in prison in Moscow. Okulicki died in 1946 and it is widely believed that he was murdered. See Stypułkowski (1989).

30   These figures do not refer exclusively to ethnic Poles, but we must assume that they constituted the majority by some margin.

31   The IPN investigates crimes against the Polish nation, and there is a voluminous literature on the subject, which includes work on (and unfortunately conflates) structural and subjective violence. Greater analytical rigour would productively contribute to the ongoing debate about the totalitarian nature of the communist systems that existed in eastern Europe and elsewhere and would engage with the contention, made most forcibly by Leszek Kołakowski, that Marx's theory was not innocent. See Kołakowski (1974 and 2005).

32   Despite the transports of December 1946, which saw overcrowded, unheated trains transport Germans west, Frank (2007: 255–6) is right to highlight the fact that, until August 1946, 'Operation Swallow' proceeded with very little loss of life, 'all the more surprising given that a large proportion of "Swallows" were aged and sick'. However, Frank's analysis does not include the losses which occurred prior to arrival at the departure points in Poland and contact with the British liaison teams. Debate on the scale of these losses continues.

33   Cited in Naimark (2001: 127).

34   See Siebel-Achenbach (1994: 133).

35   In Wrocław, a 1945 scheme to make Germans wear white armbands was abandoned when it was noted that this contributed to Poles' feeling of being a minority. See Kenney (1997: 152).

36   Cited in Naimark (2001: 134).

37   See Jerzy Laudański in AAN 1744 – Ministerstwo Bezpieczeństwa Publicznego w Warszawie: Dep. Więziennictwa 1944–55.

38   AAN MBP 1744 1 20, 3. This figure includes 13,120,481.96 złoty from the hiring out of prisoner labour, 1,317,159.63 złoty from workshops and enterprises, and 520,977.82 złoty from farms. Some organizations did not have to pay the prison service for the use of its forced labour due to the charitable nature of their activities – including the committee building a monument for the Soviet Army.

39   NA.FO 1052/323/36E 'Medical report on Operation Swallow 7 March 1946'.

40   AAN 1744 1 20, 38.

41   Cited in Kenney (1997: 153).

42   In reports and memos about Operation Swallow there is repeated concern about the lack of fit men being sent to the British zone of occupation, and the over-representation of those unable to work.

43   NA.FO 1052/323/22C.

44   Kopka (2002) maps the distribution of labour camps in Poland in the period 1944–50. In total, there were some 206 camps serving various functions. These

included forced labour camps, expulsion/repatriation camps, prisoner of war camps, holding camps and penal camps.

45 It should also be noted that PPR members in the CKŻP played a role in promulgating within Jewish milieux the idea that the Polish Government in Exile was reactionary, and implied that it was anti-Semitic. In *Biuletyn Żydowskiej Agencji Prasowej* on 14 June 1945, Michał Mirski described the Polish Government in London as reactionary and as traitors to the Polish nation and its independence. Mirski declared that 'Jews are not and will not be a toy in the hands of London reaction' (cited in Grabski 2004: 161).

46 See Hurwic-Nowakowska (1986: 30, 9). Hurwic-Nowakowska contends that the figure for June 1946 is too high, as many of those returning from the USSR were double-counted.

47 'Zagadnienie Ziem Wschodnich w świetle bezpośredniej obserwacji terenu' (AAN MSW 946: 38) quoted in Tomaszewski, J. (1985b: 113).

48 Soviet data puts the total figure at 35,961. Mironowicz (1993: 111) notes that the source data is problematic as there seem to be discrepancies in the figures. However, the limited number of Belarusian transferees is not in question.

49 The transfer agreement was subsequently extended to 15 June 1946. See Sosna (1996) for a reprint of the agreement.

50 Cited in Mironowicz (1993: 183).

51 Cited in Mironowicz (1993: 153). (Source: WAPwB, PS sygn. 19, K103 (State Archive in Białystok).)

52 See Mironowicz (2000: 47). An alternative interpretation of this order is that the MO chief simply wished to replace semi-literate functionaries with better educated people. This may have been part of the reason for the order, but it fails to acknowledge the nationality profile of the MO at the time, the form in which the demand was made and the wider nationality policy that contextualized it. So, while Polish-speaking functionaries may not have had a firm grasp of literary Polish, it is probable that their spoken Polish was 'better' than those who spoke Belarusian or its dialects as their first language. The order therefore must be seen primarily as an effort to Polonize the security service, especially given PPR sensitivities about the Party and Government being seen as not Polish enough.

53 See Mironowicz (2000: 40). This data can be found in the State Archive in Białystok, KW PZPR, sygn. 4/VI/7, k8,13,14.

54 Mironowicz (1993: 135) notes the report of Anatol Soroczyński, who states that, at the beginning of 1945, Belarusians comprised 10 per cent of the citizens' militia (MO) and 50 per cent of the Office of Public Security (UBP) in the powiat.

55 See Mironowicz (2000: 82).

56 It is worth noting that Poland's new 440 kilometre border with the Ukraine was protected during 1944 and 1945 by seven detachments (of 1,630 men each) of the newly created (July 1944) NKVD Border Force.

57 Łemkos were also targeted during Action Vistula. A report on the 'repatriation' of Łemkos from the powiats of Nowy Sącz and Nowy Targ was sent by the secretary general of the Polish Press Agency to Władysław Wolski on 6 December 1945. See Misiło 1996: 290. There are clear parallels between the treatment of Łemkos as Ukrainians and the treatment of Silesians as Germans.

58 Snyder (2003: 190) argues that the disregarding of Gomułka's order 'suggests that the decision to forcibly resettle Łemkos along with Ukrainians came from Moscow, or at least that Moscow's directives could be so interpreted'. Gomułka was very familiar with the Łemko areas in the Carpathians and, like many local officials, distinguished between Łemkos and Ukrainians. Gomułka took the view that Łemkos could be assimilated to the Polish mainstream.

59 AAN Protokoły posiedzeń Rady Ministrów RP 1945 I/58–61. Reprinted in Misiło (1996: 78) (Document 78).

60   Document reprinted in Misiło (1996: 159–62) (AAN KC PPR 295/VII-111/61–61a).
61   Document reprinted in Misiło (1996: 163).
62   In comparison, 582 Polish civilians, 811 military personnel and 603 police and government officials were killed. The total number of Ukrainians killed in the period from autumn 1944 to autumn 1947 continues to be debated, with some authors citing figures of between 8,000 and 10,000. See Jasiak (2001: 188).
63   Minutes from the conference can be found in Misiło (1996: 147–55). AAN KC PPR 295/VII 158/1–7. Representatives from the UPA were actually invited. See Jasiak (2001).
64   Cited in Misiło (1993: 65).
65   It is worth noting that Władysław Wolski, the minister responsible for repatriation affairs, visited his contact at the Soviet embassy (V. Yakovlev) without notice on the evening of 29 March 1947 to advise him what the PPR Politburo, without consulting Moscow, had decided. However, as Snyder (2003: 196) argues, cooperation between Soviet officials and Poles in March and April 1947, in relation to Action Vistula, was close. What remains unclear is the precise role played by the Soviets in initiating Action Vistula.
66   For a brief outline of the Jaworzno camp see Kopka (2002: 126–9). Jasiak (2001) suggests that 162 of these Ukranians died at the camp.
67   For further discussion of the autochthones of Opole Silesia see Berlińska (1999).
68   Violence was frequently motivated by irrational narratives – such as anti-Semitism or myths of minority members all being communists, amongst others.
69   It is worth noting that most rapes occurred during the final push to Berlin and in the immediate postwar period, with Soviet troops largely responsible. By May 1946, a British official reported that, 'In direct contrast to the stories told by Honeybee refugees [from the Russian Zone] against the Russians, very few cases of rape are reported against the Poles. In fact, only eight cases have come to the notice of this HQ since the start of Operation Swallow.' NA.FO 1052/324/18F.
70   To be clear, this is the Polish Army loyal to the Government in Warsaw, and with links to the Soviet military.
71   Kenney (1997: 144) points out that, in the first postwar year, Wrocław 'was a city without authority, one of the most dangerous places in Poland'. The Germans remaining in or returning to the area after the war had the misfortune of being scheduled for deportation, being disliked on account of the war and being in the most lawless part of Poland.
72   NA.FO 1052/475/24.
73   NA.FO 1052/475/79.
74   NA.FO 1052/475/74.
75   NA.FO 1052/323/36I.
76   NA.FO 1052/323/41B.
77   AAN 201/24/78.
78   This figure is somewhat less than the 1,500 that is frequently quoted from Dobroszycki (1973). In actuality Dobroszycki (1973: 66) qualifies the 1,500 as being 'according to general estimates', and then advises that he analysed records, reports and press cuttings to trace anti-Jewish outrages in 115 localities, in which 300 Jews were murdered and 100 wounded and missing without trace. See, for example, Gross (2000: 196).
79   Gross has since shifted his position on this issue. In his recent book 'Fear' (2006), he contends that Polish fear of Jews, as a result of Polish action against Jews during the war, fuelled postwar violence against the remaining Jewish population.
80   APŁ KWPPR 1022/69/4. Report of Leon Dąbrowski, 3 December 1945.

81 The Special Commission existed from July 1946 to March 1947.
82 The arming of Jews also helped to relieve manpower pressures affecting the security services.
83 Noted in Mironowicz (2000: 45). Records can be found at the State Archives in Białystok (APB UWB 234, 117 and 5). Also see APB UWB 515 'Spalenie wsi Szpaki, Zanie, Wólka Wygonowska, Zaleszany, Końcowizna. Meldunki i korespondencje'.
84 Some Germans also remained who performed key economic functions requiring skills which Polish the labour pool did not yet possess.
85 In his interview with Teresa Torańska in the early 1980s, Edward Ochab used the phrase 'badly born' to refer to Jews. Ochab had a record of opposition to anti-Semitism, and this comment illustrates that ethnic and national differences maintained currency at the highest levels. Ochab held a number of high positions between 1944–69, including being a member of the Central Committee of the PPR between 1946 and 1948. See Torańska (1987).

5 Securing the Church

1 Cited in Diskin (2001: 45).
2 The Decree of 25 September 1945 transferred responsibility for registering births and deaths, as well as marriages, from the Roman Catholic Church to the state.
3 Splett was nominated administrator for the Chełmno diocese on 12 December 1939. See Kersten (1991: 212).
4 Cited in Diskin (2001: 29).
5 See Curp (2001: 603), endnote 132 (AAN MZO 50: 236).
6 See Żaryn (2003: 78).
7 Cited in Dudek and Gryz (2006: 12).
8 This included General Karol Świerczewski's state funeral on 1 April 1947. In addition to the Roman Catholic rites performed, religious hymns and chants were sung. The entire ceremony was vividly described in the communist paper *Głos Ludu* the next day. See Dziewanowski (1976: 242).
9 APŁ KWPPR 1022/109/41 (Circular from PPR Voivodship Committee Propaganda Department to PPR district and town committees, 4 December 1946).
10 The monastery at Jasna Góra is the main site of Roman Catholic pilgrimage in Poland. It houses the icon 'Our Lady of Częstochowa', which is associated with several miracles.
11 See Hemmerling and Nadolski (eds) (1990). Documents 60 and 66.
12 See Gomułka's statement to the PPR's Central Committee, 10 February 1946 (Diskin 2001: 44).
13 See *The New York Times*, 10 July 1946, p. 8. Also see Checinski (1982: 22).
14 Engel compares and contrasts the level of violence against Jews and non-Jewish Government supporters, and shows that 'Jews were more at risk of being killed at different times and in different places than were government supporters' (Engel 1998: 68).
15 Cited in Gross (2006: 150). Gross notes that some Church historians writing in the 1990s supported the position of the episcopate *vis-à-vis* Kubina. These historians maintained that the Church needed to speak with one voice. Gross also highlights that a Polish historian argued in 1991 that calling for the Church to condemn anti-Semitism was equivalent 'to requesting an official endorsement by the Church of the entire system of terror that the communists had introduced in Poland'. Such an argument could only appeal, at best, to the dangerously naive.

16 Prażmowska (2004: 165) notes that a delegation, including a member of the PPR and a member of the allied Democratic Movement (SN), visited a parish priest in Kalisz with the aim of persuading him to appeal to his parishioners to honour all God's children, including Jews. The priest, a Father Martuzalski, replied that, 'lice were also created by God but we still kill them'. Also see AAN KC PPR 295/VII 149.
17 Defenders of the Church's policy during this period may contend, contrary to the documentary evidence, that the Church was, at worse, guilty of benign neglect of Poland's minority populations. Even if the historical record supported such a view (and it does not), it is necessary to point out that there is nothing benign about 'benign neglect.' Kymlicka (1995: 110) has shown that the notion of benign neglect ignores the fact that minorities face challenges which the majority does not, and benign neglect thereby compounds the difficulties that they face.
18 See Kloczowski (2000: 315–18). The publishing house PAX was registered on 3 February 1947, clearly showing to the Polish episcopate that the PAX organization had its own pro-Government agenda.
19 AAN KC PPR 295 VII 243 k47–50.
20 Cited in Siebel-Achenbach (1994: 208–09). Also see 'The Tablet' volume 192, 20 November 1948.
21 *The New York Times*, 13 June 1948, p. 8.
22 The author of the document is unknown, though Jan Żaryn contends that it was Feliks Widy-Wirski, the PPR member who oversaw propaganda during this period. See Dudek and Gryz (2006: 28).
23 AAN KC PPR 295/VII/210, 83–5.
24 In a letter dated 15 October 1947 the Secretary of the Łódź Voivodship Committee of the PPR, Marian Minor, advised Antoni Alster of the KC PPR that the Department of Culture and Art had provided 2.8 million złoty to restore Roman Catholic churches in the Łódź voivodship during 1947. See APŁ KWPPR 1022/73/36.
25 Cited in Dudek and Gryz (2006: 28).
26 See Gryz (1999: 20).
27 There can be no doubt that the PZPR expressed increased antipathy towards religious instruction in schools in the late 1940s. Dudek and Gryz (2006: 31), for example, contend that strong evidence of this can be found in the rapid increase in the number of schools under the patronage of the 'Workers' Society of Friends of Children' (Robotnicze Towarzystwo Przyjaciół Dzieci (RTPD)), which did not provide any religious instruction. However, what is surprising is not so much the expansion in the number of such schools, but their very limited number. In 1947, for example, there were six such schools, 31 in 1948, and only 100 in 1949. The RTDP merged with the 'Peasants' Society of Friends of Children' (Chłopskie Towarzystwo Przyjaciół Dzieci (CTPD)), forming in May 1949 the Society of Friends of Children (Towarzystwo Przyjaciół Dzieci (TPD)), and the number of schools with no religious teaching did increase. The state also attempted to limit the number of priests involved in the teaching of religion in schools, contending that many priests were using the classroom to promulgate reactionary views.
28 See Kenney (1997: 331). Kenney also outlines the religious outlook of workers, pointing out that some workers turned in their party cards after Pius XII's encyclical on communism in 1949.
29 See the letter from Wyszyński and Sapieha to Bierut, 12/9/1950, in Raina (1994: 260–1).
30 Presidential Decree of 25 November 1936, Council of Ministers Ruling, 17 December 1936. Dz.U no. 88 (1936) 613, Dz.U no. 94 (1936) 659.

31 Dz.U no. 7 (1945) 20. Also, see Dz.U no. 17 (1945) 96.
32 See Urban (1994: 75). Letter from Jan Szeruda to Edward Osóbka-Morawski. AAN MAP 1053.
33 See Urban (1994: 73). AAN MAP 1057. Letters from Bishop Adamski to Vice-Voivod Ziętka, 20 February and 27 March 1945.
34 See Urban (1988), who provides an overview of the activities of the Christian Ecumenical Council. The Council of Protestant Churches helped to co-ordinate aid from Protestant Churches overseas. After 1947 these overseas contacts, especial with Churches in the West, increasingly became a political liability for Protestant Churches in Poland. See Tomaszewski (1991).
35 See Tomaszewski (1991: 51). AAN MAP 1059 (Memoriał na podstawie obserwacji podczas objazdu Mazur 12–22 August 1945).
36 AAN MAP 1072. Letter from the Ministry of Justice to the Ministry of Public Administration, 6 February 1946.
37 See Tomaszewski (1991: 57). AAN MAP 1072.
38 Poland also gifted £12,000 sterling to the Constantinople Patriarchate.
39 These policies were part of the Promethean project in which the Polish state sought to exploit nationality issues against the Soviet Union during the interwar period. See Snyder (2005).
40 The change in Moscow's position coincided with the shift in Polish nationality policy. It is highly likely that the policy changes were related. In the earlier period, the contesting of autocephaly aligned with the policy of population transfers and showed the Orthodox faithful that they had no future in Poland. After 1948, with the state assuming control of minority organizations and institutions, the recognition of autocephaly coincided with the Polish desire to 'support' and monitor minority populations such as Belarusians/Orthodox.
41 This is still the case for many in the region today, with many identifying themselves as 'tutejszy' (from here/local). See Sadowski (1991 and 1995). Also see Fleming (2003).
42 PUST A7.7.2.
43 Cited in Syrnyk (2007: 228/229). Second letter is dated 28 June 1948.
44 Cited in Hałagida (2003: 92). This support was proposed as a strategy to further undermine the Greek-Catholics, who were seen as an underground organized by Ukrainian nationalist agents.

6 Rupturing homogeneity? Class and national identities

1 The Poles prepared for the meeting called by Stalin from early July 1947. Gomułka, the Polish Deputy Prime Minister, had been advised that the meeting was to facilitate the exchange of views and opinions and to establish an international press and information organ, not an instrument of Soviet control over European communist parties. See Kersten 1991: 407. It was a direct response to the perceived threat that Moscow saw in the Marshall Plan. Representatives from the communist parties of the Eastern bloc attended, together with representatives from the communist parties of France and Italy.
2 This shift is clearly seen in relation to the Belarusian population in Poland. As noted in Chapter 4, virtually all Belarusian schools were closed down between 1944 and 1947, a period characterized by *hard* ethno-nationalism. Population transfers/expulsions coincided with Belarusian quietism and affiliation to Polish majoritarian norms. The shift to *soft* ethno-nationalism, with its emphasis on integration, created space for the opening of Belarusian schools in 1949, which helped to aid assimilation and allowed the state to monitor the population closely. During the same period, Jewish institutions were brought under state control.

3 The structure of centripetal and centrifugal aspects of the PPR/PZPR's nationality policy, however, was preserved in this shift from hard to soft ethnonationalism, only expressed in a different way. Minorities were encouraged to assimilate rather than being *explicitly* targeted for exclusion and social anger, but they remained at risk of being identified as insufficiently Polish by both the PZPR (and factions within it) and the wider society through the course of the PRL. Representational violence (stereotypes and *idées fixes*) sustained the marginalization of various communities.

4 The British did not accept any further expellees under 'Operation Swallow' after 3 January 1947. Nevertheless, transports from the interior of Poland continued to move Germans to the departure points. By the end of January conditions at the holding camp at Szczecin were becoming critical and, in March 1947, typhoid broke out. With the fraudulent January elections in Poland, the political reasons for the British to continue 'Operation Swallow' had been removed. The Poles, for their part, maintained pressure on the British to accept more Germans, even going so far as to offer a 'final instalment' of expellees. The British remained steadfast in their refusal, though it was not until 26 July 1947 that the Poles were officially notified that the British had fulfilled their agreed obligations and that the transfer programme had been completed. NA.FO 1049/984 83/74/47.

5 It is worth noting that the (Warsaw) Polish Government's displeasure with British policy had been expressed in January. On 31 January 1947 a presidential order evicted the British Council, a non-political body promoting cultural exchange between Britain and Poland, from its premises at Gornośląska street in Warsaw. British Council official C.G. Bidwill saw this as part of an 'anti-British campaign', and argued that 'it appeared that this was a deliberate political attempt to curtail, or close down our work' (NA.BW 51/14 L/8/27). The Foreign Office had considered using the British Council as a way to apply some form of pressure on the Polish Government. However, in May of that year Bidwell wrote to the British Embassy rejecting Robin Hankey's secret suggestion that the British Council take a more partisan line, and stating that it was important that the British Council 'maintain [its] non-political stance' (NA.BW 51/14 POL 6/8/2).

6 NA.FO 371/64225 C10155 and C12054.

7 *The New York Times*, 17/9/1947 p. 14. NA.FO 371/56673 N9045 'Report on leading personalities in Poland, 1946'.

8 NA.FO 371/64225 C12054.

9 NA.FO 371/64226 C12192. The translation is the Foreign Office's.

10 AAN PPS 235/XIX/129 (microfilm 2244/12). The British party included Arthur Allen, Fred Lee, Henry White and George Thomas, among others.

11 NA.FO 371/64226 C13197. The translation is the Foreign Office's. Letter from Polish Military Mission to the Control Council in Berlin, 11 August 1947.

12 The Polish representative in Bad Salzuflen, M. Gondowicz, reported as early as November 1946 that Westphalian Poles requested that Polish books be sent to them. See MSZ 6 1727 107/115 (Polska Misja Wojskowa w Berlinie).

13 The rifts between Malthusian notions of 'over-population' and Marxist notions of 'reserve army of labour' reflect radically different conceptions of social organization. So, while the PPR's propaganda did not explicitly discuss the finer theoretical points of the Malthusian/Marxist debate, the notion that the Second Republic was a failure (among other reasons, due to the fact that Poles had to migrate to find employment) was highlighted and found resonance with the public. For a discussion of the limits of Malthusian notions of 'over-population', see Harvey (2001: 38–67).

14 NA.FO 1052/458 (17).

15 NA.FO 371/64226 C13641.

16 NA.FO 371/64225 C11831.
17 NA.FO 371/64225 C12090. Robin Hankey arrived in Warsaw in July 1945 and remained at the British embassy until March 1946, when he returned to London to head the Foreign Office's Northern Department. For a discussion of Hankey's contribution to Anglo–Polish diplomacy see Rothwell (1990).
18 NA.FO 371/64225 C13478.
19 NA.FO 371/64225 C10409.
20 NA.FO 371/64226 C13830.
21 NA.FO 1052/458 (54).
22 NA.HW12/318.
23 Kulczycki (1997: 251) discusses the interwar policy.
24 MSZ 6 1725 107/214. Report of K. Laskowski, 6 October 1947.
25 NA.FO 371/64225 C11831. Also, see Persson (2001) chapter VIII.
26 NA.FO 371/64226 C15789.
27 NA.FO 371/64226 C13830. Letter from Eric Cullingford to Manpower Division Headquarters, 15 October 1947.
28 NA.FO 371/64226 C16403. It is worth noting that Gomułka made his speech following the failure of the fifth Council of Foreign Ministers (made up of the Powers occupying Germany – France, the UK, the USA and the USSR), which took place in London during November and December 1947.
29 MSZ 6/88/6 33. Letter from Brigadier Staveley, Entries and Exits Branch, Intelligence Division Headquaters to General-Consul, Polish Mission, Berlin, dated 28 January 1948. Applicants to move to Poland had to initiate their application for travel documents at the office of the local civil administration. The applicant required a certificate from the manpower authorities stating that the applicant was not employed in essential work and a letter from the Polish authorities stating that an entry visa to Poland would be provided. In addition, applicants to leave Germany had to secure a certificate from the local administration stating that any goods that they wished to take with them were their property, and a certificate of clearance from the tax office. The formalities took between 4 and 5 weeks. MSZ 6/88/6 29. Letter from the Revenue Branch, Finance Division (British Element) to Colonel Marecki, Berlin, dated 19 January 1948.
30 MSZ 6/88/6 31.
31 AAN 200 II/79/1.
32 AAN 200 II/79/4.
33 AAN 200 II/79/5.
34 AAN 200 II/79/6.
35 AAN 200 II/79/9.
36 AAN 200 II/79/10.
37 MSZ 6/88/6 50.
38 AAN 200 II/79/25.
39 MSZ 6/88/6 68.
40 The refugees from Greece were made up of two groups of approximately equal size – ethnic Greeks and ethnic Macedonians. Differences and tensions between the two groups were noticed almost immediately by the Polish authorities responsible for them, and the Poles admitted that 'there are frequent conflicts of a national kind which our Polish workers and comrades do not always understand' (KCPZPR 1354 237 XXII 416 p. 25). As early as 1949, divisions within the refugee community between ethnic Greeks and ethnic Macedonians were detected. That year a report reached the KC PZPR declaring that, '[t]he Greek comrades are extremely cautious about the Macedonian comrades. Often, however, under the shield of cautiousness, is displayed great Greek chauvinism' (AAN KC PZPR 1354 237 XXII 416 p. 25). The Poles' privileging of the Greek

Communist Party and the dominant perception of the refugees as Greek probably exacerbated the ethnic tensions in the refugee milieu. The problems between the two groups of refugees only disappeared when most of the Macedonians emigrated to the Yugoslavian republic of Macedonia between 1958 and 1968.

41 For an analysis of minorities during the PRL see Mironowicz (2000). For an extended discussion of the refugees from Greece see Wojecki (1989), Pudło (1995), Fleming (2008).

42 The record of the October 1944 Moscow conference can be found at NA.FO800/414. Churchill's account of the meeting can be found in Churchill (1985 vol. 6: 198).

43 The Greek Civil War went through three phases – October 1943–February 1944, December 1944–February 1945 and 30 March 1946–16 October 1949. The first phase witnessed the two anti-German resistance forces fighting each other. During the second phase, beginning in December 1944, the communist-backed National Liberation Front (EAM) and National People's Liberation Army (ELAS) fought with the Greek Government and allied British forces in central Athens. On 12 February 1945 the EAM, ELAS and the Communist Party of Greece concluded the Varkiza agreement with the Greek Government and the British. This was the first time since 1942 that the 'balance of power in Greece as a whole swung suddenly and decisively against the Left' (Mazower 2000: 6). After the signing of the Varkiza agreement, significant purges of Leftists and resistance fighters took place, paving the way for the third round of the Civil War. The lack of moderation on the part of the Greek Government (for example, the rigged plebiscite allowing the King to return in 1946) and the concomitant persecution of Leftists, stimulated the formation of the Democratic Army of Greece (the successor to ELAS). This army was controlled by the Communist Party of Greece. In March 1946, the Civil War entered its third phase. From this date until October 1949, the Democratic Army of Greece, backed by Yugoslavia under Tito, fought the reformed National Army, which was aided by the USA, in a brutal war that saw atrocities committed by both sides. See O'Ballance (1966) and Gerolymatos (2004).

44 The Communist Party of Greece only found out about the 'naughty document' in 1952.

45 Nikos Zachariadis became the General Secretary of the Communist Party of Greece in 1934. From that date, according to Gerolymatos (2004: 128), 'the policies of [the Party] were practically dictated by the Soviet Union via the Third Communist International' and the 'senior leadership of the Communist Party identified exclusively with Moscow and any deviation resulted in purges'. During the Nazi occupation, Zachariadis was interned and subsequently transferred to the concentration camp at Dachau.

46 Due to the cost of fighting the Second World War and the debts thereby incurred by early 1947, Britain's financial difficulties were becoming acute and she could no longer maintain all her overseas commitments. The British Embassy in the United States advised the US State Department on 21 February 1947 that Britain could not continue to financially support the Greek Government, and expressed the hope that the USA would provide aid, pointing out that, 'unless Greece can obtain help from outside there is certain to be widespread starvation and consequent political disturbance in the present year' (FRUS 1947: 33). The situation in Greece helped to shape the Truman Doctrine, announced in March 1947. See FRUS 1947: 98.

47 Voglis (2000: 81) observes that 'it is difficult to estimate the number of executions, since there are no official documents from the government side', and goes on to argue that between 3,000 and 5,000 executions took place. The lowest esti-

mation is provided by British official sources, which claim that, between 1946 and 1949, 3,033 people were executed under the authority of the extraordinary court-martials.

48 APŁ KWPPR 1022/146/26.
49 AAN KC PZPR 1354 237 XXII 416 pp. 1–4.
50 The evacuation of children from Greece is still the subject of much debate. Gerolymatos, (2004: 230) argues that 'almost 28,000 were abducted or forced to flee Greece with the communist forces . . . [and] . . . faced a dreary life in the orphanages of the Eastern Bloc countries', whereas research conducted by van Boeschoten (2000: 132) found that 'most of the children wanted to leave for abroad and some even left in secret, against the will of their parents'. The reasons given include hunger and fear of the war, the desire to be with other children, to escape a shepherd's life and to be educated.
51 APŁ KWPPR 1022/109/150.
52 AAN KC PZPR 1354 237 XXII 416/53.
53 AAN KC PZPR 1354 237 XXII 419 p. 9.
54 AAN KC PZPR 1354 237 XXII 422 p. 126. It is worth noting that the refugees were described as 'repatriants'. This can be explained in one of three ways. First, it was merely an administrative slip made by an official used to dealing with repatriants; second, it was an attempt to sustain secrecy on the issue of Greek refugees; or third, it was the author's attempt to indicate to colleagues that the Greeks required assistance that was not inferior to that extended to actual repatriants, such as those from France, Belgium and Westphalia. In 1949, the programme's budget amounted to 228,769,662 złoty and in 1950 to 22,075,490 (new) złoty. See AAN KC PZPR 1354 237 XXII 422 p. 127 for a full breakdown of funding figures.
55 Beloyannis was arrested in December 1950 and accused of treason. He refuted this charge by highlighting his activities during the Nazi occupation. He was also accused of being a member of the Communist Party of Greece, which had been made illegal following the flawed 1946 election (boycotted by the Left). The trial was politically significant, given the fact that Beloyannis was a political commissar in the Greek Democratic Army.
56 Dz.U 1965 no. 15, item 77, art. 13, 1 (art. 14, 1).
57 For further details relating to the split in the PPR see Kersten (1991: 438–40, 450–6). Also see Głuchowski (2004: 365–84).
58 This refers exclusively to nationality *policy*. After 1948, insufficient fidelity to the line promoted by Moscow often resulted in the accusation of national deviation or nationalism. Elsewhere in east-central Europe, in Czechoslovakia and Hungary in particular, prosecution and purging of the communist party swiftly followed. In contrast, in Poland, the main 'nationalist', Władysław Gomułka, was excluded from power, only to return triumphantly in 1956.

7 Conclusion

1 Cited in Gutman (2001: 16).
2 It is worth noting that during the course of the PRL Poland provided sanctuary to Left-wing activists and fighters from many different countries, including those from several Latin American states.
3 See Arendt (1970: 53).
4 The stereotypes of Jew-communist and Belarusian-communist assisted the state-wide ethno-nationalist project, for example.

Bibliography

Agamben, G. (1998) *Homo Sacer: Sovereign Power and Bare Life*, trans. D. Heller-Roazen, Stanford, CA: Stanford University Press.

Agamben, G. (2003) *State of Exception*, trans. K. Attell, Chicago, IL: University of Chicago Press.

Aleksiun-Mądrzak, N. (1995) 'Nielegalna emigracja Żydów z Polski w latach 1945–1947 (część I)', *Biuletyn Żydowskiego Instytutu Historycznego*, No. 3/95 (175–8): 67–90.

Aleksiun-Mądrzak, N. (1996) 'Nielegalna emigracja Żydów z Polski w latach 1945–1947 (część II)', *Biuletyn Żydowskiego Instytutu Historycznego*, No. 3/96 (179): 17–32.

Aleksiun-Mądrzak, N. (1997) 'Sytuacja Żydów w Europie Wschodniej w latach 1945–1947 w świetle raportów przedstawicieli dyplomatycznych Wielkiej Brytanii', *Biuletyn Żydowskiego Instytutu Historycznego*, No. 1/97 (181): 65–76.

Anders, W. (1949) *An Army in Exile: The Story of the Second Polish Corps*, London: Macmillan.

Anderson, B. (1991) *Imagined Communities: Reflections on the Origin and Spread of Nationalism* (2nd edn), London: Verso.

Andrzejczuk, M. (2007) 'Kościół prawosławny w PRL w okresie stalinowskim', *Białoruskie Zeszyty Historyczne*, Białystok, 2007: 117–58.

Arendt, H. (1948/1973) *The Origins of Totalitarianism*, San Diego, CA: Harcourt Brace and Company.

Arendt, H. (1970) *On Violence*, London: Harcourt Brace and Company.

Azcarate, P. de (1945) *League of Nations and National Minorities: An Experiment*, New York: Carnegie Endowment for Peace.

Bachmann, K. and Kranz, J. (1997) *Przeprosić za wypędzenie? wypowiedzi oficjalne oraz debata prasowa o wysiedleniu Niemców po II wojnie światowej*, Kraków: Znak.

Balbus, T. (2003) *Ludzie podziemia AK-WiN w Polsce południowo-zachodniej, 1945–1948*, Wrocław: Instytut Pamięci Narodowej, Oddział we Wrocławiu.

Bán, A.D. (ed.) (1997) *Pax Britannica: Wartime Foreign Office Documents Regarding Plans for a Postbellum East Central Europe*, Boulder CO: Social Science Monographs.

Banasiak, S. (1963) *Działalność osadnicza Państwowego Urzędu Repatriacyjnego na Ziemiach Odzyskanych w latach 1945–1947*, Poznań: Instytut Zachodni.

Banasiak, S. (1965) 'The settlement of the Polish western territories 1945–47', *Polish Western Affairs*, VI: 121–49.

Bauer, Y. (1970) *Flight and Rescue: Brichah. The Organized Escape of the Jewish Survivors of Eastern Europe 1944–1948*, New York: Random House.

Baziur, G. (2003) *Armia Czerwona Na Pomorzu Gdańskim 1945–1947*, Warszawa: IPN.

Bell, P. (1990) *John Bull and the Bear: British Public Opinion, Foreign Policy and the Soviet Union, 1941–1945*, London: Edward Arnold.

Benjamin, W. (1997) 'Critique of Violence' in *Walter Benjamin: Selected Writings*, vol. 1: 236–52. Cambridge MA: Belknapp Press of Harvard University Press.

Berendt, G., Grabski, A. and Stankowski, A. (2000) *Studia z Historii Żydów w Polsce po 1945 roku*, Warszawa: Żydowski Instytut Historyczny.

Berlińska, D. (1999) *Mniejszość niemiecka na Śląsku Opolskim w poszukiwaniu tożsamości*, Opole: Instytut Śląski.

Bieschoff, R.F. (1942) *Nazi Conquest Through German Culture*, Cambridge, MA: Harvard University Press.

Birchall, I.H. (2004) *Sartre against Stalinism*, Oxford: Bergham Books.

Bogacki, A.C.J. (1991) *A Polish Paradox: International and National Interest in Polish Communist Foreign Policy, 1918–1948*, Boulder, CO: East European Monographs.

Borodziej, W. and Lemberg, H. (eds) (2000) *Niemcy w Polsce 1945–1950. Wybór Dokumentów*, vol. 1, Warszawa: Neriton.

Bosco, A. and Navari, C. (eds) (1994) *Chatham House and British Foreign Policy 1919–1945: the Royal Institute of International Affairs during the inter-war period*, London: Lothian Foundation.

Bouscaren, A.T. (1963) *International migrations since 1945*, New York: Praeger.

Bramwell, A.C. (ed.) (1988) *Refugees in the Age of Total War*, London: Unwin Hyman.

Brock, P. (1969) 'Polish Nationalism', in Lederer, I.J. and Sugar, P.F., *Nationalism in Eastern Europe*, pp. 310–72, Seattle, WA: University of Washington Press.

Bromke, A. (1962) 'Nationalism and Communism in Poland', *Foreign Affairs*, July 1962.

Bromke, A. (1967) *Poland's Politics: Idealism v Realism*, Cambridge, MA: Harvard University Press.

Bourke, J. (2007) *Rape: A History from 1860 to the Present Day*, London: Virago.

Bühler, P.A. (1990) *The Oder-Neisse Line: A Reappraisal Under International Law*, New York: Columbia University Press.

Bullen, R. and Pelly, M.E. (1985) *Documents on British Policy Overseas: Conferences and Conversations: London, Washington and Moscow*, London: Routledge.

Butler, R. and Pelly, M.E. (eds) (1984) *Documents on British Policy Overseas: The Conference at Potsdam July – August 1945*, London: Routledge.

Cała, A. (1998) 'Mniejszość żydowska' in Madajczyk, P. (ed.) *Mniejszości narodowe w Polsce*, Warszawa: ISPPAN.

Carey, J.P.C. (1948) *The Role of Uprooted People in European Recovery: An International Committee Report*, Washington DC: National Planning Association.

Chałupczak, H. and Browarek, T. (1998) *Mniejszości Narodowe w Polsce 1918–1995*, Lublin: UMCS.

Checinski, M. (1982) *Poland: Communism, Nationalism, Anti-Semitism*, New York: Karz-Cohl Publishing.

Checinski, M. (1983) *Terror and Politics in Communist Poland*, Research Paper 13, Jerusalem: The Soviet and East European Research Center, the Hebrew University of Jerusalem.

Chodakiewicz, M.J. (2003) *After the Holocaust: Polish–Jewish Conflict in the Wake of World War II*, Boulder CO: East European Monographs.

Churchill, W.S. (1985) *The Second World War: Triumph and Tragedy*, vol. VI, London: Penguin.

Ciechanowski, J.M. (2002) *The Warsaw Rising of 1944*, Cambridge: Cambridge University Press.

Ciechanowski, J.S. (ed.) (2005) *Intelligence Co-operation between Poland and Great Britain during World War II, Volume II, Documents*, Warsaw: The Head Office of the State Archives.

Ciesielski, S. and Borodziej, W. (1999) *Przesiedlenie ludności polskiej z kresów wschodnich do Polski 1944–1947*, Warszawa: Neriton, Instytut Historii PAN.

Clastres, P. (1987) *Society Against the State*, trans. R. Hurley and A. Stein, New York: Zone Books.

Clastres, P. (1994) *Archeology of Violence*, trans. J. Herman, New York: Semiotext(e).

Claude, I. (1955) *National Minorities: An International Problem*, Cambridge, MA: Harvard University Press.

Claudin, F. (1975) *The Communist Movement: From Comintern to Cominform*, Harmondsworth: Penguin.

Cobben, A. (1970) *The Nation State and National Self-determination*, New York: Crowell.

Connor, W. (1984) *The National Question in Marxist–Leninist Theory and Strategy*, Princeton NJ: Princeton University Press.

Conquest, R. (ed.) (1986) *The Last Empire: Nationality and the Soviet Future*, Stanford, CA: Stanford University Press.

Coutouvidis, J. and Reynolds, J. (1986) *Poland 1939–1947*, Leicester: Leicester University Press.

Curp, T.D. (2001) 'The politics of ethnic cleansing: The PPR, the PZZ and Wielkopolska's nationalist revolution 1944–1946', *Nationalities Papers*, 29, 4: 575–603.

Czerniakiewicz, J. (1987) *Repatriacja ludności polskiej z ZSRR 1944–1948*, Warszawa: PWN.

Czykwin, E. (2000) *Białoruska mniejszość narodowa jako grupa stygmatyzowana*, Białystok: Trans Humana.

Datner, H. (1994) 'Szkoły Centralnego Komitetu Żydów w Polsce w latach 1944–1949', *Biuletyn Żydowskiego Instytutu Historycznego*, No. 1–3 (169–171): 103–20.

Davies, N. (1981) *God's Playground: A History of Poland*, Oxford: Clarendon.

Davies, N. (1997) 'Polish National Mythologies' in G. Hoskings and G. Schoplin (eds) *Myths and Nationhood*, London: Hurst & Co.

Davies, N. (2003a) *Rising '44: The Battle for Warsaw*, London: Macmillan.

Davies, N. (2003b) *White Eagle, Red Star: the Polish Soviet War 1919–1920 and the miracle on the Vistula*, London: Pimlico.

Davies, N. (2006) *Europe at War 1939–1945: No simple victory*, London: Macmillan.

Davies, N. and Polonsky, A. (eds) (1991) *Jews in Eastern Poland and the USSR 1939–1946*, London: Macmillan.

Deak, I., Gross, J.T. and Judt, T. (eds) (2000) *The Politics of Retribution in Europe: World War II and its Aftermath*, Princeton, NJ: Princeton University Press.

Degen, R. (2005) *Kancelaria wojewódzkich urzędów administracji ogólnej na Ziemiach Odzyskanych w latach 1945–1950*, Warszawa: DiG.

Deighton, A. (1990) *The Impossible Peace: Britain, the Division of Germany and the Origins of the Cold War*, Oxford: Clarendon Press.

Diskin, H. (2001) *The Seeds of Triumph: Church and State in Gomułka's Poland*, Budapest: CEU.

Dobroczyński, M. (1996). *Niemcy, Polska, Rosja: bezpieczeństwo europejskie i współpraca*, Warszawa: Centrum Badań Wschodnich Uniwersytetu Warszawskiego.

Dobroszycki, L. (1973) 'Restoring Jewish life in post-war Poland', *Soviet Jewish Affairs*, vol. 3, no. 2: 58–72.

Dubicki, T. Nałęcz, D. and Stirling, T. (eds) (2005) *Intelligence co-operation between Poland and Great Britain during World War II, Volume I: The Report of the Anglo-Polish Historical Committee*, London: Vallentine Mitchell.

Dudek, A. (1995) *Państwo i Kościół w Polsce 1945–1970*, Kraków: PiT.

Dudek, A. (2002) *Mechanizm i instrumenty propagandy zagranicznej Polski w latach 1946–1950*, Wrocław: Atla 2.

Dudek, A. and Paczkowski, A. (2005) 'Poland' in K. Persak and Ł. Kamiński, (eds) *A Handbook of the Communist Security Apparatus in East Central Europe 1944–1989*, Warsaw: IPN.

Dudek, A. and Gryz, R. (2006) *Komuniści i Kościół w Polsce 1945–1989*, Kraków: Znak.

Dudek, A. and Zblewski, Z. (2008) *Utopia nad Wisłą: Historia Peerelu*, Warszawa: Park.

Dyczok, M. (2000) *The Grand Alliance and Ukrainian Refugees*, Basingstoke: Macmillan in association with St. Antony's College, Oxford.

Dziewanowski, M.K. (1976) *The Communist Party of Poland: An Outline History*, Cambridge, MA: Harvard University Press.

Eberhardt, P. (2000) *Przemieszczenia ludności na terytorium Polski spowodowane II wojną światową*, Warszawa: PANIGiPZ.

Eberhardt, P. (2004) *Polska i jej granice z historii polskiej geografii politycznej*, Lublin: UMCS.

Egit, J. (1991) *Grand Illusion*, Toronto: Lugus.

Engel, D. (1991) 'An early account of Polish Jewry under Nazi and Soviet Occupation presented to the Polish Government in Exile, February 1940' (pp. 172–82) in N. Davies and A. Polonsky (eds) *Jews in Eastern Poland and the USSR 1939–1946*, London: Macmillan.

Engel, D. (1998) 'Patterns of Anti-Jewish Violence in Poland, 1944–1946' in *Yad Vashem Studies*, vol. 26: 43–85.

Engel, D. (2005) 'After the Holocaust: Polish–Jewish Conflict in the Wake of World War II' in C. Freeze *et al.* (eds) (2005) *Polin: Studies in Polish Jewry*, vol. 18: 424–9, Oxford: Littman.

Engelking, B. (2001) *Holocaust and Memory – The Experience of the Holocaust and its Consequences: An Investigation Based on Personal Narratives*, trans. E. Harris, ed. G.S. Paulsson, London: Leicester University Press in association with the European Jewish Publication Society.

Engels, F. (1993) *The Condition of the Working Class in England*, Oxford: Oxford University Press.

Federal Ministry for Expellees, Refugees and War Victims (1960) *Documents on the Expulsion of the Germans from Eastern-central Europe: The Expulsion of the German Population from Czechoslovakia*, vol. IV, Bonn: Federal Ministry for Expellees, Refugees and War Victims.

Fein, H. (1979) *Accounting for Genocide: National Responses and Jewish Victimization during the Holocaust*, London: Macmillan.

Fijałkowska, B. (1999) *Partia wobec religii i kościoła w PRL 1944–1955*, Olsztyn: UWM.

Finney, P.B. (1995) '"An Evil for all Concerned": Great Britain and Minority Protection after 1919', *Journal of Contemporary History*, 30/3: 533–51.

Fleming, M. (2003) *National Minorities in Post-Communist Poland*, London: Veritas.

Fleming, M. (2007) 'Seeking labour's aristocracy? The "Westphalian incident" and Polish nationality policy in the immediate aftermath of war', *Nations and Nationalism*, 13, 3: 461–79.

Fleming, M. (2008) 'Greek "heroes" in the Polish People's Republic and the geo-politics of the Cold War 1948–1956' in *Nationalities Papers*, 36, 3: 375–97.

Foster, A.J. (1984) 'The Politician, Public Opinion and the Press: The Storm over British Military Intervention in Greece in December 1944', *Journal of Contemporary History*, 19, 3: 453–94.

Frank, M. (2006) 'The New Morality: Victor Gollancz, "Save Europe Now" and the German Refugee crisis, 1945–46', *Twentieth Century British History*, 17, 2: 230–56.

Frank, M. (2007) *Expelling the Germans: British Opinion and Post-1945 Population Transfer in Context*, Oxford: Clarendon Press.

Friedlander, H. and Milton, S. (eds) (1995) *Archives of the Holocaust: An International Collection of Selected Documents*, vol. 10, pt 2, London: Garland.

Friszke, A. (2003) *Polska: Losy Państwa i Narodu 1939–1989*, Warszawa: Iskry.

Gądek, M. (2008) (ed) *Wokół Strachu: Dyskusja o Książce Jana T. Grossa*, Kraków: Znak.

Geertz, C. (1973) *The Interpretation of Cultures*, London: Fontana.

Gellner, E. (1983) *Nations and Nationalism*, Oxford: Blackwell.

Gellner, E. (1994) *Encounters with Nationalism*, Oxford: Blackwell.

General Sikorski Historical Institute (1961 and 1967) *Documents on Polish–Soviet Relations 1939–1945*, London: GSHI.

Gerolymatos, A. (2004) *Red Acropolis, Black Terror: The Greek Civil War and the Origins of Soviet–American Rivalry, 1943–1949*, New York: Basic Books.

Glassheim, E. (2001) 'The mechanics of ethnic cleansing: The expulsion of Germans from Czechoslovakia, 1945–1947' in P. Ther and A. Siljak (eds) *Redrawing Nations: Ethnic Cleansing in East-Central Europe, 1944–1948*, New York: Rowman and Littlefield.

Głowacki, W. (1946) 'Zagadnienie repatriacji Polaków obywateli niemieckich' *Przegląd Zachodni*, No. 3: 238–57.

Głuchowski, L.W. (2004) 'Gomułka writes to Stalin in 1948' in A. Polonsky (ed.) *Polin: Studies in Polish Jewry*, vol. 17: 365–82, Oxford: Littman.

Głuchowski, L.W. (2009) 'A Critical Analysis of the Activities of the Polish Military Intelligence Service, 1945–1961' in L.W. Głuchowski and A. Polonsky (eds) *Polin: Studies in Polish Jewry*, vol. 21: 93–149, Oxford: Littman.

Gollancz, V. (1947) *In Darkest Germany*, London: Gollancz.

Gontarczyk, P. (2003) *Polska Partia Robotnicza: Droga do Władzy (1941–1944)*, Warszawa: Fronda.

Goodwin-Gill, G.S. (2000) 'The experience of displacement: refugees and war' in J. Bourne *et al.* (eds) (2000) *The Great War 1914–45: Lightning Strikes Twice*, London: Harper Collins.

Góralski, W.M. (2006) *Polish–German Relations and the effects of the Second World War*, Warsaw: Polish Institute of International Affairs.

Gordon, R. (2001) 'A response to Hannah Arendt's Critique of Sartre's Views on Violence' in *Sartre Studies International*, vol. 7, no. 1: 69–80.

Górski, K. (1946) 'Zadanie historiografii polskiej na Pomorzu' in *Przegląd Zachodni*, No. 2: 138–46.

Goss, K. 2001 'Struktura wyznaniowa mieszkańców byłego województwa białostockiego', *Pogranicze: Studia Społeczne* X: 114–36, Białystok: Uniwersytet w Białymstoku.

Grabski, A. (2004) Działalność komunistów wśród Żydów w Polsce (1944–1949), Warszawa: Trio.

Grabski, A., Pisarski, M. and Stankowski, A. (1997) *Studia z dziejów i kultury Żydów w Polsce po 1945 roku*, Warszawa: Trio.

Gregory, D. (2004) *The Colonial Present*, Oxford: Blackwell.

Grosby, S. (2005) *Nationalism: A Very Short Introduction*, Oxford: Oxford University Press.

Gross, J.T. (2000) 'Stereotypes of Polish–Jewish Relations after the War: The Special Commission of the Central Committee of Polish Jews' in A. Polonsky (ed.) *Polin: Studies in Polish Jewry*, vol. 13: 194–205, Oxford: Littman.

Gross, J.T. (2001) *Neighbors: The Destruction of the Jewish Community in Jedawbne, Poland*, Princeton, NJ: Princeton University Press.

Gross, J.T. (2002) *Revolution from Abroad: The Soviet Conquest of Poland's Western Ukraine and Western Belorussia*, Princeton, NJ: Princeton University Press.

Gross, J.T. (2006) *Fear – Anti-Semitism in Poland after Auschwitz: An Essay in Historical Interpretation*, Princeton, NJ: Princeton University Press.

Gryz, R. (1999) *Państwo a Kościół w Polsce 1945–1956 na przykładzie Województwa Kieleckiego*, Kraków: Nomos.

Guibernau, M. (1996) *Nationalisms: the Nation-State and Nationalisms in the Twenty-first Century*, Cambridge: Polity Press.

Guibernau, M. (2004) 'Antony D. Smith on nations and national identity: a critical assessment', *Nations and Nationalism*, 10: 125–42.

Gutman, I. (2001) 'Introduction', *Więź – Thou shalt not kill: Poles on Jedwabne*, pp. 9–16, Warsaw: Więź.

Hałagida, I. (2003) *Ukraińcy na Zachodnich i Północnych Ziemiach Polski 1947–1957*, Warszawa: IPN.

Hammond, T.T. (1975) *The Anatomy of Communist Takeovers*, London: Yale University Press.

Harvey, D. (1999) *The Limits to Capital*, Oxford: Blackwell.

Harvey, D. (2001) 'Population, resources and the ideology of science', in D. Harvey *Spaces of Capital: Towards a Critical Geography*, pp. 38–67, London: Routledge.

Hemmerling, Z. and Nadolski, M. (1990) *Opozycja antykomunistyczna w Polsce 1944–1956: wybór dokumentów*, Warszawa: Ośrodek Badań Społecznych.

Hirsch, H. (1999) *Zemsta Ofiar: Niemcy w obozach w Polsce 1944–1950*, Warszawa: Volumen.

Hobbes, T. (1991) *Leviathan*, ed. R. Tuck, Cambridge: Cambridge University Press.
Hobsbawm, E. (1992) *Nations and Nationalism since 1780: Programme, Myth, Reality*, Cambridge: Cambridge University Press.
Hobsbawm, E. and Ranger, T. (1984) *The Invention of Tradition*, Cambridge: Cambridge University Press.
Holler, J. E. (1963) *The German Expellees: A Problem of Integration*, Washington DC: Population Research Project, The George Washington University.
Hoover, H. and Gibson, H. (1942) *The Problems of Lasting Peace*, New York: Doubleday, Doran and Company.
Horowitz, D.L. (2001) *The Deadly Ethnic Riot*, Berkeley: University of California Press.
House of Commons (1944–1950) *Parliamentary Debates (Hansard)*, London: HMSO.
Huener, J. (2003) *Auschwitz, Poland and the Politics of Commemoration, 1945– 1979*, Athens: Ohio University Press.
Hurwic-Nowakowska, I. (1986) *A Social Analysis of Post-war Polish Jewry*, Jerusalem: Shazar Centre for Jewish History.
Ichijo, A. and Uzelac, G. (eds) (2005) *When is the Nation? Towards an Understanding of Theories of Nationalism*, London: Routledge.
Iwaniuk, S. (ed.) (1998) *Białorusini i stosunki polsko-białoruskie na Białostocczyźnie 1944–1956: Wybór Dokumentów*, Białystok: Białoruskie Towarzystwo Historyczne/Orthdruk.
Iwaniuk, S. (2005) 'Represje polskiego podziemia wobec ludności białoruskiej na Białostocczyźnie po lipcu 1944' in J. Milewski and A. Pyżewska (eds) *Stosunki Polsko-Białoruskie w Województwie Białostockim w Latach 1939–1956*, Warszawa: IPN.
Izdebski, Z. (1946) 'Podstawy weryfikacji ludności na Śląsku Opolskim' in *Zaranie Śląskie*, 1946, 1–2.
Jabłoński, K.H. (1981) 'Legalizacja Związków Wyznaniowych w PRL' in *Studia Prawnicze* 4(7): 69–90.
Jakubowski, G. (2002) *Sądownictwo Powszechne w Polsce w latach 1944–1950*, Warszawa: IPN.
Jankowiak, S. (2004) 'Wysiedlenia Niemców z Polski po II wojnie światowej' in *Pamięć i Sprawiedliwość*, 2(6): 139–60.
Jankowiak, S. (2005) *Wysiedlenie i emigracja ludności niemieckiej w polityce władz polskich w latach 1945–1970*, Warszawa: IPN.
Janowicz, S. and Chmielewski, J. (2000) *Nasze Tysiąc Lat*, Białystok: Othdruk.
Janowicz, J. (2004) *Likwidacja oficjalnego nazewnictwa miejscowości Białostocczyzny pochodzenia białoruskiego przez administrację rządową w latach 1921–2004: Dokumenty, komentarze*, Białystok: Scripta Manent.
Jarząbek, W. (2005) 'Miejsce Polski w polityce międzynarodowej w latach 1944– 1947' in *Pamięć i Sprawiedliwość*, 2(8): 71–88.
Jasiak, M. (2001) 'Overcoming Ukrainian Resistance: The Deportation of Ukrainians within Poland in 1947' in P. Ther and A. Siljak (eds) *Redrawing Nations: Ethnic Cleansing in East-Central Europe, 1944–1948*, New York: Rowman and Littlefield.
Jeżewski, H. (1942) *Granice wielkiej Polski*, Lwów: Wyd.św. Barbary.
Kalicki, W. (1999) *System propagandy politycznej oficjalnej PPS 1944–1948*, Wrocław: Wydawnictwo Uniwersytetu Wrocławskiego.

Kamiński, Ł. (2000) *Polacy wobec nowej rzeczywistości, 1944–1948*, Toruń: Wyd. A. Marszałek.

Kamiński, Ł. and Persak, K. (eds) (2005) *A Handbook of the Communist Security Apparatus in East Central Europe, 1944–1989*, Warsaw: IPN.

Kamiński, M.K. (2005) *W obliczu sowieckiego ekspansjonizmu: Polityka Stanów Zjednoczonych i Wielkiej Brytanii wobec Polski i Czechosłowacji 1945–1948*. Warszawa: Neriton/Instytut Historii PAN.

Kaps, J. (ed.) (1952) *The Tragedy of Silesia 1945–46: A Documentary Account with a Special Survey of the Archdiocese of Breslau*, trans. G.H. Hartinger, Munich: Christ Unterwegs.

Kaufman, E. and Zimmer, O. (2004) '"Dominant ethnicity" and the "ethnic-civic" dichotomy in the work of A.D. Smith' in *Nations and Nationalism*, 10: 63–78.

Kaufman, J. (1998) *A Hole in the Heart of the World: The Jewish Experience in Eastern Europe after World War II*, London: Penguin.

Kedourie, E. (1965) *Nationalism*, London: Hutchinson.

Kemp, W.A. (1999) *Nationalism and Communism in Eastern Europe and the Soviet Union: A Basic Contradiction?*, Basingstoke: Macmillan.

Kemp-Welch, A. (2008) *Poland under Communism: A Cold War History*, Cambridge: Cambridge University Press.

Kenney, P. (1997) *Rebuilding Poland: Workers and Communists 1945–1950*, London: Cornell University Press.

Kenney, P. (2000) 'Whose Nation? Whose State? Working-Class Nationalism and Anti-Semitism in Poland, 1945–1947' in A. Polonsky (ed.) *Polin: Studies in Polish Jewry*, vol. 13: 224–35, Oxford: Littman.

Kersten, K. (1964) 'The transfer of German population from Poland 1945–7', *Acta Poloniae Historica*, X: 27–47.

Kersten, K. (1974) *Repatriacja Ludności polskiej po II wojnie światowej*, Warszawa: Wydawnictwo Zakład Narodowy imienia Ossolińskich.

Kersten, K. (1986) *Narodziny systemu władzy: Polska 1943–1948*, Paris: Libella.

Kersten, K. (1991) *The Establishment of Communism in Poland, 1943–1948*, trans J. Micgiel and M. Bernhard, Berkeley: University of California Press.

Klafkowski, A. (1963) *The Potsdam Agreement*, Warsaw: Polish Scientific Publishers.

Kloczowski, J. (2000) *A History of Polish Christianity*, Cambridge: Cambridge University Press.

Kłosiński, K. (2000) *Nowa mentalność: życie codzienne w szkołach 1945–1956*, Warszawa: Trio.

Kochanowski, J. 2001 'Gathering Poles into Poland: Forced migration from Poland's former eastern territories' in P. Ther and A. Siljak (eds) *Redrawing Nations: Ethnic Cleansing in East-Central Europe, 1944–1948*, New York: Rowman and Littlefield.

Kochavi, A.J. (2001) *Post-Holocaust Politics: Britain, United States and Jewish Refugees 1945–1948*, Chapel Hill: University of North Carolina Press.

Kołakowski, L. (1974) 'My Correct Views on Everything: A Rejoinder to Edward Thompson's Open Letter to Leszek Kołakowski' in *The Socialist Register*, vol. 11 http://socialistregister.com/socialistregister.com/files/SR_1974_Kolakowski.pdf (accessed 4 April 2008).

Kołakowski, L. (2005) *Main Currents of Marxism*, London: Norton.

Kopka, B. (2002) *Obozy pracy w Polsce 1944–1950: Przewodnik encyklopedyczny*, Warszawa: Nowa Karta.

Korbonski, A. (1965) *The Politics of Socialist Agriculture in Poland 1945–1960*, New York: Columbia University Press.

Kousoulas, D.G. (1975) 'The Greek Communists Tried Three Times and Failed' in T.T. Hammond (ed.) *The Anatomy of Communist Takeovers*, pp. 293–309, London: Yale University Press.

Kraft, C. (2001) 'Who is a Pole, and who is a German? The Province of Olsztyn in 1945' in P. Ther and A. Siljak (eds) *Redrawing Nations: Ethnic Cleansing in East-Central Europe, 1944–1948*, New York: Rowman and Littlefield.

Kulak, J. (1998) *Białostocczyzna 1944–1945: w dokumentach podziemia i oficjalnych władz*, Warszawa: Instytut Studiów Politycznych PAN.

Kulczycki, J. (1997) *The Polish Coal Miners' Union and the German Labor Movement in the Ruhr, 1902–1934: National and Social Solidarity*, Oxford: Berg.

Kulczycki, J. (2001) 'The national identity of the "natives" of Poland's Recovered Lands' in *National Identities*, 3, 3: 205–219.

Kulińska, L. (1999) *Narodowcy: z dziejów obozu narodowego w Polsce w latach 1944–1947*, Warszawa: PWN.

Kulińska, L. et al. (2001) *Narodowcy: myśl polityczna i społeczna Obozu Narodowego w Polsce w latach 1944–1947*, Warszawa: PWN.

Kulisher, M. (1947) *Europe on the Move: War and Population Changes 1917–47*, New York: Columbia University Press.

Kurcz, Z. (1995) *Mniejszość niemiecka w Polsce*, Wrocław: WUW.

Kymlicka, W. (1995) *Multicultural Citizenship*, Oxford: Clarendon.

Laitin, D. (2007) *Nations, States, Violence*, Oxford: OUP.

Lane, A.B. (1948) *I Saw Poland Betrayed*, Indianapolis, IN: Bobbs-Merrill.

Lane, T. (2004) *Victims of Stalin and Hitler: The Exodus of Poles and Balts to Britain*, London: Palgrave.

Lawrence, B.R. and Karim, A. (2007) *On Violence: A Reader*, London: Duke University Press.

Lenin, V.I. (1988) *What is to be done?*, London: Penguin.

Libionka, D. (2007) 'Kwestia żydowska w Polsce w ocenie Delegatury Rządu RP i KG ZWZ-AK w latach 1942–1944' in B. Engelking et al. (eds) *Zagłada Żydów: pamięć narodowa a pisanie historii w Polsce i we Francji: Wybrane materiały z kolokwium polsko-francuskiego, Lublin, 22–23 stycznia 2004*, Lublin: Wydawnictwo Uniwersytetu Marii Curie-Skłodowskiej.

Linowski, J. (1987) *Trudne powroty: losy żołnierzy polskich na Zachodzie, 1945–1949*, Warszawa: Wydawnictwo Ministerstwa Obrony Narodowej.

London, L. (2000) *Whitehall and the Jews 1933–1948. British immigration policy, Jewish Refugees and the Holocaust*, Cambridge: Cambridge University Press.

Lotarski, S.S. (1975) 'The Communist Takeover in Poland' in T.T. Hammond (ed.) *The Anatomy of Communist Takeovers*, pp. 339–67, London: Yale University Press.

Luxemburg, R. (1976) *Rosa Luxemburg: The National Question*, H. Davis (ed.), New York: Monthly Review Press.

Łepkowski, T. (1984) 'Myśli o historii Polski i Polaków' *Zeszyty Historyczne*, 68: 120–9.

Łodziński, S. (1998) 'Polish citizenship: Ethnic boundaries and issues of citizenship in Polish society' in B. Balla and A. Sternberg (eds) *Ethnicity, Nation, Culture*, Hamburg: Kramer.

Macartney, C.A. (1934) *National States and National Minorities*, London: Oxford University Press.

McDermott, K. and Agnew, J. (1996) *The Comintern: A History of International Communism from Lenin to Stalin*, Basingstoke: Macmillan.

Machcewicz, P. (1996) 'Anti-Semitism in Poland in 1956' in A. Polonsky (ed.) *Polin: Studies in Polish Jewry*, vol. 9: 170–83.

Madajczyk, P. (1996) *Przyłączenie Śląska Opolskiego do Polski 1945–1948*, Warszawa: ISPPAN.

Madajczyk, P. (ed.) (1998) *Mniejszości narodowe w Polsce*, Warszawa: ISPPAN.

Madajczyk, P. (2001) *Niemcy polscy 1944–1989*, Warszawa, Oficyna Naukowa.

Madajczyk, P. (2004) 'Mniejszości narodowe w Polsce po II wojnie światowej' in *Pamięć i Sprawiedliwość*, 2(6): 37–56.

Marecki, J. and Musiał, F. (eds) (2007) *Nigdy Przeciw Bogu: Komunistyczna bezpieka wobec biskupów polskich*, Warszawa/Kraków: IPN.

Marrus, M. (1985) *The Unwanted: European Refugees in the Twentieth Century*, New York: Oxford University Press.

Marx, K. and Engels, F. (1992) *The Communist Manifesto*, Oxford: Oxford University Press.

Mazower, M. (ed.) (2000) *After the War was Over: Reconstructing the Family, Nation and State in Greece, 1943–1960*, Princeton, NJ: Princeton University Press.

Melchior, M. (1990) *Społeczna Tożsamość Jednostki: w świetle wywiadów z Polakami pochodzenia żydowskiego urodzonymi w latach 1944–1955*, Warszawa: Uniwersytet Warszawski.

Mevius, M. (2005) *Agents of Moscow: The Hungarian Communist Party and the Origins of Socialist Patriotism 1941–1953*, Oxford: Clarendon Press.

Micgiel, J. (1992) *Coercion and the Establishment of Communist Rule in Poland 1944–1947*, New York: unpublished PhD thesis, Columbia University.

Michlic, J. (2006) *Poland's Threatening Other: The Image of the Jew from 1880 to the Present*, Lincoln: University of Nebraska Press.

Michlic-Coren, J. (2000) 'Anti-Jewish Violence in Poland, 1918–1939 and 1945–1947' in A. Polonsky (ed.) *Polin: Studies in Polish Jewry*, vol. 13, 34–61.

Mikołajczyk, S. (1948) *The Pattern of Soviet Domination*, London: Sampson Low, Marston & Co. Ltd.

Milewski, J.J. and Pyżewska, A. (eds) (2005) *Stosunki Polsko-Białoruskie w Województwie Białostockim w latach 1939–1956*, Warszawa: IPN.

Miner, S.M. (2003) *Stalin's Holy War: Religion, Nationalism and Alliance Politics, 1941–1945*, London: University of North Carolina Press.

Mironowicz, E. (1991) 'Białorusin-Komunista', *Przegląd Kresowy*, 1: 29–30.

Mironowicz, E. (1991) 'Białorusin-Konformista', *Przegląd Kresowy*, 4: 19–20.

Mironowicz, E. (1993) *Białorusini w Polsce 1944–1949*, Warszawa: PWN.

Mironowicz, E. (2000) *Polityka narodowościowa PRL*, Białystok: Wydanie Białoruskiego Towarzystwa Historycznego.

Misiło, E. (1993) *Akcja 'Wisła'*, Warszawa: Wydawnictwo 'Archiwum Ukraińskie'.

Misiło, E. (1996) *Repatriacja czy deportacja: Przesiedlenie Ukraińców z Polski do USRR 1944–1945 Tom 1 – Dokumenty*, Warszawa: Wydawnictwo 'Archiwum Ukraińskie'.

Monticone, R. (1986) *The Catholic Church in Communist Poland 1945–1985. Forty Years of Church–State Relations*, New York: Columbia University Press.

Motyka, G. (ed.) (2005) *Służby Bezpieczeństwa Polski i Czechosłowacji wobec Ukraińcow*, Warszawa: IPN.

Motyka, G. and Kosiewski, P. (eds) (2000) *Historycy polscy i ukraińscy wobec problemów XX wieku*, Kraków: Universitas.

Mouffe, C. (2005) *On the Political*, London: Routledge.

Musiełak, M. (1986) *Polski Związek Zachodni 1944–1955*, Warszawa: PWN.

Naimark, N.M. (1992) 'Revolution and Counterrevolution in Eastern Europe' in C. Lemke and M. Marks (eds) *The Crisis of Socialism in Europe*, Durham, NC: Duke University Press.

Naimark, N.M. (2001) *Fires of Hatred: Ethnic Cleansing in Twentieth-Century Europe*, Cambridge, MA: Harvard University Press.

Naimark, N.M. and Gibianski, L. (1997) *The Establishment of Communist Regimes in Eastern Europe, 1944–1949*, Boulder, CO: Westview Press.

Namysło, A. (2004) 'Instrukcja MBP dla rozpracowania partii i organizacji działających w społeczeństwie żydowskim z 1946 r', in *Pamięć i Sprawiedliwość*, 2(6): 341–58.

Neyman, L. (1941) *Szaniec Bolesławów*, Warszawa: Szaniec.

Nimni, E. (1991) *Marxism and Nationalism: Theoretical Origins of a Political Crisis*, London: Pluto.

Nimni, E. (1995) 'Marx, Engels and the National Question', in W. Kymlicka (ed.) *The Rights of Minority Cultures*, pp. 57–75, Oxford: Oxford University Press.

Nitschke, B. (2004) *Wysiedlenie czy wypędzenie? Ludność niemiecka w Polsce w latach 1945–1949*, Toruń: Marszałek.

Noskowa, A. (2005) 'Na drodze do stworzenia PKWN – rola Moskwy' in *Pamięć i Sprawiedliwość*, 2(8): 31–50.

O'Ballance, E. (1966) *The Greek Civil War*, New York: Praegar.

Ossowski, S. (1967) 'Zagadnienia więzi regionalnej i więzi narodowej na Śląsku Opolskim', in S. Ossowski, *Z zagadnień psychologii społecznej*, Warszawa: PWN.

Ost, D. (2005) *The Defeat of Solidarity: Anger and Politics in Postcommunist Poland*, London: Cornell University.

Paczkowski, A. (1993) *Referendum z 30 czerwca 1946 roku: Przebieg i wyniki*, Warszawa: ISPPAN.

Paczkowski, A. (2001) '*Żydzi w UB próba weryfikacji stereotypu*', in T. Szarota. (ed.) *Komunizm, Ideologia, System, Ludzie*, pp. 192–204, Warszawa: Neriton.

Paczoska, A. (2002) *Dzieci Jałty: Exodus ludności polskiej z Wileńszczyzny w latach 1944–1947*, Toruń: Marszałek.

Paczoska, A. (2004) 'Oskarżeni o separatyzm. Działania tajnych służb PRL wobec działaczy kaszubskich w latach 1945–1970' in *Pamięć i Sprawiedliwość*, 2(6): 205–32.

Patrick, M. (1991) *Politics and Religion in Eastern Europe: Catholicism in Hungary, Poland and Czechoslovakia*, London: Polity Press.

Paulsson, G.S. (2000) 'The Demography of Jews in Hiding in Warsaw, 1943–1945' in A. Polonsky (ed.) *Polin: Studies in Polish Jewry*, vol. 13: 78–103.

Paulsson, G.S. (2002) *Secret City: The Hidden Jews of Warsaw, 1940–1945*, London: Yale University Press.

Pelly, M.E., Yasamee, H.J. and Hamilton, K.A. (1991) *Documents on British Policy Overseas: Eastern Europe, August 1945–April 1946*, London: Routledge.

Penkalla, A. (1995) 'Stosunki polsko-żydowskie w Radomiu' *Biuletyn Żydowskiego Instytutu Historycznego*, no. 3/95 (175–8): 57–66.

Penkalla, A. (2000) 'Poles and Jews in the Kielce Region and Radom, April 1945–February 1946' in A. Polonsky (ed.) *Polin: Studies in Polish Jewry*, vol. 13: 236–52.

Persson, H.A. (2001) *Rhetorik und Realpolitik: Grossbritannien, die Oder-Neisse-Grenze und die Vertreibung der Deutschen nach dem Zweiten Weltkrieg*, Berlin: Berlin Verlag Arno Spitz.

Piesakowski, T. (1990) *The Fate of Poles in the USSR 1939–1989*, London: Gryf Publications.

Pisuliński, J. (2004) 'Polityka władz wobec społeczności ukraińskiej w latach 1944–1956', *Pamięć i Sprawiedliwość*, 2(6): 161–84.

Polish Ministry of Foreign Affairs (1941) *The Polish White Book*, New York: Polish Ministry of Foreign Affairs.

Polish Ministry of Information (1941) *The German Fifth Column in Poland*, London: Hutchinson.

Polish Ministry of Preparatory Work Concerning the Peace Conference (1944/45) *Information Notes*, London.

Polonsky, A. (ed.) (1976) *The Great Powers and the Polish Question 1941–45: A Documentary Study in Cold War Origins*, London: LSE.

Polonsky, A. (ed.) (2005) *Polin: Studies in Polish Jewry*, vol. 17, Oxford: Littman.

Polonsky, A. and Drukier, B. (1980) *The Beginnings of Communist Rule in Poland*, London: Routledge.

Polubiec, Z. (1984) *Polska Partia Robotnicza: Dokumenty 1942–1948 programowe*, Warszawa: Książka i Wiedza.

Porter, B. (2000) *When Nationalism Began to Hate: Imagining Modern Politics in 19th Century Poland*, Oxford: Oxford University Press.

Potichnyj, P.J. (ed.) (1980) *Poland and Ukraine: Past and Present*, Toronto: The Canadian Institute of Ukrainian Studies.

Prażmowska, A. (1995) *Britain and Poland, 1939–1943: The Betrayed Ally*, Cambridge: Cambridge University Press.

Prażmowska, A. (2004) *Civil War in Poland 1942–1948*, London: Palgrave.

Proudfoot, M.J. (1957) *European Refugees 1939–52: A Study in Forced Population Movement*, London: Faber and Faber.

Pudło, K. (1995) 'Grecy i Macedończycy w Polsce 1948–1993: Imigracja, przemiany i zanikanie grupy', *Sprawy Narodowościowe*, Seria Nowa. IV, 1(6): 133–51.

Raina, P. (1994) *Karol Maria Splett: biskup gdański na ławie oskarżonych*, Warszawa: Książka Polska.

Rees, L. (2008) *World War Two Behind Closed Doors: Stalin, the Nazis and the West*, London: BBC Books.

Reynolds, D. (2004) *In Command of History: Churchill Fighting and Writing the Second World War*, London: Allen Lane.

Reynolds, D. (2006) *From World War to Cold War: Churchill, Roosevelt, and the International History of the 1940s*, Oxford: Oxford University Press.

Romanow, Z. (1999) 'Ludność rodzima na Pomorzu Zachodnim po II wojnie światowej' in K. Kozłowski (ed.) *Ludność rodzima i polska na Pomorzu Zachodnim VII–XX wiek*, Szczecin: Wydawnictwo Archiwum Państwowego 'Dokument' w Szczecinie.

Ross, G. (ed.) (1984) *The Foreign Office and the Kremlin: British Documents on Anglo–Soviet Relations 1941–1945*, Cambridge: Cambridge University Press.

Rothwell, V. (1982) *Britain and the Cold War 1941–47*, London: Cape.

Rothwell, V. (1990) 'Robin Hankey' in J. Zametica (ed.) (1990) *British Officials and British Foreign Policy 1945–50*, pp. 157–88, Leicester: Leicester University Press.

Sadowski, A. (1991) *Narody wielkie i małe: Białorusini w Polsce*, Kraków: Trans Humana.

Sadowski, A. (1995) *Pogranicze Polsko-Białoruskie: Tożsamość mieszkańców*, Białystok: Trans Humana.

Salomon, K. (1991) *Refugees in the Cold War*, Lund: Lund University Press.

Sanford, G. (2005) *Katyn and the Soviet Massacre of 1940: Truth, Justice and Memory*, London: BASEES/Routledge.

Santoni, R.E. (2003) *Sartre on Violence: Curiously Ambivalent*, University Park: Pennsylvania State University Press.

Sartre, J.P. (1982) *Critique of Dialectical Reason*, trans. A. Sheridan-Smith, London: Verso.

Save Europe Now (1948) *Save Europe Now 1945–48: Three Years' Work*, London: Gollancz.

Schechtman, J.B. (1946) *European Population Transfers: 1939–1945*, New York: Oxford University Press.

Schechtman, J.B. (1949) 'The Polish–Soviet Exchange of Population', *Journal of Central European Affairs*, IX: 289–314.

Schechtman, J.B. (1953) 'Postwar population transfers in Europe: a survey', *The Review of Politics*, XV, 4: 151–78.

Schieder, T. (ed.) (1953) *Dokumentation der Vertreibung der Deutschen aus Ost-Mitteleuropa, Vol I/1: Die Vertreibung der deutschen Bevölkerung aus den Gebieten östlich der Oder-Neisse*, Bonn: Bundesministerium für Vertriebene.

Schieder, T. (ed.) (1956) *Documents on the Expulsion of the Germans from Eastern-Central Europe: A Selection and Translation from Dokumentation der Vertreibung der Deutschen aus Ost-Mitteleuropa*, Bonn: Federal Ministry for Expellees, Refugees and War Victims.

Schimitzek, S. (1966) *Truth or Conjecture: German Civilian War Losses in the East*, Poznań: Zachodnia Agencja Prasowa.

Schmitt, C. (1976) *The Concept of the Political*, New Brunswick, NJ: Rutgers University Press.

Schoenberg, H.W. (1970) *Germans From the East: A Study of their Migration, Resettlement, and Subsequent Group History Since 1945*, The Hague: Martinus Nijhoff.

Sebag-Montefiore, S. (2004) *Stalin: The Court of the Red Tsar*, London: Pheonix.

Seniuta, A. (1974) *Obywatelstwo i jego regulacja prawna w PRL*, Wrocław: PWN.

Seton-Watson, H. (1961) *The East European Revolution*, New York: Praeger.

Shlomi, H. (1991) '"The Jewish Organising Committee" in Moscow and the "Jewish Central Committee" in Warsaw, June 1945–February 1946: Tackling Repatriation' in N. Davies and A. Polonsky (eds) *Jews in Eastern Poland and the USSR 1939–1946*, London: Macmillan.

Shore, M. (2006) *Caviar and Ashes: A Warsaw Generation's Life and Death in Marxism, 1918–1968*, London: Yale University Press.

Siebel-Achenbach, S. (1994) *Lower Silesia: From Nazi Germany to Communist Poland 1942–1949*, New York: Macmillan/St Antony's College, Oxford.

Sienkiewicz, W. and Hryciuk, G. (2008) *Wysiedlenia, wypędzenia i ucieczki 1939–1959, Atlas Ziem Polski: Polacy, Żydzi, Niemcy, Ukraińcy*, Warszawa: Demart.

Sitek, A. (1986) *Organizacja i kierunki działalności kurii administracji apostolskiej Śląska Opolskiego w latach 1945–1956*, Wrocław: published PhD, S.Sitek.

Smith, A. (1986) *The Ethnic Origins of Nations*, Oxford: Blackwell.

Smith, A. (1991) *National Identity*, London: Penguin.

Smith, A. (1995) *Nations and Nationalism in a Global Era*, Cambridge: Polity.

Snyder, T. (2003) *The Reconstruction of Nations: Poland, Ukraine, Lithuania, Belarus, 1569–1999*, London: Yale University Press.

Snyder, T. (2005) *Sketches from a Secret War: A Polish Artist's Mission to Liberate Soviet Ukraine*, London: Yale University Press.

Sosna, G. (1996) *Sprawy narodowościowe i wyznaniowe na Białostocczyźnie 1944–1948 w ocenie władz Rzeczypospolitej Polskiej: Wybór dokumentów*, Ryboły: Orthdruk.

Stankowski, A. (1997) Emigracja Żydów z Pomorza Zachodniego w latach 1945–1960' in A. Grabski, M. Pisarski and A. Stankowski (eds) (1997) *Studia z dziejów i kultury Żydów w Polsce po 1945 roku*, pp. 83–142, Warszawa: Trio.

Stelmachowska, B. (1946a) 'Polska kultura ludowa czynnikiem zespalającym Ziemie Odzyskane' in *Przegląd Zachodni*, No. 12: 979–90.

Stelmachowska, B. (1946b) 'Ostyli obyczaj rodzimy na Ziemach Odzyskanych' in *Przegląd Zachodni*, No. 1: 9–21.

Stettinius, E. (1950) *Roosevelt and the Russians: The Yalta Conference*, London: Jonathan Cape.

Stola, D. (1995) *Nadzieja i Zagłada: Ignacy Schwarzbart – Żydowski przedstawiciel w Radzie Narodowej RP, 1940–1945*, Warszawa: Oficyna Naukowa.

Stola, D. (2000) *Kampania antysyjonistyczna*, Warszawa: ISPPAN.

Strang, W. (1955) *The Foreign Office*, London: Allen and Unwin.

Strang, W. (1956) *Home and Abroad*, London: Andre Deutsch

Strauchold, G. (2001) *Autochtoni Polscy, Niemieccy czy . . . Od Nacjonalizmu do Komunizmu 1945–1949*, Toruń: Marszałek.

Stypułkowski, Z. (1989) *Zaproszenie do Moskwy*, London: Polska Fundacja Kulturalna.

Subcommittee of the Committee on the Judiciary (1950) 'Expellees and Refugees of German Ethnic Origin', Report of a Special Subcommittee of the Committee on the Judiciary, 81st Congress, HR 2nd Session, Report No. 1841, 24 March 1950, Washingtion DC.

Subtelny, O. (2001) 'Expulsion, Resettlement, Civil Strife: The Fate of Poland's Ukrainians 1944–1947' in P. Ther and A. Siljak (eds) *Redrawing Nations: Ethnic cleansing in East-Central Europe, 1944–1948*, New York: Rowman and Littlefield.

Sugar, P.F. and Lederer, I.J. (1969) *Nationalism in Eastern Europe*, Seattle: Washington University Press.

Sworakowski, W. (1944) 'An error regarding East Galicia in Curzon's Note to the Soviet Government' in *Journal of Central European Affairs*, IV: 3–26.

Sword, K. (1996) *Deportation and Exile: Poles in the Soviet Union, 1939–48*, London: Macmillan in association with School of Slavonic and East European Studies, University of London.

Sychowicz, K. (2005) 'Kościół katolicki w województwie białostockim wobec podziemia antykomunistycznego w latach 1945–1953' in *Pamięć i Sprawiedliwość*, 2(8): 125–42.

Syrnyk, J. (2007) *Ludność ukraińska na Dolnym Śląsku 1945–1989*, Wrocław: IPN.

Szaynok, B. (1994) 'Początki osadnictwa żydowskiego na Dolnym Śląsku po II wojnie światowej (maj 1945–styczeń 1946)' *Biuletyn Żydowskiego Instytutu Historycznego*, No. 4/94 (172–4): 45–64.

Szaynok, B. (2000) 'The Bund and the Jewish Fraction of the Polish Workers' Party in Poland after 1945' in A. Polonsky (ed.) *Polin: Studies in Polish Jewry*, vol. 13: 206–23, Oxford: Littman.

Szaynok, B. (2004) 'Komuniści w Polsce (PPR/PZPR) wobec ludności żydowskiej (1945–1953)' *Pamięć i Sprawiedliwość*, 2(6): 185–204.

Szaz, Z.M. (1960) *Germany's Eastern Frontiers: The Problem of the Oder-Neisse Line*, Chicago: Henry Regnery Co.

Szczerbiński, H. (2003) *Ludność niemiecka w Polsce w latach 1944–1980: Sytuacja Ekonomiczna, Prawna i Polityczna*, Warszawa/Toruń: Wydawnictwo Regionalny Ośrodek Badań i Dokumentacji Zabytków.

Szcześniak, B.A. and Szota, Z.W. (1973) *Droga do nikąd. Działalność Organizacji ukraińskich Nacjonalistów i jej likwidacja w Polsce*, Warszawa: MON.

Szmeja, M. (2000) *Niemcy? Polacy? Ślązacy! Rodzimi mieszkańcy Opolszczyzny w świetle analiz socjologicznych*, Kraków: Universitas.

Taborski, B. (1996) 'Moja wojna' *Zeszyty Historyczne* 118: 45–94, Paris: Instytut Literacki.

Tarka, K. (1998) *Litwini w Polsce 1944–1997*, Opole: WUO.

Terry, S.M. (1978) 'The Oder-Neisse Line Revisited: Sikorski's Program for Poland's Post-war Western Boundary 1939–42' in *East Central Europe*, 5/1: 39–68.

Ther, P. (2001) 'A century of forced migration: The origins and consequences of "Ethnic Cleansing"' in P. Ther and A. Siljak (eds) *Redrawing Nations: Ethnic Cleansing in East-Central Europe, 1944–1948*, New York: Rowman and Littlefield.

Ther, P. and Siljak, A. (eds) (2001) *Redrawing Nations: Ethnic Cleansing in East-Central Europe, 1944–1948*, New York: Rowman and Littlefield.

Tłomacki, A. (2003) *Akcja 'Wisła' w powiecie bielskim na tle walki politycznej i zbrojnej w latach 1944–1947*, Biała Podlaska: Calamus.

Tomaszewski, H.R. (1991) *Wyznania typu ewangeliczno-baptystycznego, wchodzące w skład Zjednoczony Kościół Ewangeliczny, w latach 1945–1956*, Warszawa: Słowo i Życie.

Tomaszewski, J. (1985a) 'Belorussians in the eyes of the Poles, 1918–1939' *in Acta Poloniae Historica*, 51: 102–22.

Tomaszewski, J. (1985b) *Rzeczpospolita wielu narodów*, Warszawa: Czytelnik.

Tomaszewski, J. (2000) 'From internationalism to nationalism? Poland 1944–1996', in A. Goldman *et al.* (eds) *Nationalism and Internationalism in the post cold war era*, pp. 67–86, London: Routledge.

Torańska, T. (1987) *'Them' Stalin's Polish Puppets*, New York: Harper and Row.

United States Department of State (1955) *Foreign Relations of the United States, Diplomatic Papers: The Conferences at Malta and Yalta 1945*, Washington DC: US Government Printing Office.

United States Department of State (1972) *Foreign Relations of the United States 1947*, Washington DC: US Government Printing Office.

Urban, K. (1988) 'Chrześcijańska Rada Ekumeniczna w Polsce 1945–1950 (z historii i aktywności społecznej)' in *Zeszyty Naukowe Akademii Ekonomicznej w Krakowie*, no. 250: 35–53.

Urban, K. (1994) 'Kościół Ewangelicko-Augsburgski w Polsce 1945–1950 (z zagadnień kształtowania się struktury diecezjalno-parafialnej)' in *Zeszyty Naukowe Akademii Ekonomicznej w Krakowie*, no. 437: 65–80.

van Boeschoten, R. (2000) 'The Impossible Return: Coping with Separation and the Reconstruction of Memory in the Wake of the Civil War' in Mazower, M. (ed.) *After the War was Over: Reconstructing the Family, Nation and State in Greece, 1943–1960*, Princeton, NJ: Princeton University Press, 2000.

Van den Berghe, P. (1978) 'Race and ethnicity: a sociobiological perspective' in *Ethnic and Racial Studies*, 1(4): 401–11.

Voglis, P. (2000) 'Between negation and self negation: Political prisoners in Greece, 1945-1950' in Mazower, M. (ed.) *After the War was Over: Reconstructing the Family, Nation and State in Greece, 1943–1960*, Princeton, NJ: Princeton University Press.

Walicki, A. (1982) *Philosophy and Romantic Nationalism: The Case of Poland*, Oxford: Clarendon.

Walicki, A. (2001) 'Traditions of Polish Nationalism in Comparative Perspective', *Dialogue and Universalism*, vol. 1, XI, no. 4: 5–50.

Wenklar, M. (ed.) (2007) *Koniec jałtańskich złudzeń: Sfałszowane wybory 19/1/1947*, Kraków: IPN.

Wierzbicki, M. (2000) *Polacy i Białorusini w zaborze sowieckim*, Warszawa: Volumen.

Wierzbicki, M. (2004) 'Białorusini polscy w okresie przełomu (1939–1945)' in *Pamięć i Sprawiedliwość*, 2(6): 83–114.

Wilpert, F. (1964) *The Oder-Neisse Problem: Towards Fair Play in Central Europe*, New York: Edition Atlantic-Forum.

Wiskemann, E. (1956) *Germany's Eastern Neighbours: Problems Relating to the Oder-Neisse Line and the Czech Frontier Regions*, New York: Oxford University Press.

Wojecki, M. (1989) *Uchodźcy Polityczni z Grecji w Polsce 1948–1975*, Jelenia Góra: Karkonoskie Towarzystwo Naukowe.

Woodhouse, C. (1976) *The Struggle for Greece 1941–1949*, Chicago, IL: Ivan R Dee.

Woźnicka, Z (2004) 'Emigracja i podziemie Polskie w konfrontacji ze Związkiem Sowieckim po 1945 roku' in Z.J. Kapery (ed.) *Wkład Polskiego Wywiadu w Zwycięstwo Aliantów w II Wojnie Światowej: Akta Konferencji Naukowej, Kraków 20–22/10/2002*, Kraków: Wydawnictwo Polskiej Akademii Umiejętności.

Wrona, J. (2004) 'System polityczny w Polsce w latach 1944–1947' in *Pamięć i Sprawiedliwość*, 2(8): 51–70.

Zaremba, M. (2001) *Komunizm, legitymizacja, nacjonalizm: Nacjonalistyczna legitymizacja władzy komunistycznej w Polsce*, Warszawa: TRIO.

Zayas, A.M. de (1975) 'International Law and Mass Population Transfers', *Human Rights Law Journal*, 16: 207–28.

Zayas, A.M. de (1977) *Nemesis at Potsdam: The Anglo-Americans and the Expulsion of the Germans – Background, Execution, Consequences*, London: Routledge.

Zayas, A.M. de (1993) *The German Expellees: Victims in War and Peace*, trans. J.A. Koehler, Basingstoke: Macmillan.

Zmijewski, N. (1991) *The Catholic-Marxist Ideological Dialogue in Poland 1945–1980*, Aldershot: Dartmouth Publishing.

Zway, I. (1998) *The Crime of Being German: The Losers*, Lewes: Lewes Book Guild.

Zwolski, M. (2005) 'Deportacje internowanych Polaków z województwa białostockiego 1944–1945' in *Pamięć i Sprawiedliwość*, 2(8): 89–108.

Żaryn, J. (2003) *Dzieje kościoła katolickiego w Polsce 1944–1989*, Warszawa: Neriton.

Żurko, J. (2000) *Rozsiedlenie ludności w ramach akcji 'Wisła' w dawnym województwie wrocławskim: Opracowanie materiałów źródłowych*, Wrocław: Wydawnictwo Uniwersytetu Wrocławskiego.

Žižek, S. (2008) *Violence*, London: Profile Books.

Index

Action Vistula 38, 91–2, 98, 119, 121–22
Adamski, Stanisław 105, 117
Alster, Antoni 138, 139
Alter, Wiktor 27
American Jewish Joint Distribution Committee 70
Anders, Władysław 6, 51
anti-Semitism 53, 69–70, 79, 86, 96, 143–44; Catholic Church 107; during population transfer 37; WiN 97
Atlantic Charter 28
Attlee, Clement 28
Auschwitz-Birkenau 92

Belarusians: in PPR 89; stereotyped 35, 58, 59; transferred to the East 68; transfers 35
Beloyannis, Nikos 140
Beneš, Edvard 80
Berman, Adolf 70, 79
Berman, Jakub 9, 11, 12, 67, 105, 111
Bevin, Ernest 43, 66, 125–27, 129
Bierut, Bolesław 4, 10, 43, 68, 112, 114
Bourdillion, Francis 128
Breitinger, Hilarius 102
Brichah 44, 49
Broniewski, Władysław 137
Brystygierowa, Julia 112
Bund 27, 39, 50, 70
Bursche, Juliusz 116
Butler, R.A. 6
Byrnes, James 66, 67, 72, 109

Caritas 104, 112, 114
Cavendish-Bentinck, Victor 4, 43, 60
Churchill, Winston 7, 27, 28, 30, 67, 132; assurances to Poles 30; Greece 135; meeting with Polish leaders in 1944 28; on Curzon line 1944 28; on post-war Polish frontiers 30; pressure on Poles 29; speech to Commons 28/9/44 29; support for transfers 30–1
CKŻP 70, 86, 96, 97
Cold War 1, 20, 114, 141–2, 146
COMECON 10
Cominform 9, 10, 125, 141, 146
Comintern 11, 12, 63
Concordat 102, 106, 113
Congress of Autochthones 72
Control Commission 44, 46, 12–7, 131–2
Council of Experts 72, 93
Curzon line 23, 28, 30, 47, 68, 149; Churchill's support 28; history 28; Stalin's ultimatum to Polish delegation 29; Tehran Conference 27

Dean, Pat 131
Dimitrov, Georgi 12, 13, 14, 63, 154
Dłuski, Ostap 137, 139
Dmowski, Roman 25, 41, 63

Eden, Anthony 7, 28, 135; assurances to Poles 30
Egit, Jacob 49, 84, 97
elections: 1947 55; eastern Poland 1939 5
Engels, Friedrich 15
Erlich, Henryk 27

ethno-nationalism: of Catholic clergy 123; centrifugal and centripetal aspects 3,4, 166; hard and soft 21, 89, 126, 134; legacy 100

Finder, Paweł 12, 13
Foreign Research and Press Service 8, 25
Fornalska, Małgorzata 13

Gedvilas, Mečislovas 33
Germans: general conditions 46; in labour camps 84; number expelled/ transferred 43; Polish opinions 24; population 42; stigmatised 84; benefits to the PPR 83; Savery's proposal 8, 23; transfer/expulsion 43; view of FRPS 8; wild expulsions 42; work 85: *see also* 'Operation Swallow'
Gestapo 6, 13
Gloch, Feliks 117
Gomułka, Władysław 4, 9–10, 13–14, 58, 63, 68, 82, 89, 127, 131: condemnation of 146; demands removal of Germans (May 1945) 65; ethno-nationalism 65; Our relations with the Germans 63
Gottwald, Klement 80
Government in Exile 55, 62, 70, 79, 86, 99: assessment of public mood in 1944 64; declaration by Wasilewska (ZPP) 14; fall of government coalition 29; identification of a fifth column 22; influence in DP camps 41; influence on Western Allies 6; on national homogeneity 27, 33; pressured on the Curzon line 30; refutes 'secret' document 62; RJN policy 64; Western recognition of 50; withdrawal of recognition 55; 1942 response to Vatican 103
Grabski, Stanisław 28, 41, 47, 51, 66–7
Grabski, Władysław 71
Greek political refugees 136
Greek-Catholic Church 118–20

Halifax, Lord 8, 23
Hankey, Robin 129–30
Hitler, Adolf 11, 117

Hlond, August 103, 109, 113–14, 120–123: meeting with German bishops 106; receives reports from WiN 107; support for the new Polish borders 110
Holocaust 50, 59
Home Army 31, 56, 68, 74, 81, 90: members deported 39
homines sacri 75, 148

Institute for National Remembrance 1
Izdebski, Zygmunt 72, 73

Jaroszewicz, Piotr 103
Jasna Góra 106, 111
Jaworzno 92, 98, 119
Jewish Religious Congregation 86
Jews: exit from Poland *see Brichah*; government policy towards 49; productivisation 49, 70; return from the East 36, 48; stereotyped 58, 60
Jeżewski, Henryk 25
Józewski, Henryk 12, 26, 121
Jóźwiak, Franciszek 13

Kahane, Rabbi 70
Kaławsk 20, 44, 46, 83, 95, 99: British personnel stationed 7; overcrowding 44; screenings 45
Kalinowicz, Aleksander 122
Karski, Jan 63
Kashubians 15, 17, 71, 74
Katyń 6, 27
Kenchington, Brigadier 40, 45–6
Kielce pogrom 50, 79, 96–7, 107
Kirkpatrick, Ivone 5
Knoll, Roman 25–27, 61– 63, 87: on Belarusians 26; on Jews 27; on Ukrainians 26
Kołakowski, Leszek 144
Kowalski, Aleksander 13
KPP 10, 12, 63
KPRP 10
KRN 14, 41, 47, 48, 70, 79, 121
Krushchev, Nikita 33
Kubina, Bishop 107

labour camps 34, 81, 84–5, 136
land reform 1, 20, 56, 64, 66, 82, 93, 104

Landau, Dolek 49
Laudański, Jerzy 84
Lenin, Vladimir Ilich 15
Lewandowski, Kazimierz 132
Lithuanians 39, 71, 154
Luxemburg, Rosa 15
Lwów Congress of Cultural Workers 17

Łemkos 89, 119, 154

Mabbott, John 8, 25
Marecki, Colonel 132–34
Marshall plan 141
Marx, Karl 15, 16
Mazurians 15, 17, 71, 73, 117
Mikołajczyk, Stanisław 28–30, 51, 67,
    82, 102, 109, 154; exit from
    Government in Exile 29; flight from
    Poland 55; depicted as a Western
    stooge 127
Minc, Hilary 4, 57, 58, 63–4
miners 85, 93, 129, 130–133
Modrzejewski, Roman 36
Modzelewski, Zygmunt 33, 126, 127,
    130
Mołojec, Bolesław 12, 13
Molotov, Vyacheslav 135
Moscow Conference 29, 33
Mossor, Stefan 39, 91–2

Nałkowska, Zofia 137
National Democracy 41, 59–61, 63
nationalism: theories 14
nationality policy: centrifugal aspects 3,
    147–48, centripetal aspects 3, 147–8;
    KPP 10
Nazi occupation 6, 12, 60, 64, 88, 116,
    137
Neyman, Lech 25
NKVD 20, 31, 53, 55, 90, 97, 108, 115,
    148: arrest of professors in 1939 6;
    deportations 39; 'repatriation' of
    Belarusians 121
Nowotko, Marceli 12, 13
NSZ 60, 77

Ochab, Edward 49, 73
Oder: as border line 8, 25, 29, 42–3,
    66–7, 110, 114

Olechnowicz, Mścisław 132
Operation PUR 50
Operation Swallow 7, 20, 43, 95, 126,
    127, 131; calls for cessation 44; exit
    of Jews 49; lack of skilled males 85,
    134; organisation of 43; Polish
    attempts to restart 46; suspended 46;
    third report 44
Orthodox Church 120, 121, 123: in the
    'Recovered Territories' 122;
    organisation 120; Soviet policy
    towards 119; State policy towards
    120; Uniate clergy 118
Osóbka-Morawski, Edward 14, 33, 48,
    117
Ossowski, Stanisław 93
Ostrowska, Kazimiera 41

PAX 108, 109
Piasecki, Bolesław 108, 109, 122
Piaskowski, Stanisław 84, 104
Piast Poland 70, 74, 81, 104
Pietkiewicz, Jan 132
Piłsudski, Józef 10, 11
Piontek, Bishop 103, 104
Pius XII 102, 103, 109, 120
PKWN 14, 87: abolition of religious
    oath of office 102; establishment of
    33; first anniversary parade 106; land
    reform 56; manifesto 69; Soviet
    recognition of 50; transfer
    agreements 33
pogrom 79, 96, 97, 107: *see* Kielce
    pogrom; Kraków 59
Poles: repatriated from the West 40;
    transfer from the East 36, 47
Polish Military Mission 44–5, 129,
    131–2
Polish Society of Friends of Democratic
    Greece 137
Polish–British relations 7, 8, 27,
    126
Polish–Soviet War 28
Polonisation 68; and the Roman
    Catholic Church 105; and Protestant
    Churches 119
Ponomarenko, Panteleimon 33
Potsdam Conference 7, 31, 42–44, 83,
    85, 95, 99, 126

PPR: establishment of 12; hostility to the Roman Catholic Church 111; membership 12, 88; relations with the Roman Catholic Church 101; slogans 65; social anger *see* social anger; 'What are we fighting for?' 13

PPS 12, 48, 55, 65–6, 77, 102, 138, 146

Prawin, Jakub 45, 85, 129, 130: transfer of Germans 46

prisoners of war 40, 43, 68

prisons 79, 82, 84, 136, 140

Progressive Catholics 108

property restitution 53, 96

Protestant Churches 101, 115, 118: marginalization 117; special council 117; transfer of churches from 104

PSL: activists and anti-Semitism 59, 62; harassed 55, 64, 66, 82, 127; position on referendum questions 56

PUR 18, 35, 36, 37, 41, 49, 87, 90: administrative control 34; complaints 36–7; establishment 34; logistical difficulties 36

PZPR: nationality policy 142; support for refugees 138, 139

PZZ 71, 74

Radkiewicz, Stanisław 4, 112: hostility to the Roman Catholic Church 112

representational violence 76, 78, 80–1, 100

ritual murder (myths of) 96, 107, 108

RJN 64

Rola-Żymierski, General 14, 105

Roman Catholic Church 20, 100–02, 110–16, 120, 148; incorporation of the 'Recovered Territories' 103

Romer, Tadeusz 25, 28, 33, 61, 62

Roosevelt, Franklin Delano 27–28

Sapieha, Adam Stefan 104, 105, 107

Sapieha, Michał 34, 36–7, 114

Save Europe Now 46

Savery, Fred 8, 22–25, 61

Schenk, Rabbi 70

Schonfeld, Solomon 70

Seeds, William 5, 6

Serov, Ivan 108, 168n29

Sikorski, Władysław 6, 22

Silesians 15, 17, 71

social anger 2, 80–1, 100, 122, 123, 141, 144–48: definition of 53; PPR/PZPR 4, 67

Sommerstein, Emil 70

Soviet Army 4, 14, 20, 27, 42, 53, 55–58: deportation of Poles 39, 85; letter of welcome from bishop 105

Soviet soldiers: excesses 37, 39, 58, 97, 99

Soviet Union 12, 14, 26, 39, 64, 121, 154: 1920 war 10; acceptance of refugees 140; British response to invasion of Poland 5, 6; deportations 58; election in Poland 1939 5; internationalism 142; PPR/PZPR 10; primacy in relation to Poland 30; transfer agreement 33

Special Commission 96

Splett, Karl Maria 102, 105

Spychalski, Marian 14, 45

Stalin, Joseph Vissarionovich 14, 31, 54, 62, 135, 148: Churchill's 'naughty document' 135; conversation with Roosevelt 28; creation of initiative group 12; ethno-nationalism 3; Greek Communists 136; influence on PPR 4, 13; liquidation of KPP 11; May (1926) error 10, 11; meets members of KRN 14; purge of KPP 11; stance on Curzon line 29; talks with Churchill at Tehran 27

Staveley, Brigadier 132

Strang, William 8, 24

structural violence 76–81: Poles 81–83; Germans 83–86; Jews 86–87; Belarusians 87–89; Ukrainians 89–93; autochthonic populations 93,94

subjective violence 76; targeted at various population groups 94–99

Świerczewski, Karol 91

Szczecin 85, 95, 99: British personnel stationed 7, 20; Gomułka's 7/9/1947 speech 127; Jews leaving Poland 49; responses to referendum questions 56; screenings 45; wild expulsions 42

Szeruda, Jan 116, 117
Szklarska Poręba 9, 125
Szuldonfrei, Michał 70
Szybek, Leon 132
Szymanko, Roman 132

Tehran Conference 27
Todys, Czesław 140
Treaty of Riga 10, 26
Turowicz, Jerzy 104
Tuwim, Julian 137

Ukrainians *see* Action Vistula:
    Jaworzno camp 92; transferred
    to the East 68; victims of violence
    38
UNRRA 40, 41, 45, 57: aid 57;
    repatriation campaign of 1947 40
UPA 38, 89–92

Valedenskii, Dionysius 120
Vatican 20, 101–103, 106, 109, 110, 114:
    decree forbidding Catholics joining
    communist parties 113
Versailles Treaty 22

Warsaw Uprising 27, 60, 151n10
Wasilewska, Wanda 13
Western Allies 33, 42, 69: accused of
    being pro-German 146; Polish
    Government in Exile 6, 30;
    recognition of Government of
    National Unity 55; support for Soviet
    Union 30
Westphalians 127–134
WiN 60, 77, 97, 107
Witos, Wincenty 10
Wolski, Władysław 34, 36, 37, 50, 132:
    co-operation with UNRRA 40; MAP
    conference 10/2/1048 132; reports to
    Council of Ministers on Ukrainian
    transfers 89; Westphalians 126
Wyszynski, Andrei 34
Wyszyński, Stefan 113, 114

Yalta Conference 1, 4, 30

Zachariadis, Nikos 136
Zhdanov, Andrei 9
Zionist 39, 45, 48, 50
ZPP 13, 14